I0815996

PRAISE FOR *THIS THUG'S LIFE*

"I have known Mo for years, and his memoir captures exactly what it's like to sit down and listen to the man tell stories: he really brings us back to the '90s—and to Tupac—in full color. His voice is authentic, honest and uniquely his. I learned new things about Mo, Pac, and the Shakurs, but most of all I loved being brought back to that unique and beautiful time in our lives."

—Jada Pinkett Smith, Emmy-award winning actress, producer and *New York Times bestselling author*

"*This Thug's Life* is both testimony and tribute. A son's remembrance, a brother's reflection, and a man's reckoning with legacy. Mopreme Shakur shares a deeply personal look at love and survival from inside the Shakur family. *This Thug's Life* reminds us that truth, like art, always finds its way home."

—Regina King, Academy and Emmy Award winning actress, director, and producer

"This powerful and profound memoir is a beautiful letter and labor of love sent by the inimitable Mopreme Shakur to all of us who cherish Truth and Justice! He comes from a revolutionary Black family of nobility that includes his little brother Tupac Shakur who forever changed global youth culture with his artistic genius. This book is an instant classic!

—Cornel West, philosopher, political activist, and *New York Times* bestselling author

If you think this is going to be a salacious tell-all book, think again. Mopreme has gifted us an epic love letter to his extended family, to the movement, to Hip Hop, to the ancestors who carried the culture through captivity and Jim Crow, into the streets of Queens,

Cali and beyond. Fearlessly honest and often funny as hell, *This Thug's Life* is the real thing: True. Heartfelt. Undiluted. Genius.

—Robin D. G. Kelley, historian and author of *Freedom Dreams: The Black Radical Imagination*

"I've known Mopreme for 35 years. He has always been someone to go to when you wanna cut through the bullshit and find out what's really going on. No exaggerations. No self-aggrandizement. He's always solid. Plus, he's an amazing storyteller- which can be hard when you're limited by those principles. If you wanna know Tupac's story, the best way would be to listen to Tupac tell it. The second-best way is through his brother Mo."

—Boots Riley, filmmaker and rapper

"This is a beautiful story of legacy and liberation, brotherhood and artistry, *resilience* and survival. Told as only a Shakur could...with revolutionary love, community, and fearless honesty. I am proud to call Mo my brother, comrade, and friend."

—Ray Luv, rapper, producer, and songwriter

"Mopreme Shakur — and his memoir *This Thug's Life* — have it all: smooth, sincere, and above all, substantive. This is an intimate look at the zenith of hip-hop that only a true insider can provide. Anyone who's interested in music, politics, and the vital intersection between the two should read this book. It's an up-close look at the making of legends and brothers in music."

—Peter DiStefano, guitarist – Porno for Pyros, The Psychedelic Furs, Lance Herbstrong

"I've known Mo for years, but reading this, I realized how much I never really knew him. I've had the privilege of meeting both his parents, and now I understand how deeply their love and struggle shaped him. What moved me most is Mo's strength, his ability to persevere through everything when most would fold. This book is reflective, raw, and full of truth. Behind the legend is a man I've been lucky to call a friend, and his story reminds us that greatness is born from pain, and that love is still the last word."

—Carey W. Hayes, screenwriter, producer and co-creator of The Conjuring franchise

"*This Thug's Life*, the autobiography of Mopreme Shakur, big brother to Tupac Shakur and a rap pioneer in his own right, is the most important book to date about the Shakur family. Written with beautiful honesty and unapologetic passion, it is the story we have been waiting for, about Tupac, about Mopreme's own incredible journey, about American and hip-hop history, about the movements for change, then and now. Any current or previous book that claims to tell this whole story is inauthentic. Mopreme has gifted us with raw truths, because he was fully there, because he fully lived it. That is why *This Thug's Life* is a book for the ages, one that will be read and studied and passed around for years to come. It is that timely and that timeless, and an instant classic."

—Kevin Powell, Grammy-nominated poet and Tupac Shakur biographer

"Mopreme Shukur's *This Thug›s Life* connects important behind the scenes stories and insights into the worlds of Hip Hop, entertainment, Black Power, and Revolution. Shakur's life and family connections provide him the unique position to illuminate the life and meaning of his brother and his musical collaborator Tupac Amaru Shakur, as well as his father revolutionary activist, health worker, and political prisoner Dr. Mutulu Shakur. Mopreme's memoir allows the reader to relive joyous and challenging moments of our cultural and political history. This powerful story will contribute to much of what is known about the revolutionary Shakur family and their impact on revolutionary Black movements and Black music."

—Akinyele K. Umoja, activist scholar and author of *We Will Shoot Back*

THIS THUG'S LIFE

AN UNAPOLOGETICALLY BLACK STORY

MAURICE "MOPREME" SHAKUR

WITH TALIA C. RODRÍGUEZ-SHAKUR

KENSINGTON PUBLISHING CORP.

kensingtonbooks.com

DAFINA BOOKS are published by

Kensington Publishing Corp.
900 Third Avenue
New York, NY 10022

All Kensington titles, imprints, and distributed lines are available at special quantity discounts for bulk purchases for sales promotions, premiums, fund-raising, educational, or institutional use. Special book excerpts or customized printings can also be created to fit specific needs. For details, write or phone the office of the Kensington sales manager: Kensington Publishing Corp., 900 Third Avenue, New York, NY 10022, attn: Sales Department; phone 1-800-221-2647.

Library of Congress Control Number is available

First hardcover printing: March 2026
ISBN: 978-1-4967-6058-6

ISBN: 978-1-4967-6060-9 (e-book)

10 9 8 7 6 5 4 3 2 1

Printed in the United States of America

The authorized representative in the EU for product safety and compliance
is eucomply OU, Parnu mnt 139b-14, Apt 123
Tallinn, Berlin 11317, hello@eucompliancepartner.com

To all the people who have ever felt powerless, alone or on the outside, to the brothas and sistas in the pen, all the political prisoners and all the lost souls who strive for a better day. Straight ahead!

I may be a nigga, but for sure I ain't your nigger . . .

I'M WRITING this note because my editor asked me to address my use of THE N-WORD. And yeah, I do use the word liberally. Even so, my first response was, uuugh I have a volume of work that speaks for itself on this issue—songs, album titles and even a whole group name. Plus, I talk about it in this very book. My thinking was, my people know what I mean even if they don't agree with me. But then, maybe you're not coming from the same place and even if you are, it wouldn't hurt for me to elaborate.

Now, let it be known: I love niggas. And you don't necessarily have to be Black to be *my* nigga.

I'ma take it way back. The transatlantic slave trade and the hundreds of years of chattel slavery that followed is a singular event in human history. There is no event that was so devasting to a single people. This is not an invitation to compare other people's painful histories. Humanity can be cruel and there is no shortage of genocides, wars, forceful dislocations, torture, human trafficking, rape and denigration in our history. And miss me with the argument that slavery existed before and after the transatlantic slave trade. That is an argument that is utterly insincere in its simplicity—slaves were (are), of course, prisoners of war, enslaved after their people were conquered, trafficked for sex, imprisoned, incarcerated . . . countless examples of forcing people into labor. What makes the transatlantic slave trade, and chattel slavery that developed from it, different is that enslaved people and their descendants, for generations, were confined to the conditions of their enslavement. It was unique in human history for being both inter- and transgenerational. And what sets it aside from all the many horrors that humanity is capable of is also the sheer scope and scale of it. Measuring it against other events in human history is a foolish task. It quickly devolves into an absurd measurement of pain and atrocity that only trivializes the trauma of all the pain being measured.

The multigenerational and systematic dislocation, murder, torture, rape, denigration and forced labor that was the transatlantic slave trade and chattel slavery that followed for hundreds of years after the trade ended, has no parallel. And the colonization of Africa followed for centuries after that, as did segregation and the Jim Crow South. On our backs, from our bodies, intergenerational wealth was built and capitalism developed. Globally. But though it's from us, it's largely not for us. The US emerged as the most powerful player in the game of capitalism, again, from us but largely not for us.

And from this, nigger—a uniquely ugly word intended to denigrate and dehumanize people even if the shackles are no longer there. Anti-Black racism is global, but that shit starts here. My people took their word, their hatred, their ugliness and made it ours with our own terms. I may be a nigga, but for sure I ain't your nigger. Then we did something transcendent and beautiful with all that trauma and ugliness, we stretched its boundaries and redefined its use. We made it multipurpose, multifaceted and inter-contextual. We made it a whole new word and dared those that use it for hate to show us who they are.

And still, there is a debt that we are owed, for the generations of forced labor that built this wealth, for the PTSD (Post-Traumatic Slavery Disorder) and for the largest defamation of character that birthed this word. N.I.G.G.A.—Never Ignorant Getting Goals Accomplished. I'll stop using it when we get reparations . . . maybe. But I'll never stop loving niggas.

CONTENTS

INTRODUCTION

My father was a leader, a prominent figure in the movement for the liberation of Black people, a political prisoner for thirty-seven years in a country that doesn't admit we have them: Mutulu Shakur.

My baby brother is the greatest rapper of all time, a legendary and transcendent figure whose music will outlive us all by generations: Tupac Shakur.

And me? Maurice, Little Mutulu, Mogie, Mocedes, Mopreme, 'Preme . . . I've been known by a lot of names by a lot of people. I'm the eldest son, the big brother, a father, a husband, a writer, a creative, a man who can pen a volume of stories in a single line all set to a bangin' beat. I made my mark in this world with my pen. I'm Mopreme Shakur, ya heard? I'm the big homie. I'm Mo. I'm the only surviving member of the venerable and legendary hip hop groups T.H.U.G. L.I.F.E. and Outlaw Immortalz, both of which I founded with my baby brother Tupac.

And I'm a lot of firsts: I'm my mother's first child and only son. Sharan Harding had me as a teen and grew to become one of the kindest and most generous people I've ever known. To the extent that I am kind, it is because of my mother.

I'm the first child of a man who is admired and respected by many, a man so driven by his love for his blind mother, Delores Porter ("DP," as she was known), that it compelled him to advocate for the liberation of all Black people. He was a man ahead of his time, treating addiction with acupuncture and compassion, fighting alongside revolutionaries to upend colonialism and imperialism, and loving people so much that he eventually sacrificed his own freedom for the cause. And I was there, as a shorty, soaking up all the things that made him respected and that made him loved.

While a teen and already a community organizer himself, my father chose his own spiritual fathers. Salahdeen El Hajj Shakur was one of these men, and he became much more to my father as the patriarch of the Shakur clan. He also chose Herman Ferguson and Sonny "Abubadika" Carson as political mentors and spiritual fathers. All three men became no different to me than if they were my family by blood. Lumumba, Zayd, and Wakil were Salahdeen's sons; they became my father's brothers, and so they were my uncles. Assata was my father's sister, so she is my aunt. Afeni became a Shakur before marrying my father. And chosen family can also become blood. When Afeni and Mutulu married, her son from a previous relationship, Tupac, became my brother; and then they had a child together, my sister Sekyiwa. In between is my brother Ayize. Then my father married Makini, from whom I have a sister, Nzingha, and brother, Chinua. We would later discover another brother, Tyrone. We don't half step: They are my siblings, my brothers and my sisters.

And just like we don't half step, we don't distinguish aunts and uncles by choice or by blood. The brother of my father is my uncle, his sister is my aunt, and their children are my cousins. Fulani Sunni-Ali, Ahmed Obafemi, and Bilal Sunni-Ali—they are my aunt and uncles and their children are my cousins. Cecilio Chui Ferguson, Sekou Odinga, Watani Tyehimba, Shaheem Jabbar, Churne Lloyd, Adbul Majid, and Sharon Howell, Nehanda Obafemi, Yaasmyn (Yas) Fula, Yuri Kochiyama, Nobuko Miyamoto are my uncles and aunts. So their children are my cousins. The young people my father mentored and took under his wing, they're my brothers, sisters, godbrothers, godsisters. There are many more in this massive, and massively impressive, Shakur clan. But these names and relationships will help you make it through this journey that is my story.

My life is the intersection between the story of a man you should have read about in your American history books but didn't, and a superstar you think you know but don't.

I put in the work. I'm also the first of my family in the music business with a hit record. And then I teamed up with my baby brother and my life becomes the stuff of legend. As a society, we're just starting to consider how and who tells the stories that are important to us as a people. My story comes from the culture—from the inside.

That story? It's one of a Black child who was raised to embrace and love my Blackness, and who went on to create art aimed at helping others love our Blackness, too. As a creative bunch—a bunch of Black creatives—I just wanna warn you that as you come on this journey with me, you will encounter a lot of names. You may not be sure how to pronounce them. Or you may wonder, was so-and-so once called something else? And you may also wonder, how did they keep all these things straight, manage all these relationships, hold all this shit together? Well, to the extent that we did, it was love. It was always our love that has endured throughout these relationships, our love for each other, our love for our art, our love for our Blackness, no matter how messy that may be. But in order to help you through this, I'm going to give you some more background, to the best of my ability, on how all these groups and people fit together.

Digital Underground is a rap group and collective, with a massive and intensely creative membership that is held together by the leadership of the late and legendary Shock G (whom Pac and I called "Shocka Locka"), Money B ("Mon"), and DJ Fuze. They're massively talented, hugely influential, vast in membership, and crucial in giving Pac his start in the industry. Frankly, they're massively important to me, too, and Mon would later name me as an official member.

Underground Railroad was similarly a collective, but it was broader. It was centered in music, rap specifically, but it was also a cultural collective whose affiliations expanded beyond the musicians who brought us together. It was basically everybody that was down with us, regardless of their role. A key member of Underground Railroad was Deon "Big D The Impossible" Evans, who was a prolific music producer. Ray Luv, Raw Fusion, The Live Squad, Jeremy, many members of Digital Underground, Pee-Wee, Big Money Otis, LaQuincy McCarty, Shock G, Dank, Wiz, J-Dee (of Da Lench Mob), Stretch, Maj and I were all down with Underground Railroad.

Some of the groups and collectives overlapped with albums, which is one way to organize them in your mind. The overlap between groups and albums is more obvious in some cases than others. Underground Railroad was before and around the time of *2Pacalypse Now*, my brother's first solo album. 50 N.I.G.G.A.Z. was a group we wanted to be a movement, as in, one good one in each state and we have a movement. It corresponded with the album *Strictly 4 My N.I.G.G.A.Z.*, the latter a backronym for Never Ignorant Getting Goals Accomplished. The members of 50 N.I.G.G.A.Z. were Tupac, me (as "Wyked" at the time), Mouseman, Man Man (as manager), and Mike Cooley (as manager). Because we were thinking about building a movement, the members were not limited to musicians.

The Have-Notz were a group of young artists, teens at the time, that Pac was working with. We all had a dedication to developing young artists. And as a teen, Pac, even more so than I, developed his skills alongside other youth in groups that were mentored by adults. His friendship with his mentor Leila Steinberg in Marin, while he was in high school, is an important example of this. But truly, we were raised to look out for those younger than us, and that continued as a through-line in our artistry as adults. The Have-Nots were one of those groups. I don't actually know all of the members, because Pac met kids he adopted into The Have-Nots all the time, all over the place, and we weren't together every moment. A few I remember are Jesse, Man Man's little brother John, Arrington, and Reese.

At a certain point, our family began to turn to us for support for some of our younger cousins. As an adult looking back on it now, it seems insane that we, barely adults—me in my mid-twenties and Pac in his early twenties—were taking responsibility for our teenage cousins who were minors at the time. But there isn't much "regular" about us, and we were happy to have them with us. Katari and Malcolm came out first. Katari Cox is Aunt Glo's son; Aunt Glo was Afeni's sister. Malcolm is the son of Aunt Glo's close friend. Then our cousin Yafeu Akiyele Fula, who we called "Yaki," came out. Yaki was a cousin through both of his parents, as they were both members of the Black Panther Party (BPP). His father, Sekou Odinga, who was BPP, BLA (Black Liberation Army), and also RNA (Republic of New Afrika), was one of my father's codefendants. Sekou was arrested when Yaki was four and would eventually serve thirty-two years. Yaki's mother is Yaasmyn Fula, and she was very close with Afeni; the two of them raised their children together for a period of time. Actually, because Yaki and Tupac spent their formative years in the same household, we saw Yaki as a cousin-brother. I called him "the Young Prince," because he really was like our little brother. Yaki eventually brought out some of his childhood friends from New Jersey. The first of those friends was Mutah.

We made a group of the younger guys. This was pretty much overlapping with the album *Strictly*, and just as we, the older ones who were colleagues and peers, had 50 N.I.G.G.A.Z., their group was called the Young Thugz. They each had their rap monikers, of course: Katari was "K-Dog," Malcolm was "Big Malcolm" or "Big Malc," and Yaki was "Young Hollywood."

When 50 N.I.G.G.A.Z. morphed into T.H.U.G. L.I.F.E., Pac created a label for it. That was Out Da Gutta. T.H.U.G. L.I.F.E. was our first group that actually had a deal on a label that Pac owned, and would be the only one to release an album on that label. The plan was for the group to put out continuous volumes, and we did switch up members over the course of recording because this was the project that we, Pac and I, worked on for the longest period of time. We recorded for almost three years. The members were Tupac, me (for the first time as Mopreme), Big Syke, Macadoshis, and Rated R. Johnny J was crucial to the group as a producer. Warren G produced as well, and Live Squad—Stretch and Maj—worked on the album. There were others who didn't end up making it on the album. For example, Pac really wanted a female member, and Yani was an early member, but she didn't continue to record with us.

Concurrent to T.H.U.G. L.I.F.E., but a little towards the latter half of recording, the little homies morphed from Young Thugz into Dramacydal. It was all the members of Young Thugz, basically, with their same names: K-Dog (Katari), Big Malcolm, Lil' Mu (Mutah) and Young Hollywood (Yaki), plus some new members. I worked on Dramacydal's recordings and was charged with executive producing some of their work as a veteran artist, in addition to being a member of T.H.U.G. L.I.F.E. Upon Pac's release from jail, and when he signed to Death Row Records, me, Pac, and Syke from T.H.U.G. L.I.F.E. merged with the members of Dramacydal to form the Outlaw Immortalz.

In the Outlaw Immortalz, Tupac famously called himself Makaveli. And he gave us each an alias of an embattled leader. He gave me the name Komani, after the Iranian revolutionary leader Ayatollah Khomeini, and Big Syke became Mussolini, but both of us continued to use Mopreme and Syke at the same time. Katari, who was previously K-Dog, became Kastro. Mutah, who was known as Lil' Mu, became Napoleon. Yaki, who had been known as Young Hollywood, became Kadafi. Malcolm, Big Malc, became E.D.I. Mean after Idi Amin. Fatal, who was a childhood friend of Yaki's, came out to Los Angeles after Pac was released from prison. Pac decided to put him in the group and named him Hussein Fatal, after Saddam Hussein. Storm was the only woman in the group, but Pac never gave her an alias. Noble was a friend of Yaki's and Mu's from New Jersey who came out in 1996, joining last, and was also without an alias. At one point, Fatal and Yaki had a duo, Fatal-N-Felony. This was concurrent to the Outlaw Immortalz.

Eventually, when Tupac was making moves to leave Death Row, he created a new label—Euphanasia. Yaki's mom, our aunt Yaasmyn, helped with the administration and formation according to Pac's wishes.

Throughout it all, in all our work and in all the ways we articulated ourselves, we were young men struggling to make our voices heard and our people proud under the scrutiny of the media and, very literally, the government. And we were soaring to the heights when tragedy struck and my brother was murdered. With no closure and my father in prison for thirty-seven years, I've had to pick myself up and move through this life without them. My story is one of resilience, of finding joy in the most vulnerable of spaces.

I've been a lot of things to a lot of people. I've seen the unbelievable. I've done the unimaginable. But the one thing I haven't done, and what I'm about to do for you, is tell my story—unvarnished and real. It's a uniquely and unapologetically Black story. My life has all the drama of epic historical fiction: political intrigue, violence, complicated relationships, rags to riches, fame, tragedy, and love. So much love.

I'd like to show you all of it—but mostly the love.

CHAPTER 1

YOUNG LOVE

Every parent-child relationship is marked by contradictions, and mine were no different: My childhood was full of unpredictable experiences that somehow lived without conflict within me. Where do I even begin? It all started, as these things usually do, with my parents, high school sweethearts who in this case had *very* different backgrounds. Though both sides of my family have roots in North Carolina and made their way to New York during the Great Black Migration, their respective upbringings were remarkably different, even if they shared a lot of cultural experiences. Their paths would diverge down the road, but when they were younger, the shared experience of living in the same neighborhood was enough for them to find common ground. It usually is, when two teenagers find each other attractive.

At the time my parents met at sixteen years old, my father, Jeral Williams, was already a budding activist and organizer. To hear my mother tell it, he was charismatic and charming, the coolest cat out there. He always dressed sharp and was well-put-together. He would wear leather driving gloves and these groovy hats, putting together a fit, often with colors that would clash on other people but somehow didn't on him. He pulled off looks that nobody else could. But under that slick exterior, he was a kid forced to take on responsibility well beyond his years: His mother began losing her vision when he was young; by the time she was twenty-five, she was blind. He had to be her eyes, doing the shopping and trying to access whatever resources were available in the sixties to help a blind, single mother. There weren't a lot. This was before "The War on Poverty," so there was some support for disabled people that she could access, but no system set up for a single, blind mother trying to take care of her family. They often relied on charity from the community and loved ones. It was this struggle—taking care of his mother, watching her try to take care of her kids—that awakened my father to the broader struggles of Black and poor people. The awakening started, as luck would have it, right around the time he met my mother.

My mother's family were mostly civil servants. My maternal grandmother had moved to New York for a better life, and she aspired to be part of the bourgeoisie, centering most of her social circle around the church. She was a nurse with five children: my mother Sharan; my Aunt Jean, who also became a nurse; my Uncle Joey, who was an all-around hustler and street cat; my Uncle Harold, who was a social deviant; and my Aunt Mona, who isn't much older than I am.

My mother was and is a critical thinker. The first time she met my father, she'd just been kicked out of class for refusing to stand for the national anthem—this was in 1966. She was visibly upset and went off down the hill, on the corner of Hillside and 168th Street, which was literally downhill from Thomas Edison and Jamaica High, the two high schools that sat across the street from one another. Edison was all boys at the time and was up until the mid-1980s. It was also one of the top high schools in the city, and probably the best public school in Queens. You had to test into the school. I eventually went to Edison.

My father went to Edison and my mother, who was also very smart, went to Jamaica High, probably because girls couldn't attend Edison at the time. Of course, none of those particulars mattered to the teens, who would all congregate "Down the Hill." Jeral, as he was known at the time, was already there, speaking to the other kids about RAM (Revolutionary Action Movement), which he had already joined. RAM was a clandestine organization in the early days of Black Liberation/Empowerment movements, one of the organizations being watched by J. Edgar Hoover's FBI. I would discover later that this was around the time that the FBI opened a file on my dear old dad. He was sixteen.

So this young activist and organizer, my dad, was doing his thing, talking to all the other kids. But he stopped when he saw my mother walk through the crowd in distress. Jeral was never one to leave a pretty girl crying. You could say they got along well: A year after they met, when they were seventeen, I was born.

My grandmother, meanwhile, had no capacity to tolerate anything that interfered with her middle-class aspirations and image. And there came my mom, pregnant and a potential high-school dropout. My grandmother would have none of it. She gave my mom a choice: Get a place and raise me on her own or stay at home to finish school and make other arrangements for me. Raising an infant by herself wasn't an option at the time; she just didn't have the resources, and although my father would have been involved, neither did he. He resented my grandmother for what he saw as pressuring my mother into taking me away from him, but the truth is he was too young and already increasingly too involved in activities that would eventually, and ironically, take him away from me in a much more substantive way.

So, when I was three weeks old, my mother sent me down to live with my Aunt Joanna, my grandmother's aunt, whom I called Aunt Jo, and Uncle Gene in Fayetteville, North Carolina. I would live with them until I was five.

Aunt Jo was a deeply religious woman, highly involved in the church, praying and playing spirituals on her organ every day. We had nothing, materially speaking. It was a very simple, rural life. Aunt Jo had an acre and a half that ran alongside Highway 210, upon which my Uncle Gene had built a two-bedroom house with a porch. There was a plot of land with vegetables that she would grow, and a small group of pine trees with a clearing where I would play. We had an outhouse and a well, and since we had no running water, we either had to get water from the well to use a pot in the house or make our way to the outhouse in order to go to the bathroom. What scared me quite a bit as a little dude was going to the outhouse at night. Of course, there were no lights. Eventually, Uncle Gene made me my own chair that I could use inside, with a hole cut out on the bottom and a big pot underneath. But I had to make sure I had water from the well in the pot, so when I took a poop, it wouldn't stick to the sides. In order to take baths, I would get water from that same well, Aunt Jo would heat it up on the stove, and I would take a bath right there in the living room in the big tin tub. Come to think of it, my aunt and uncle must have bathed there, too, but I never saw it.

Like a true country girl, my Aunt Jo hardly ever wore shoes unless she had to. She was a deeply religious woman, so much so that she was scared to death of frogs but would pick a snake up with her bare hands because she felt it represented the devil—and she didn't fear the devil. I, on the other hand, did not like snakes. I did not want to fuck around with no snakes.

But damn, we lived in a house full of love. I never felt deprived, or like I was missing anything material. The love got me through. Aunt Jo would always call me Shelton, my middle name, "Ooh, Shelton, you're gonna be a prize fighter with those shoulders!" She loved giving me Mountain Dew and baking all kinds of desserts like coconut pie, chocolate cake, and molasses bread, always giving me the bowl so I could lick it clean. I definitely have Aunt Jo to blame for kick-starting my lifelong sweet tooth.

And I'll never forget how she took my feelings—and their intensity—seriously, no matter my age. When I earnestly believed, at four years old, that my babysitter Jackie was my girlfriend, Aunt Jo sat me down and explained that Jackie had a boyfriend, and what that meant. I never did like Jackie's boyfriend. But I still remember how Aunt Jo treated my crush with all the seriousness of a grown man planning to propose to his partner.

My Uncle Gene, meanwhile, was a master woodworker who once carved a rifle stock out of a single piece of wood. He carved me my own chair, a ukulele, and a golf putter sized for a toddler. I was always amazed by what he could do. We'd play games together that only made sense in a small home in the South with no running water. In one, Jo would lift the kitchen table off the ground and then drop it back down. The thud would send roaches running out of the table, and I would laugh and scream and see how many I could stomp before they disappeared again. It was like an interactive whack-a-mole that doubled as pest control. I always had a blast, and still remember the satisfying crunch whenever I got one.

Aunt Jo also played piano for the church, and it was important to her that I was involved in music, too. I was too young to join the choir, but my Aunt Jo still put me on stage at our family church as a soloist to sing "In Times Like These" at four years old. Even when I was older and making my way in the music industry, she'd ask me, "Shelton, are you still singing those blues?" She understood in a way that so many other people don't that rap has a musical, lyrical connection to the blues. They carry a shared ability to comment upon the human condition, particularly the darker and more despondent, uglier, heavier parts of our experiences. That she could see that so clearly and so simply just tickled me. Still does.

Aunt Jo had a *great* sense of humor, and loved retelling the story of the time her friend brought over the boy she was taking care of—this friend called him "her boy," but that don't mean he was her son. It just so happened that when they came in, I was eating my cereal for breakfast. It was the South, so the door was open with just the screen door shut. When they arrived, Jo just hollered for them to come in. And when they did, that little boy saw me at the table eating my cereal, and chose, the little mothafucker—I'm irritated right now thinking about it—just chose to stick his hand in my cereal. Not once, but twice!

I'd had enough. I proceeded to push away from the table, grab him by the collar, and push him all the way into the corner of the house and just started beating and beating and beating him with my right hand. Aunt Jo would always bust out laughing when she got to this part of the story. I loved seeing her gold tooth as she mimicked the noises I was making: "Kapow! Kapow! Kapow!" She would imitate her friend: "Oh 'Anna! Oh 'Anna, come get your boy! He's whooping on my boy! 'Anna come get your boy!" My Aunt Joanna just said, "Well, he shouldn't've bothered him while he was eating." There wasn't a better sound in my life than my Aunt Jo's laughter. I still think about it and smile.

Aunt Joanna was my whole damn heart. My Uncle Gene and I were close, too, but my Aunt Jo was my buddy. I would call her my mama, even though she told me to call her Jo. She'd filled that role for my mom in those early years, but it wasn't like my real mom was totally absent. Aunt Jo would take me to get my picture taken to show off every missing tooth and new outfit so she could send them back to New York to my mother, and my mother would call all the time so that I could hear her voice. I got to spend my young years in the South, but even though Aunt Jo raised me as her own, it was always made clear to me that my mother was in New York waiting for me to come back.

When I was five, I was old enough to require a little less time- and energy-intensive care, which meant it was time for my mom to come and bring me back home to New York with her. I did *not* want to go. My mother was very present in my life, even when I was gone, but that did not mean that I wanted to go with her. I really didn't trust leaving the comfort of my childhood with Aunt Jo, and I was too little to understand anything other than her caring for me. It was a very serious moment, and Aunt Jo dealt with it very seriously. She got down on one knee at my level and grabbed both my wrists and said, "Now, Shelton, it's time for you to go back with your mama now, okay? I love you, and Daddy Gene loves you, but your mama loves you, too. So it's time to go back with her, okay?"

I was *very* unsure about this proposition, but I trusted Aunt Jo. I would have done anything for her. I said, "Okay, Jo. I don't wanna go, but if you say go, I'll go." She proceeded to tell me how I could come back every summer and always visit, and that I always had a home there. But right then, I knew I was in for a big change.

Back in New York, my father was eager to see me. After my birth, his life had continued to diverge from my mother's, and they had separated at some point. Their separation never seemed contentious, but I wasn't there to witness the breakup, and even if I had, I probably would've been too young to understand it. By 1972, New York was *different*, even in the five years since I'd been born. The awakening that began as my father witnessed his mother's struggles had grown into Afrocentrism, a worldview that believes Black people should center their lives around African traditions and values, regardless of where they live. He developed allegiances with radical and progressive movements like Pan-Africanism (the belief that all peoples of African descent should be unified) and tri-continental leftism (basically a critique of racism and imperialism in all its forms). He came under the tutelage of Salahdeen Shakur, who was active in Malcolm X's sphere both before and after the Nation of Islam, and converted to Islam, taking the name Mutulu Shakur.

I would understand later that my father was a founding member of the provisional government of the Republic of New Afrika. It's an interesting thing, to say the least, that I realize there's a history to be explained in order for you to understand what I mean. What's odd to me is that this is necessary at all, because it's a part of our history—a part of American history, a part of world history—that we should all know. But most of us are unfamiliar for very deliberate reasons that have to do with where we learn our history, who gets to tell that history, whose history gets told, and why. I'll get to the RNA, but I think I should back up a little bit to Afrocentrism and Black Liberation.

I understand Afrocentrism and Black Liberation from my lived experiences, from my father and the community of people who raised me. Centering the culture and history of African peoples throughout the Black Diaspora came naturally to me by way of the life my family lived. It seemed obvious to me that Black folks have certain through-lines that connect us. And as a child, I understood there were certain images and styles that embodied Afrocentrism. They were present around me all the time, so that I didn't often think about their meaning as a political statement until later in life: Afros; Afro picks; braids; red, black and green; the outline of the African continent; the Black Power fist; dashikis; kufis; jewelry from many African traditions; Black Panther posters . . . *red, black, and green and green and red, black and green, right on!* I think you get the idea. For me, to love Black people is to love myself. And I saw so much love that started from my father and my mother and radiated out into a vast and diverse community of Black folks from different walks of life together in common purpose. Afrocentrism is something I felt and not something I thought about from an intellectual perspective until I was a teen.

Black Liberation, which starts with the idea of Black self-sufficiency and that we should be free to be in charge of our destinies, our own media, our own businesses, our own farms, essentially own the products of our own ideas and labor, was similarly obvious to me. I didn't have to un-think the means by which systems remove us from that ownership as a child, because I was watching my dad and his comrades build their own systems for themselves. Now, Black Liberation as a movement and a set of ideas around which to organize, was much bigger than what my individual experiences were as a child. In the sixties, there began to grow a broad and diverse culture of people critical of the reformist methods and piecemeal successes of the civil rights movement. The textbooks will say it was a counterculture that began in opposition to MLK Jr. and faith-based organizations, and that it was largely due to the rise of Malcolm X following his departure from the Nation of Islam. My father was indeed a follower of Malcolm X through his relationship with Salahdeen Shakur, who had done security for Malcolm X before Malcolm was assassinated. Salahdeen was the patriarch of the Shakur clan, and Mutulu took the Shakur name and converted to Sunni Islam. But I take exception to the notion that Black Liberation, Black Power, was a counterculture.

From my experience, these two approaches to attaining equality were concurrent, not counter, to each other. As I mentioned, by the time my father, a sixteen-year-old Jeral Williams, met my mother, he had been begun organizing for RAM, which was a Black nationalist, Marxist-Leninist organization that applied the teachings of Mao to the American Black experience. RAM was founded in 1962 and was a secular organization that did count Malcolm X as a member. Before RAM, there were Trotskyist and Marxist Black activists organizing around labor and a firm foundation in Black nationalism that had been in dialog throughout the U.S. and Caribbean for decades. Black Liberation is not a counterculture within the Civil Rights Movement. It is a school of thought firmly rooted in the Black experience beyond and predating the Civil Rights Movement, going back to before Marcus Garvey when the first slaves rebelled on this land, if you ask me. And you're reading my book, so I figure you are.

Now I realize that we're talking about labor, working people, Black folks, poor folks, and it should be no surprise that this isn't in many high school U.S. history textbooks. Mutulu often said that this country has such disdain for poor people that our social safety nets are designed to humiliate and denigrate the very people who need to access them. These are the conditions my father and his comrades rose up against, and there was no way they were going to go about it without the understanding that they are entitled to be treated with dignity. And that, for me, is the root of Black Liberation and of Black Power—that we aren't going to ask to be treated equally and will instead move through this world with the knowledge that it's already ours to embrace and that we will demand it with dignity and power in any circumstance it is denied.

In this context, the founding of the Republic of New Afrika is pretty logical. In 1968, when Mutulu was not yet eighteen years old and I was still a toddler living in North Carolina with Aunt Jo, the founders of the RNA met in Detroit to form a provisional government. They renounced their U.S. citizenship, produced a declaration of independence, a constitution, a framework for governance, and named their leadership. The first president was Robert F. Williams, an activist with the NAACP who was living in exile after arming his chapter in response to state-sanctioned Klan terrorism, and who also was the first person to identify as a Black Nationalist. Williams and Mutulu were part of a generation that lived through the assassination of many of our leaders, through Emmett Till and countless other lynchings. See, they never gave us our forty acres and a mule. It was obvious they didn't want to live with us, no way. Now, "they" aren't all white people, and "they" may not even all be white. But "they" is enough of the population to make life difficult for us, and you know exactly who they are. So it was only logical that the Republic of New Afrika sought an independent nation made of five Black-majority states in the southeast (Louisiana, Mississippi, Alabama, Georgia, and South Carolina, with adjoining areas in North Florida and East Texas), reparations, and the right to the self-determination which was denied at the end of the Civil War—to decide for themselves the nation of their citizenship. My father was now a New Afrikan.

My mother, meanwhile, was at Baruch College, with her eyes set on a career as a civil servant. She continued to center herself around my grandmother as the familial matriarch, which meant the Black Baptist church. It wasn't just that my father had different cultural touchpoints now. *Everything* that he centered his life and his beliefs around was different. They never really talked about their separation with me, but I gather it was in no small part because they simply grew apart and into different spheres. They still believed a lot of the same things, but they had a marked difference of opinion on how to go about achieving their goals: reform vs. revolution.

The hustle of New York was entirely new to me. My mom was putting in the work, though, really focused on finishing school to make a better life for us. She would take me to classes with her sometimes, and I loved sitting in the big lecture halls. They made me feel grown, and I would just sit and soak it all in. She also had to navigate the system to see what support she could get as a single mom in college. I remember one time, we were at the office with the social worker, and they were clearly not helping her like we needed. I just remember her saying, "Well, fine, then! You take care of him." And she got up and stomped out of the office, leaving me sitting there in shock! I watched through the window as she stormed down the street and the social worker chased after her. Eventually, she came back and they sorted something out. On the way out, my mother held my hand and whispered, "You know I wasn't going to leave you, right?" The hustle was for sure different, but I was for sure loved.

Still, that love wasn't expressed the same then as it had been by Aunt Jo. Back in North Carolina, I basically had all of Aunt Jo's time and attention, all of the time. That was not the case for either my mother, who was finishing up college while holding down a job, or my father, who was actively engaged in the community. He would have me with him, running around the city, meeting various people. They were from all walks of life, but they were all interconnected in the way they understood family to be beyond blood, in service to the people. They would all call me "little brother." They were largely a community of healers and revolutionaries, so they would randomly grab me and massage my neck or massage my palm, or ask to look at my tongue. Of course, Aunt Jo would take me to the doctor if I was sick. My father's community, on the other hand, were concerned about my wellness on a daily basis, and in a way that was focused less on treating illness and more on supporting life and wellness. It was a community that was focused on *us*, collectively. I wasn't the focus of anyone's full attention; I was part of a group of people that were all watching out for one another.

I hung out with my dad a lot, but I was living with my mother, who was balancing college and motherhood. We relied a lot on my mother's family for help. We all lived in my grandmother's house at first: my mother and I, my Aunt Mona, my Uncle Harold, my grandmother, and my grandmother's husband, Pop Pop. But they had their own lives, too, which led to me becoming very self-sufficient very early on. Of course, the South had already prepared me for that. You don't play "stomp the roach" or take your well water in for your bath without learning some self-sufficiency. I remember one time, we were headed out somewhere and my Aunt Mona expected me to carry something that was clearly too big for me. I said, "I tan't tote it." Everybody was rolling! They thought the idea of this little boy unable to carry some load was just about the most hilarious thing. Thing is, if I couldn't even say "I can't hold it," what made them think I could actually hold the damn thing? I was five, fuck them. That was life in the city compared to being down South. There wasn't much time for me to adapt. I had to just figure it out. And I grew to like that.

"Figuring it out" meant learning who these new family members were and how to act around them, too. When my mother brought me back from North Carolina, and before she let my father take me, I spent a little time starting to get to know my aunts and uncles. My Aunt Jean, who was older than my mom, and my Uncle Joey, who was just younger than my mom, were out of the house already. As far as the kids went, my Uncle Harold and my Aunt Mona were still in the house, and they were in their teens. The closest male to my age was my Uncle Harold. One of the earliest memories I have in New York was hanging out in front of the house with Aunt Mona and Uncle Harold and several kids from the neighborhood. I was the new addition to the family, so everybody was coming by to meet me and hang out. I hadn't been around any of them before, so I was just experiencing another part of my family.

One of those family members was my Uncle Joey. Now, although he was legally an adult at the time, there's no means by which I would consider my time with him as having been supervised, but he did take care of me in his own unique way. My Uncle Joey seemed to take to me. He wasn't much younger than my mom, and he also knew my father, who knew all of the streets and all the players in them. I didn't know whether he liked me because of that, or he just liked me. We would play around; I'd swing on his arms. We'd take trips walking around the neighborhood and go to the store.

I *loved* hanging out with my Uncle Joey. He had a big, out-of-shape Afro. Very seldom did I see that 'fro maintained. It would be sticking out over here, or sticking out over there. He drank a lot and did drugs, but everybody loved him. They were also scared of him;

no one wanted to piss him off. He was built like a football player—about six-one with big, broad shoulders like boulders. He was only in his early twenties, but even then you could see the streets were taking their toll. He had lost a couple of teeth and walked with a limp. Still, he was the man.

One day, he took me with him to what I thought was going to be the store. We went walking three or four blocks up to the boulevard. I'm thinking we're going to go into the corner store and he's going to buy me something, but no. We busted a left instead of a right and walked into the pool hall. This is one place on the boulevard I hadn't been yet, and for very good reason: I was five. Uncle Joey put his arm around me, and I looked around. There were, of course, no children in the room; nothing but a bunch of old hustlas and niggas smoking and drinking, listening to soul music. We didn't go fully into the pool hall, just stood near the front entrance.

I see Uncle Joey looking around and he decides to make this announcement: "Ay! This my nephew Maurice, ya hear me? And don't none of y'all fuck with him!" My eyes popped open. I'm like, *Uncle Joey, what the hell are you so mad about?* I stood there thinking, *Okay, now what?* My Uncle Joey said, "Yeah, yeah!" And I'm thinking, I love my Uncle Joey, but was that shit necessary? Nobody had threatened me, nobody hit me, no one even cursed at me. He just wanted mothafuckas to know that I was his nephew. The funny thing was, there was no response or engagement of any kind from anybody in the room. Instead, there were moans and groans and a few, "Oh, come on, Joe." I thought the whole episode was totally unnecessary. But I love the hell out of my Uncle Joey for it still, to this day. He wanted to claim me as his nephew. That's some real family shit.

And then there was my Uncle Harold. Now, I don't know what the diagnosis for my Uncle Harold was, but that motherfucker was *off*. I'd call him a sociopath or a psychopath or one of those paths, but I'm not an expert. Big picture, he was a nutball Black man who was about six-one, light skinned with this dusty brown hair—like it wasn't black, it wasn't brown. It was like the color of rodent fur if rodents were nappy. There were weird highlights in it and he left it in a little 'fro. That might have been why he wore cowboy hats—along with matching cowboy boots and belt buckle, of course. He also blasted country music from his car *in Queens, New York*, and had a bizarre infatuation with Hitler. He was *obsessed* with Nazi paraphernalia. He would watch old war films with Nazis in them and try to learn German. Of course, the Allies were the heroes, but his dumbass was rooting for the Nazis. He would talk to me in German and try to get me to learn German as well. I still remember some German words and sentences to this day.

Everyone in the neighborhood knew him as "the crazy guy," ever since he was a teen. My Uncle Harold was honestly and truly the oddest Black man I have ever met or known. He might even be the oddest Black man you'd ever met, if you'd known him. The shitty part is that he was also my mother's favorite brother.

All I know is, he had no regard for my life, even as a child when my well-being was in his hands. The very first time I met him, he waited until we were alone and then hung me out of a second-story window by my ankle. I was five. And yet it seemed like from the beginning, my Uncle Harold was assigned to babysitting duties. Aunt Jo had taught me good manners and to respect my elders, and I was told that my uncles were my elders, even though they weren't exactly adults. Uncle Harold acted like he liked me, but he had a weird way of showing it. I had to be about six years old and my Uncle Harold, with a smile on his face, would say, "Ay, yo! Watch this!" and then grab me and choke me out. Right there in front of everybody. Sometimes it was a headlock, sometimes he would choke me with his hands. Most times he choked me until I passed out. The first time, I remember he choked me with his hands, and when I came to, all of these people I didn't know yet were yelling at him. "Leave that boy alone! What the fuck are you doing? Harold, you need to stop playing before you hurt him." It turns out that the ones yelling at him would later turn out to be my longtime friends: Randy (Ran Chan), Tony, Dave, Steve (Whip Whop), and Mimi (Steve's sister).

I was young, but I can still remember so clearly that feeling of confusion when I started to come to. This dude is supposed to be my uncle, my elder, and he's done something to me that caused these strangers to yell at him. I didn't feel like I was really hurt, but I had never been unconscious before. I was more confused than anything else.

I wish I could say that was the only time that Harold harmed me, but it was far from it. Another time, he was playing around with a ski pole, twirling it around, swishing it, pretending like it was a sword and shit. He was trying to impress everybody and I thought I was part of his audience. Now, looking back, it's clear that I wasn't an audience member, I was his target. Eventually he got tired of showing off and stabbed me in the head with the ski pole. I wasn't aware of the danger at all—the last thing I expected was to be hurt by my uncle. When he hit me in the head with it, blood started trickling down my face. And I'm just saying to myself, *He just hit me with a stick. Why'd he hit me with a stick?* I still have that little scar on my forehead to this day. My mother was always at school and my grandmother was always at work. I don't even remember what, if anything, they said to me or my uncle when they saw my face. Looking back, it's hard to wrap my brain around how unsupervised we were at times. But as a single mom, my mother would need to rely on Harold to watch me. And he had her fooled. She thought he was such a good guy because he would spend time with the kids, but what they didn't see was how manipulative and evil he was.

CHAPTER 2

REVOLUTIONARY LOVE

On the flip side, I didn't have much interaction with my father's family by blood—meaning, his mother and his siblings. But I spent a lot of time with the family he was building. Mutulu had taken the name Shakur because of Salahdeen, and Salahdeen was the patriarch of the clan, which meant that Salahdeen's children—Lumumba, Assata, and Afeni—all became his siblings. All I knew was that my father was a soldier, which he always impressed upon me. What he meant, I came to understand, was that he was a leader in the Black Liberation Army. The '70s was right in the middle of a groundswell of movements and organizations focused on civil rights and the liberation of Black people, partnering with groups that focused on overlapping causes like anti-war, anti-poverty, anarchists, anti-fascists, socialists, communists, anti-colonialism, and on and on and on. The Black Liberation Army was the armed force defending the Republic of New Afrika and the Black Panthers, of which Afeni was a proud member. Afeni, at the time that I met her as my father's wife, had successfully defended herself as a member of the Panther 21 against federal charges of planting bombs in various parts of the city—all while out on bail and very, *very* pregnant with her son Tupac.

I hung around my dad as much as I could during this time and usually quietly observed his meetings. I didn't know what sayings like "power to the people" and "free the land" meant when I first heard them, but their meanings slowly revealed themselves. I just wanted to learn. My mother was alternately amused and dismissive about my father's beliefs, but mostly she was patient. I only remember her putting her foot down a few times, saying that I wasn't allowed to go somewhere with him or attend a certain meeting. She didn't believe all the same things that my father did, but she wasn't opposed to me learning about them.

And I wasn't the only kid who hung around: Afeni had her young son, Tupac, from a previous relationship. I can remember the first time my father walked him over to me and said, "This is your brother. Hold his hand." I was five then and Tupac was between one and two: old enough to walk and just starting to talk. Even as a little one, Tupac had his distinctive, raspy voice. Like a lot of little ones, he couldn't say his L's, so he would call my father Mutulu "Tudu." I absolutely loved being a big brother.

Around the time my mom transferred from Queensborough Community College to Baruch College, where she finished her degree, she decided to give my father custody of me for a period of time. My father hadn't had any time with me for the first five years of my life, and it was only weekends and little visits for my first year in New York. My father lived in Harlem at the time, on 122nd and Morningside, across from Morningside Park, and I moved in with Afeni, Tupac, and him. It was a brownstone apartment, and we were on the second floor. I found Afeni to be very interesting. She was a beautiful dark-skinned woman who seemed no-nonsense. It always looked to me like she had a lot on her mind. She was very intense. So, I tried real hard to be on my best behavior with her, because I really wanted her to like me. I would come to find out later in life that she saw that in me at that tender age and saw that I "always wanted to be a good boy."

Even better, as a part of the whole deal, I got a baby brother. I was older, but it didn't matter. We played constantly. He would run up to me and just karate chop me anywhere, anytime. He would hit me anywhere he could reach me. Mind you, he was significantly smaller than me, but I could see really early that little dude had the heart to fight. Because my father introduced me to Tupac as Mutulu—I was always Little Mutulu with my father's family—and it was hard for the little dude to get out all them consonants, he would call me "Tulu," which sounded like "Tudu." I called him "Paqui." We had fun. Mutulu would take us to Morningside Park to hang out and play while he played paddleball. He would swoop me and Pac up and go to Lincoln Detox, where he was working at the time. If we didn't go to work with him, he would drop us off at the Lesanes', Afeni's sister's house in the Bronx.

My father, meanwhile, had been developing what would become a lifelong devotion to holistic healing, particularly using food as medicine—things that are now embraced within the wellness movement but looked strange to others at the time. He would make me eat whole lemons and oranges, peel and all. It was just awful, but he knew it was good for my immunity. He would massage the pressure points on my hand, which I did not understand and disliked because it kinda hurt. But Pops was ahead of his time. He was a healer, and believed that advocating for people in the way he felt they should be cared for meant taking the same holistic approach to health as he did to freedom and equality. It was one and the same thing, and he was always motivated by love. People followed my father because they knew he loved them. He would talk to my cousins when their behavior was counterproductive—not to judge them or chastise them, but to find a way for them to channel their energy into something that served their own interests. That's some powerful shit to see as a little one.

It was important to him that his kids were part of the culture, too. There were always African drumming circles in the park, and we'd stop and listen whenever we had the time. And Mutulu enrolled us in Black Panther karate school. I remember how excited Pac and I were on our first day. We were watching all the kids dressed in their gis, performing their moves. They looked fucking *sharp*. We wanted to know where our gis were! Mutulu was like, "Naw. Just strip down to your underwear and get out there." We looked at each other. There was no way we were going to go out there and practice in our BVDs!

But Mutulu was quite persuasive. We weren't happy about it, but we went out there and practiced karate in our underwear.

Just before I came back to NYC, my father, the Panthers, and the Young Lords—an organization fighting for, among other things, the independence of Puerto Rico—had taken over the drug rehabilitation center at Lincoln Hospital in the Bronx, which had the most deplorable conditions. *The New York Times* quoted a community member once who called it the Butcher Shop, and the name stuck. The Butcher Shop was supposed to have been condemned, but without the will to build a hospital to serve the community, the city left it operating. The care was appalling, but it was the only hospital for Black and brown folks in the South Bronx. In 1970, a group consisting mostly of non-medical staff who were also members of the Young Lords and Black Panthers occupied Lincoln Hospital in what was known as The Takeover. After negotiating with the city and the administration, they received a number of concessions that improved care, most notably a patient's bill of rights—which became the blueprint for the patient's bill of rights we still have in the U.S. today. The city and administrators also agreed to allow certain programs to continue under the control of the community. One of those programs was Lincoln Detox, the hospital's detoxification clinic, which prior to that was simply dispensing methadone. The community was wary of methadone, viewing it as equally addictive as heroine with worse lifestyle outcomes because it tied you to the particular clinic for regular doses instead of actually detoxifying—liquid handcuffs.

This was all around the time my dear old dad had begun to pursue acupuncture and sought to educate himself so he could use it in the community. The first time he saw it in use was in Chinatown when he was with Nobuko Miyamoto, herself an accomplished artist and activist. Nobuko and Mutulu were both close with Yuri Kochiyama, who was previously a member of RAM and also one of the founding members of the RNA, who had a very close friendship with Malcolm X, holding him in her arms as he lay dying. Mutulu had a deep network and he, Walter Bosque (a Young Lord who worked at Lincoln Hospital as a phlebotomist), Richard Delaney (a friend and former roommate), and Richard Bird (upon whom the titular character in Gordon Parks Jr.'s *Super Fly* is largely based), sought out a place to learn, but acupuncture was illegal in New York at the time. Plus, there weren't really programs as much as apprenticeships, which were long. On top of that, there was a language barrier—the masters didn't speak English or Spanish, and Mutulu, the Richards, and Walter didn't speak Chinese. They learned what they could in New York, but they were limited by the circumstances of the time. They eventually found a school in Montreal and went there to learn.

My father was seeing young men coming back from Vietnam addicted to heroin, and he saw the system's response to opioid addiction with methadone as equally problematic, just switching one addiction for another. He was a great believer in the potential of acupuncture, and after studying in Montreal, he went on to study in China and eventually got licensed in California, which had a licensure program at the time; he believed that Eastern medicine was something we needed to utilize more in the West, especially as it related to addiction treatment. Even with acupuncture illegal in New York at the time, they were going to put it to use to prove its effectiveness.

By this time, the Black Panthers and Young Lords had taken over Lincoln Hospital, kicked out the bureaucrats, and made certain demands of the city. Beyond demanding free, universal healthcare—the first to prominently link it to basic human rights—they also demanded that the city not allow a methadone clinic, so that they could treat addicts with acupuncture instead. They obviously didn't get universal healthcare, but the city negotiated the rest with hospital administrators, some of whom were members of the Young Lords and the same chapter of the Black Panthers as Afeni.

In 1972, Zayd Shakur, Salahdeen Shakur's son, referred Mutulu to Cleo Silvers, the hospital's administrator, herself a member of the Young Lords and the Bronx Chapter of the Black Panthers, and the chief community negotiator during The Takeover, asking her to bring him on as the medical director of the detox clinic. By the time I had returned from down South, Cleo had taken him on, and my father was the medical director of Lincoln Detox, responsible for educating practitioners in techniques of inner-ear acupuncture and coordinating the political education that they were combining with the acupuncture into a therapeutic protocol. As a result, my father would often take us with him to Lincoln Detox. The way everyone there treated him and talked to him, it was clear that he was the man.

This part is amazing, and just one of the million reasons why my dad was the shit. They started treating over two hundred patients a day, combining a five-point protocol that used points on the inner ear with group therapy in the form of political education classes. My dad developed this new protocol out of necessity—on the one hand, to comply with the ever-shifting demands of the city council and those administrators who were actively trying to undermine their work. But on the other hand, because it *worked*, essentially combining their version of talk therapy, political education, and massage with a known acupuncture treatment for addiction. It was groundbreaking and truly healing for the community, particularly for the recovering addicts—many of whom went on to learn the protocol and treat other patients themselves. My dad had been inspired by the barefoot doctors of China: each one, teach one. There was a lot of political intrigue and bullshit going on while my dad was there, but one thing that was for sure is that Mutulu saw to it that a lot of people got the treatment they needed. So much so that one of the doctors the hospital and city administrators required to "oversee" their work subsequently stole the protocol, in complete contradiction to the community-based healing for which they were fighting.

As an adult, I now understand how radical my father was. I mean, just saying this sounds crazy: Back in the '70s, my father saw that methadone was just as toxic and addictive as heroin and decided to take over a clinic to use a combination of inner-ear acupuncture, massage, and therapy instead. Goddamn, the balls he needed to have! And he was *right*, too: This protocol would eventually become the blueprint for the National Acupuncture Detoxification Association (NADA), an addiction treatment protocol that's now used all over the world. It's worth noting that the founder of NADA is the guy who stole this protocol, never properly credited my dad for his work until 2021, and has never compensated him to this day. But as a kid, I didn't know or appreciate any of that. I just saw my father walking around in a setting where he was clearly respected, clearly in charge, clearly a leader, and that love and respect was passed down to us as kids. Pacqui and I would drink the little cups of Tang that they had for the addicts that were jonesing. It was full of vitamin C, but there was also so much sugar! It's the sugar that the addicts needed, and we kids loved it, too. We would run around on that sugar high and just talk to the people, and I've been told that they really liked having us kids there because it normalized drug rehabilitation, which so often felt taboo.

The city shut down Lincoln Detox in 1979, when the program came into the crosshairs of a political environment that was very much threatened by the idea of Black empowerment. In particular, a young Chuck Schumer, at the time a council member, had a particular bug up his butt about the political education aspect, which he called an effort to radicalize the population. Of course, they also accused the clinic of various financial improprieties, but you can never trust bureaucrats to keep an honest ledger when there's a political motivation. There was also a close relationship between any Democrat on the rise, particularly in New York at that time, and the Rockefellers, an extremely powerful political family that was also heavily invested in pharmaceuticals, including methadone.

It didn't take my father long, however, to open up another community clinic called BAAANA (Black Acupuncture Advisory Association of North America). They set up in a brownstone in Harlem on Strivers' Row and continued practicing holistic healthcare. It was so unique. They no longer had city funding, so they took on paying patients and were entirely community funded. They held seminars on healthy eating and juicing. They continued political education, but were able to expand it because they were no longer beholden to the city's regulations. It became, because it could be, more organically connected to the political and cultural organizations they were allied with at the time. It was a hub of . . . everything.

When I was with my father, my Blackness was always affirmed and valued. We felt connected to our ancestors and learned about African—specifically West African—traditions that were new and outside the realm of the Black Christian American cultural boundaries of my mother's family. They never denied our Blackness, but it was always framed within the boundaries of a dominant white society and its customs. My mother's family centered our Black *American* roots. My father chose to center the things that were specific to our Black African ancestors. As different as this may seem, it didn't feel foreign. It felt affirming to have Blackness rooted at the center of our experiences. I loved wearing my kufi and dashiki. I loved learning songs about African liberation and self-determination. And I felt love for the good of a community that was broader than my immediate family or blood relatives. We celebrated Kwanzaa, and learned about its seven principles: *Umoja* (unity), *Kujichagulia* (self-determination), *Ujima* (collective work and responsibility), *Ujamaa* (cooperative economics), *Nia* (purpose), *Kuumba* (creativity), and *Imani* (faith). These were all principles that appealed to my sense of honor and decency, and were in line with how my mother's family also aspired to live our lives in the community as Christians in the Baptist faith. To this day, this dual upbringing imparts within me an unflinching and unapologetic love and acceptance for my Blackness, the Blackness of others, and all the diversity of those expressions and culture.

Now, it's not necessarily that my mother's family disagreed with Mutulu in principle. They didn't mind—even appreciated—him and his community teaching me about what it means to be Black and to come from rich African cultural traditions. But they knew how threatening the principle of Black liberation was—is—to the white establishment, and they were dismissive of the idea that it could find success. Honestly, they were scared of what it would mean to fight for it, even though, ironically, many would look at the land my mother's family kept in North Carolina from slavery times as the very model of self-determination. They kept the deed as a communal property amongst family members unless and until they had to parcel it out—that's cooperative economics. And others might look at how they did everything possible to keep parcels of the land amongst family members as collective work and responsibility. But my mother's family, all things considered, would always stop short of holding the system or establishment to account if it meant an armed struggle. And that was the road my father was heading down.

I was enrolled in first grade as Mutulu Shakur. Kids are shitty—there was a whole song about my name. They would sing, "Mutulu, caca doodoo. Mutulu, caca doodoo." Which is fucked up, but also, admittedly, hilarious. How could a budding wordsmith like me not appreciate the rhyme? It wouldn't have mattered if the rhyme wasn't funny, anyway, because I had already seen how people respected my father. I was unflappable in my pride. I was Mutulu Shakur's son. One of my favorite memories in life are the mornings when my dad would walk me and Pacqui to school. It was a clear, solid routine: Pac would be on one side holding his hand and I was on the other side holding his other hand, as we walked down the streets of Harlem. I liked it because it was the first time I had experienced being walked to school. But also, there was a particular paternal camaraderie that Pac and I were experiencing that I had only seen on TV up until then.

It wasn't all fun. Another paternal aspect was discipline. One time, I got in trouble in school because there was a pretty little Latina girl I liked, we called them Spanish back then. I remember being annoyed because she was not paying me any mind, and she chose instead to play with this little Latino—who wasn't my friend yet, so I couldn't play with them. That's some kid logic for you. And some more kid logic: I figured out a solution. One day, while he was on the monkey bars, I proceeded to push him off because I wanted to play with the young lady. It seemed perfectly reasonable to me. But not to my father. Mutulu was *pissed*. I remember him having a talk with me, saying, "What you did was wrong. You know it was wrong, don't you? So, you got a choice: You can get your beating now or get your beating in the morning before school."

Of course, I delayed it. But when the time came, he was very direct about it. He asked me if I was ready, and told me to come lean over his knee, old-school style. And he went to town. It wasn't abusive, but hard enough that my little thighs stung in my seat at school all that day. I got the message: Don't put your hand on nobody if they haven't done nothing to you. I wish I could say that I was a good boy after that and didn't get spanked again, but shit happens.

We also did fun stuff, like going to the movies as often as we could. One of the times Mutulu took us, he got us up in the middle of the movie and made us leave. I didn't understand why the hell we were leaving in the middle of a film that I saw him enjoying, too. I'd learn later that he thought the feds were following him. Honestly, looking back, I have no reason to disbelieve him. I'm quite sure they were.

This was the Bruce Lee era, and we were usually watching a karate film whenever we went out. At the time, Bruce Lee was it, and we were all obsessed with him and the culture. We were in Black Panther karate school, after all, and even that song was everywhere. *Everybody was kung fu fighting, huh! Those cats were fast as lightning, huh!* We would go to double-feature matinees. We would all mob out the theater doing our karate moves. One time—and I can't remember who took us, but Mutulu wasn't there—we'd seen a good one. I think it was Bruce Lee's *Enter the Dragon* or something. Pac and I had been karate fighting, waiting for Mutulu to get home so we could tell him all about it. When Mutulu got home, we were all excited. He came into our bedroom, opening our door to check on us, and he was with Big Chui. Chui was one of his lifelong friends, who would later be a codefendant in his trial. We were already in bed, but Pac and I were describing the movie to them simultaneously. We had bunk beds and, since I was older, I was on top. In my overzealousness in describing the film, I proceeded to demonstrate my favorite part: a Bruce Lee flying kick. Not thinking about the consequences, I got up and did a flying kick off my bunk bed. *Whaaaaaa!* I had the kick part down, but the landing not so much. I remember landing flat on my back. *Boom!* My head was spinning a little bit. I glanced over to my left side and saw bone sticking out of my wrist. The bone was the whitest thing I had ever seen.

My father and Big Chui flew into action. Mutulu scooped me up immediately and put me in Chui's arms. They started flying down the stairs of the brownstone and rushed me to Harlem Hospital. I ended up in a cast and my arm in a sling. I had to stay at the hospital for a week, and I was bed-bound because the sling was attached to the bed and I couldn't get up. It was a kids' ward, and all the kids that could run around, of course, did, and they would come visit me. I had a little hospital girlfriend that would come see me. She was so sweet. I remember her being so nice. Anything I wanted, she would go get it for me, because I couldn't move from the bed. She really wanted to look out for me, and it was a bit of redemption, because unlike the monkey bars incident, she liked me better than the other little guys in the ward. That made me feel good for sure.

When my mother got word that I was in the hospital, needless to say she was pissed the fuck off. She didn't care what circumstances had gotten me there. All she knew was that her son was in the hospital, that Mutulu had been in charge, and that was it. As soon as I was able to get discharged, I didn't get to go back to the house to see my father or Fe or Pac. My mother picked me up. Literally, she picked me up and carried me back home with her. I had been in bed and off my feet for so long that I'd basically forgotten how to walk. My legs were spaghetti noodles. I couldn't have weighed that much at the time, but I was dead weight. She was determined to carry me the best she could, but she was having a hard time, slipping in the snow. I remember the random brothers on the street seeing my mother struggling with me, offering their help to carry me part of the way to the train station.

That hospital trip marked the end of me living with my dad. From then on, I would see my father through weekend visits and shared custody. No more living full-time with my father, Afeni, and my brother.

My siblings would later joke (or maybe tease) that because I was born before Jeral became Mutulu I was the only child born out of love, and the rest of them came out of the struggle. Whatever that meant to them, I can tell you that when it comes to the movement—to the struggle for Black people's lives—nobody can do that work from a place that's not rooted in love. Mutulu, Afeni, and their brothers and sisters in the movement were motivated by a pure love for the people. I felt that love every day I was with them.

CHAPTER 3

HELLO JAMAICA

Now that my father no longer had custody of me, I would spend a lot time at my grandmother's house, which meant that Harold was the assigned babysitter. He stayed in the basement, which he had set up as his apartment. When he was babysitting me, he was always calling me to come down to the basement, and I would have a glimpse into his weird-ass world. He had the fun things that most kids would like: knives, pellet guns, mini-bikes, radio-controlled airplanes. He had model rockets that I liked to watch go off, and he liked showing off for the kids around the neighborhood. We had two neighbor boys, Gabby and Julio, who were around my age. I remember Harold would keep telling me to go get them, he wanted to show Gabby this, he wanted to show Gabby that. I'd pretend not to hear him call me, or say no, but Harold would threaten to shoot me with one of his pellet guns if I didn't go bring Gabby over. He'd try and buy us a bunch of junk food, too, making us feel like he was our friend.

Besides the boring war films he made me watch on TV, he would pull out the film projector and show me porn. I was very intrigued by the porn, but I knew it was wrong. It just *felt* wrong, and I didn't think I should be looking at it. But there he was, showing it to me. I was interested, sure, and I was also smart enough, I think, to feel apprehension and caution. As an adult looking back, I recognize that this was an attempt at grooming.

I guess folks in the neighborhood knew something wasn't right. Harold would take me to the store and people we knew would always warn him off of fucking with me. One time, Steve (Whip Wop) saw us and yelled at him, "Harold! Stop fucking with the boy! Leave that boy alone!" Harold had on a pair of pants, a cowboy hat, and a cowboy belt. No shirt, no shoes. Out on the streets in Queens. And Harold just takes off, chasing after Steve for yelling at him. He didn't catch him. How could he, running barefoot?

Harold would buy me all this candy. You think that's nice, huh? Well, he'd buy me all this candy and then rat me out to my mom when she got home because I was racking up a big dentist bill with all my cavities. He derived sick pleasure from my mother punishing me for eating candy when I wasn't supposed to. Some of the most unpleasant things Harold made me do would happen when my mother and grandmother were working nights, the eleven-to-seven shift. When they left for work, Harold would wake me up after my mother made me go to bed. And when he got me up, he'd torture me. He'd make me eat vinegar, hot sauce, mayonnaise, mustard, ketchup, pickle juice, and other combinations of random shit to see when I would throw up. I should have told someone what he was doing, but I didn't know this new family well, and who to trust. I didn't have Aunt Joanna and Uncle Gene anymore. My mother was always gone or working, and so was my grandmother. I felt alone. So I would throw up, clean myself up, and then he'd want to rassle, because he was supposed to be teaching me how to fight. That's what he said, at least.

But then things started getting even stranger. He'd call me, telling me to come down to the basement. He'd say, "I can't fall asleep, so I need to lay on top of you." I knew that shit was not right. But I had no one to turn to. I had to make sure I survived. I also knew that I needed to make sure he didn't do anything more than laying on top of me. He didn't take off my clothes or nothing. All I could muster up to say was, "I don't like doing this."

Then things started to escalate. I was in the basement one day with Harold when he pulled his penis out and put it to my face. I pushed it away and shook my head. He came at me again and put it closer, near my lips. I pushed it away. And he stopped. He didn't get any more aggressive than that, but from then on I knew what time it was. I knew that if I didn't stand up for myself, it was gonna get worse. I think that was the point that Harold realized he wasn't going to be able to push me around as much anymore, and he became worried that I might tell someone what he was doing to me.

That's when he started showing me his real guns. He had a black .38 revolver with a wood grip and an M1 carbine rifle from World War II which I guess he thought would impress me. He had me shoot the rifle in a closet. It was the weirdest shit, and felt dangerous. But I'd handled guns down South with my Uncle Gene, and I suppose I wasn't as impressed, excited, or frightened as Harold wanted me to be, because this motherfucker looked at me—holding the .38—and said, calm as shit, "You know I could kill your mother with this."

I was an easy target for him because I was always around, and he knew he could threaten me. I need to be clear here: I don't blame my mommy—and yes, I still call her my mommy—for working with limited childcare as she tried to finish college. She made miracles out of nothing, and I didn't tell her what was going on because I didn't know what Harold would actually do if I did. But *damn*. I cried myself to sleep because I couldn't talk to her about it. I fully believed Harold when he said he could kill my mom. But as young as I was, I was determined to survive and to bring no harm to my mother.

So by the time I was seven, Harold and I had this uneasy balance: He'd mostly stopped doing shit to me, but I knew he had his guns in the closet and was threatening to use them if I said shit about him. The only one who ever saw through Harold was my uncle Joey. My junkie, hustler, street cat, thug Uncle Joey. He would protect me whenever he was around. He didn't live with my grandmother, so he couldn't be there every time Harold acted up, but if he caught Harold fucking with me, he would go all-in: "Fight me, motherfucker, fight me! He's a kid. I'll fuck you up!" And he would. So while all my family viewed Joey as the bad seed, junkie, thief, thug, I learned a very valuable lesson: Image ain't shit. A lot of the real ones may be judged or maligned for not conforming to what "respectable" looks like, but that doesn't mean they aren't good people. Shit, every one of us is flawed. If you spend your life judging everyone who's complicated or adjusting to their own trauma, you'll be one lonely motherfucker.

Uncle Joey was an addict, and he supported his addiction in all the ways addicts do. He even robbed us on Christmas one year—all the presents just gone from under the Christmas tree. Oh, my God, it's hilarious, even though I'm still irritated to this day! All the presents were under the tree, and I was going to get a cherry red, ten-speed Scorcher bike. It had the red cushy tape on it, dope as fuck. It was too big to be wrapped, and was just sitting there, all shiny and pretty, under the tree. We came home that night, all dressed up from a church event, and all the presents were gone. There were a lot of presents, too, so there's no way he took them all in one trip. We also had one of those big consoles, like everyone had in the seventies, a big wood console that had electronics built into it. He had dragged it by the door, presumably with the intention of coming back for it, but we got home first. And dig this: My Uncle Joey actually stopped to make himself a snack. He left a mess on the counter. This guy stopped mid-caper and made himself a snack! When we got home, that's exactly how my grandmother knew it was him, because there was no forced entry. And when she saw that mess in the kitchen, it removed any doubt. It was for sure Uncle Joey. Fucking guy. I never even got to ride that bike once.

I was so mad, disappointed, but then also—of course! That's how life was, and you roll with the punches. It was the late '70s, Southside, Jamaica, Queens. Everyone had a junkie uncle. Everyone lived with a street hustler in the family. He was that guy—the guy walking through the neighborhood with a hot TV propped on his shoulder, on the way to get a few bucks to feed his addiction. But he was also my favorite uncle, and he protected me and looked out for me. My grandmother, a nurse, didn't know how to deal with his addiction. To be fair, I'm not sure we'd know how to deal with his addiction even today—it remains difficult to find that support in society. But my father always asked about Joey; my father was always problem focused and solution oriented. My father understood addiction and was working towards treating it in a way that would eventually become known as "harm reduction." He didn't judge. He saw past Joey's addiction to see a man who was good in spite of it.

My experience with Harold also taught me that you gotta have your goons—your gorillas, as I call them. Life gets gully and complicated, and when shit gets real, you need your real ones: the ones ready to do what's right, even if what's right is outside of and separate from many social norms and legal systems. When you have a mission to accomplish, you need to look at that person by your side and know they're in it for real. That *real* real is love. And that's the most powerful force in the world. It comes in more forms than most people realize.

CHAPTER 4

A TALE OF TWO LIVES

Now, we're talking about New York in the 1970s, before all the materialism of the next decade. We were financially poor, whether I was with my mom or my dad, but we were always rich in life and in love. That was a constant on both sides of my family: finding meaning in ways and places that had nothing to do with money or material possessions. With my father, the sense of purpose was the people, the community. With my mother, the sense of purpose was a formal education for a secure financial future and livelihood.

When I was in second grade, my mother moved into the projects. We were in the Redfern Projects in Far Rockaway, Queens. Think about that: Moving up meant the projects, and it *was* a step up from where we'd been before. The projects were crowded and, of course, completely neglected. There was so much crime, and it definitely wasn't the safest place for a woman with a young child. But we were finally on our own. I had to grow up real quick. I knew it was us against the world, and I had to protect and watch out for my mother as much as she had to protect and watch out for me. I'd gone from "tan't tote it" to feeling a shared sense of responsibility for my loved ones. I felt a sense of purpose in that, too.

Redfern was gully, but we were alone. It was just me and her—no extended family in the mix. I had no friends, no father around now, no aunts, no uncles, no brother. And that meant that when my mother wasn't around, it was just me. And she wasn't around a lot, because she'd finished college and had a good job with the city as a 911 operator. I became one of the many latchkey kids around the city, house keys tied around my neck and all.

It seemed like the kids in Redfern were meaner. I often played by myself. I remember someone gave me a brand-new basketball, red, white, and blue. I was only seven, so I was still little. But the bigger dudes would roll up, ask to play with my ball, and then walk away with it. I was getting bullied. I mean, it was bad. I remember getting bullied getting off the school bus, physically pushed around. It didn't take me long to realize that I didn't like this fucking place at all. Far Rockaway was right near the beach, but I never got to go to the beach. To this day I think, why didn't we go to the beach? We lived right there.

My mother has always had a natural elegance and knew how to make simple things feel elegant. She would make us simple dishes for dinner, like tuna fish on lettuce with crackers. But she would fan the crackers and boiled egg around the dish to make it look pretty. I would go to . . . I don't exactly want to call it a "date night" with my mom, but it kinda was. We'd go to a restaurant, just her and I, and we'd both dress up sharp. Good manners were a must, and also a sense of chivalry. I'd open and close doors, walk on the outside of the sidewalk, all that.

I also watched my mother go through her struggles. There were so many roaches in the apartment, it would depress her. Our first Christmas, she didn't have any money to buy me any presents. She was distraught about it, and she apologized to me for it. I honestly wasn't upset at all, because at that point in my life, I hadn't had a Christmas like my mother was trying to give me anyway. I didn't, and still don't, remember Christmas with Aunt Jo. And with my dad it was Kwanzaa. You can't miss what you haven't really had. She says I told her, "It's alright, Mommy. It'll be okay." And apparently that meant a lot to her.

There were different guys from the neighborhood who would try to get with my mom, so they would try to play cool and act like they liked me. These friends of hers would come over and hang out and listen to Marvin Gaye. One dude offered her some weed for her to sell to help her out with the bills. Side note: My mom got the measurement on the nickel bags wrong. Unbeknownst to her, they were extra fat. Needless to say, she became quite popular.

But by next Christmastime, my mother was determined that it was going to be nice for me. A day or two before Christmas Eve, my mother was trying to get all my presents ready. She was trying to do it secretly, but I knew what she was doing. It was getting late, and my mother sent me to bed. She and one of these dudes were hanging out and he was trying to be helpful, helping her put the Christmas toys together. I had put on my pajamas and gone on to bed, laid down, and was trying to go to sleep. Next thing I know, I hear my mother yelling, talking loudly, and this man talking loudly as well. I'd grown pretty keen to knowing my mother's voice when she was upset. So I popped up, opened my door, and creeped down the hallway. The hallway ended at the front door and all I was able to catch was some dude flying out the front door, slamming it shut and my mother chasing him out the door with a knife in her hand, growling and thrusting the knife into the door behind him. I asked her if she was okay, and all she said was, "Go to bed, Maurice. I'm sorry." I had never seen an adult exhibit pure rage right in front of my face before. That lesson taught me to not ever piss my mother off. I never did find out what happened between them.

Once I was back living with my mother, I began to see small hints of conflict between my parents' lifestyles. At one point, I wanted some nunchucks. My mother wasn't with the whole Chinese theme. It was a struggle just to get some Chinese slippers. She said they had no support, they were slippery, and they were cheap. "You'll put a hole in them in a week." I eventually got them and got over that hump, but now I wanted some nunchucks. I asked my mommy, but she had no idea what nunchucks were. I'd show her these badass posters with Bruce Lee, using them in the battle or hanging around his neck. She said, "Maurice, that's just a couple of sticks and a chain. You'll crack your head open." I really think she just didn't want me to have a weapon, but my plan was innocent: I wanted to get good with them and use them in karate school. I mean, Mutulu was going to get them for me, but first he wanted me to ask my mother. So after getting turned down by my mom, I went back to him and told him the bad news. He was bummed out because he was all for his little badass son kicking ass with some nunchucks. He called my mother and began the debate. I couldn't hear it all, but my mother said, "Jeral, you told Maurice he could get them nunchucks. I don't care what the hell it is. He's gonna crack his head open!" I was hugely disappointed at the time, but looking back, it was actually one of the few normal parental experiences between my mom and my dad.

After we both got turned down, I was, needless to say, very upset. But my dear old dad didn't give a fuck. Mutulu, remember, was a man of action. Next thing I know, he was coming over, and he said he had something for me. What did he have? A pair of nunchucks! I had given up on the idea, but the brilliance of my dear old dad had found a way! What he did was find me a pair of rubber nunchucks, connected with a cord in the middle instead of a chain. The shafts were rubber and were eight-sided. I was so excited, because I had never even heard of a pair of nunchucks like this. I called my mommy in to come see them and Mutulu went immediately into "calm her down" mode: "Now, Sharan, they are totally safe for him. They're made of rubber. There's no metal; there's a string in the middle here." My mom wanted to see them for herself, and she started playing with them! Eventually she handed them back and said, "Oh, Maurice, you be careful. They're still dangerous." But I got 'em!

I wanted to see myself using them, so I would use them in front of the mirror. I would take off my shirt and push my little bird chest out, get in my little stance. I started going behind my back with sound effects: *whoosh*, *whoosh!* And I would get a good roll going before realizing I was making marks on the wall, black streak marks on each side of me. I knew my mommy was gonna kill me, so I adjusted myself and got away from the wall, but then I would graze myself with them. It wasn't usually a dead-on smack, but my mom was right: It did hurt. They were rubber, but they were still hard.

It was all worth it, though. I would practice pretty often. I made a lot of black marks on the wall, but I always got them up. I had a pretty good routine and got good enough. But they didn't make it to karate class; I can't remember why. I loved those things, and I was better than anyone else my age.

I did get to use them a bit with Pac, though: After every film, me and him would karate fight in our room. All you'd hear was *pshsh, pshsh* as we threw our karate chops and kicks. But I saw that if I accidentally hit or kicked Pac too hard, he would get furious. His little temper was off the chain. He would take it personally, and often his response was to overreact. I had to work real hard to let him know I was sorry and didn't mean it. He never told on me or involved the adults, but he would attack me for real, like he was for real serious about hurting me back.

In 1974, we had settled into a routine of sorts. Mutulu would pick me up on weekends, which I looked forward to with great excitement. We would ride around together. I would run errands with him, and he would stop to see his friends in between. He wanted me to roll with him. One particular time, he informed me that we'd be spending the night at his friend's house. He said her name was Moto. He didn't remember that I had met her once before when we ran into her on the sidewalk one day in front of her house. I remembered her because she was strikingly beautiful: She had deep, dark skin with big, big clear brown eyes, a nice smile, and she seemed to like me. So, when Mutulu said we were going to be spending the night at her house, I was like, *great*.

The three of us had spent the day together, walking around the city, and eventually it was time for me to go to bed. The bedroom where I was going to be sleeping was upstairs. I went upstairs, laid down, and tried to go to sleep in this different house. But I was nowhere near asleep when I heard Moto and Mutulu clearly arguing. Curious kid that I was, I got up and went to the top of the staircase and peeped around the corner. Mutulu and Moto were in a heated conversation. They were arguing and pointing their fingers at each other for emphasis. I think they thought they were whispering, but they were really quite loud. I remember being so fascinated by seeing my father argue with someone. It was so not his way of solving conflict, and I had never seen that up to that point.

I couldn't take my eyes off of them. When I finally broke my gaze, I glanced and looked towards the left side of the room in which they were arguing. Leaning up against the wall was a military duffel bag with about ten rifles sticking out the top. I noticed they weren't the type of rifle that I used to shoot with my Uncle Gene down South. These were Army rifles, like the ones I recognized from the G.I. Joe toys. I couldn't really hear what Mutulu and Moto were arguing about, but I had a good feeling it was about those rifles leaning against the wall over there. I quietly turned around, went back to the room, and went to bed. I dared not get caught because I didn't want to make Moto mad when I was just getting to know her. I laid there wondering why the hell Mutulu needed so many rifles. I'm thinking with my kid's mind, *All you need is one. All you need is one to do some target practice. Two at the most! If you had two, you could go hunting with your friend. I hope he got one for me.* And the very last thought in that young mind thinking things through: *Man, I hope he don't get into no trouble.*

Another time that Mutulu came to pick me up, he was with Afeni and my baby sister Sekyiwa, who had just been born. Afeni sat down at the kitchen table and began breastfeeding Set. My mother was *livid.* She couldn't believe that Afeni would just whip her breast out in front of me, without covering herself up with a blanket. My mom swears that I looked at her wide-eyed, and that's the reason she told Afeni to stop. I'm not gonna say my mom was wrong, but I don't think Afeni was, either. She and my father were just ahead of their time. There are whole movements now, forty-plus years later, to ensure that women have the freedom to breastfeed their children in an environment that doesn't sexualize them. My mother was *not* ready for that in the '70s.

Even though there was a village, a community of people raising me and all the kids communally, there wasn't a whole lot of supervision. When my dad got together with Afeni, this naturally expanded the family. This happened around the same time that he expanded the family by becoming a Shakur. I became part of this massive blended family that was still growing by the time I came to live with him. I get why this can be hard to keep up with! In addition to the Shakur clan, Afeni also had her biological family—mainly her sister and extended family. Afeni's sister, Gloria Jean Cox, Aunt Glo as I called her, had a lot of children from her own blended family, and because they were my brother Tupac's cousins, they were my cousins, too. There were the Lesanes—Billy (Billy Bang), Scott, Kenny (Kenny Black), Jamala (Moo), Greg—from Aunt Glo's first marriage, and then there was TC, her husband, and their children, Mai Ling and Katari (K). There's cousin Philip, too. I'm still not sure where he falls.

When my dad dropped me and Pac off to spend time with the Lesanes, it was mostly me, Pac, and Kenny who spent time together, because we were close in age. Actually, Kenny and I are closer to the same age, and Pac was right behind us. Kenny Black was very mischievous, but fun and lovable, playing jokes on people, getting into fights in the neighborhood. When Pac and I would get there, we would end up catching the aftermath of Kenny Black. If they were after him, now they were after all three of us. Kenny would just be laughing, and me and Pac would be pissed the fuck off. What it did do is make us pretty good at fighting and sticking together.

A lot of times, I just got to hang out and play with all my cousins up in the Bronx, in the Leland Projects. One vivid memory was a weekend when Pac was running around playing with some younger kids, and I was with all the older cousins, piled in the bedroom watching TV. We were in the bedroom and Bill started talking about some pot. I was pretty innocent and naïve when it came to drugs; the only drug I kinda knew something about was heroin, and there was no way I was fucking with that. So we're in the room, Billy, Kenny, Scott, Jamala, I think even Greg was in there. One of them pulled out a little nickel bag, a little yellow envelope of weed and said, "Mutulu, you ever smoked weed?"

I'm like, "Nah, nah, not really." I was too young to even be interested. Well, somebody rolled a joint and said, "Yo, try it! Try it! Weed don't hurt you." Now, mind you, I didn't know how to smoke anything, let alone marijuana. I was trying to smoke it, and they knew I was faking, 'cause I wasn't coughing much. I inhaled a little bit, but I didn't really get high. And they were like, "How you feel?" I said I felt alright. And they showed me the envelope. "You see that on the envelope? That means there's angel dust in it." Everybody in the room started laughing. Meanwhile, I'm having an anxiety attack. I didn't fuck with drugs, but I was smart enough to know what angel dust was: PCP. I was mad at them for a long time, until I realized that they were just fucking with me. It's par for the course where they were growing up, but I didn't want to fuck with any of that shit.

The thing about being with my dad and his people is they just included us, the kids, in so much of their adult world. And I wanted to grow up like them. They didn't fuck with heroin, but they did smoke weed. Plus, I didn't realize this at the time, they did fuck with other drugs recreationally. Perhaps they thought heroin wasn't a drug that could be used recreationally. I don't know. I was too young to understand where they drew the line. I wanted to be like my dad and his friends, and I was also a young and impressionable kid who looked up to his older, badass cousins. There's a conflict here, for sure, that maybe only makes sense in the mind of a kid. At the end of the day, I was too freaked out to enjoy that hit of weed, but I would come to enjoy it later on in life.

CHAPTER 5

THE OLD HOMEPLACE

Besides spending time with my dad's family, I spent plenty of time going back down South to visit Aunt Jo and Uncle Gene. I went back every summer, starting when I was seven. My parents would both be working, so I just traveled down by myself by bus, on either Greyhound or Trailways, whichever had the best price. My mother or my grandmother would take me to Port Authority and pin a note on my coat for everyone to see. The note had all the pertinent information: my name, where I was going, and I think my mother's number and Aunt Joanna's number. It was a whole routine. We would get there early so everyone could take a look at the bus and so that I could get the closest seat to the bus driver. I put my stuff in the seat and then we'd go back outside and wait for the bus driver. My mother would introduce me to the driver, let him know where I was going, where I was going to be sitting, and I was told to listen to the bus driver. Most of them were cool and friendly. Looking back on it, I still can't believe that as an eight-year-old I was allowed to travel all that way all by myself.

I felt like I was a cool little kid. I would get to know the bus drivers, ask how things worked, how the controls worked on the bus. I think those little friendships made the eleven-hour trip more enjoyable and less dull and lonely. At the rest stops, you're allowed to get off the bus. Those were the times or situations where, if I wasn't careful, something bad could've happened. You could always kind of tell the quality of the bus driver at these rest stops, because some of them would take special care to know where I was and where I was going. In the midst of taking their own break, they would still try to look out for me. A lot of them grew to like me because I was sort of responsible, and I'd be the first one at the door waiting to re-board and they'd be happy to see me. Like, *alright, the kid listens.*

My grandmother would put food together for me for my trip. She would make some of her famous traveling sandwiches, which were fairly simple: She would toast some bread, put mayonnaise on one side, mustard on the other, and put a piece of American cheese on the toasted bread. Then she fried up some bologna. Once the bologna bubbled and got a little char on it, then she put the hot bologna right on top of the American cheese, which made it melt as she squished it with the other slice of bread. Once she squished it—which is very important—she sliced it in half diagonally and wrapped it in foil while it was still hot. By the time I unwrapped one, three or four hours into the trip, it was perfectly melted, it was moist, and almost better than a hamburger, let me tell you. She always packed four or five of those and a little of everything: a thermos with juice or Kool-Aid, a banana, an orange, some cashews—my grandmother and I both love cashews—and a piece of sweet potato pie or a Twinkie or something sweet. The thought was, to try to give me whatever possible food I would want, so I wouldn't venture out on those rest stops trying to buy food with the little money I had. It worked for the most part, but my curiosity would still make me go out.

I would take a few naps in between the snacking and the rest stops, and before I knew it, I was in Fayetteville, North Carolina. I'd get off the bus into the loving arms of my Aunt Joanna and Uncle Gene. I was still *very* attached to Aunt Joanna and Uncle Gene. Everyone around would always say that they spoiled me. They were the ones who would get me a new bike every year I came down. I wanted walkie-talkies, they got me walkie-talkies. I don't know who I was talking to, but they got them for me. My Uncle Gene would show me his rifle and how to use it and we would have target practice right off the porch, shooting at cans or a tree heading into the woods.

I was probably only down there three weeks or a month, but it felt like the whole summer. Even as a little kid, the difference in pace between New York City and the South was very noticeable. I loved being with my Aunt Joanna and Uncle Gene, but a shorty got bored with the South. I always missed them when I left, but I was always more than ready to go back to the bustle of New York when it was time to head home.

Besides my solo summers down South with my Aunt Joanna and Uncle Gene, I also went on family trips to Fayetteville, North Carolina. On these trips it would be Grandmother, her husband at the time, Reverend Holmes, my mother, my Aunt Mona, my cousin Jermaine, and sometimes my cousin Gretchen. My grandmother always had big cars—big Impalas or a Plymouth—and Reverend Holmes always had Cadillacs. There was always enough space for everyone to go if they wanted to, or if their mother made them. (My other two uncles wouldn't always come, but they eventually moved down there.) It was the same preparation ritual as when I would go by myself, but a whole lot more sandwiches, snacks, and road food. Grandmother would also fry some chicken, and we'd eat cold fried chicken on the way down. At a certain point, my grandmother actually bought a camper. She would pull it all the way down South with all of us and park it on the old family land where she planned to build a home. My grandmother actually saved the main part of our family's land from being sold after owning it since emancipation. She was proud, and we were proud of her for having the wherewithal and the ability to save it for future generations. She began tearing down the old family place and was planning to build a new one.

My great-grandparents had a huge house on this property, which spanned both sides of the freeway. I don't know what year it was built, but I know that my great-grandfather built it himself. There was a well on the property and the house was *huge*, with a tin roof. It had a raised porch and six bedrooms. They had thirteen kids so they needed the room! It wasn't the first McDaniel homeplace, which was a log cabin eight miles down the road. By the time my grandmother got the land, it had been split between various generations and family members. The piece my grandmother ended up owning had been passed to one of my great-grandmother's brothers, my Uncle David. He lived in it, but he had become an alcoholic. He would drink a bottle and just throw it out the window until there were huge piles of bottles all outside the house. There was no running water and the house was totally dilapidated. The property taxes were in arrears. My grandmother didn't actually inherit the property; she had to buy it back from the state after it was seized over the unpaid taxes. She got a bulldozer to haul all the glass out of the backyard so she could rebuild.

I also spent time with my Aunt Jean, my mother's older sister. Aunt Jean was always a real class act. She wasn't around a lot, because she had gotten married to Uncle Johnnie and had my oldest first cousin, Gretchen, who was born two years after me. Aunt Jean always had good energy. She always made me laugh. We still love the fact that she called everyone "darling," but with the old-time, mid-Atlantic, Hollywood accent from the 1940s. She was also a nurse like my grandmother, so she worked a lot.

My Uncle Johnnie was one of the coolest white dudes I ever met. He was very even-tempered, soft-spoken. He had his hobbies, like, he always kept an aquarium. He had his reel-to-reel tape recorder, with which I was fascinated. Jogging was big at the time, and he liked to jog. He and Jean seemed to have a peaceful life together. I would go spend the night with them at their first place together in Brooklyn. I liked going to their house because I got to play with my cousin Gretchen and they had the biggest dog in the world, a Great Dane named Sheba. She was the biggest dog I had ever seen. Picture this: my Uncle Johnnie had a little orange Volkswagen Karmann Ghia convertible, which we all piled into. You've got this mixed couple, with this big-ass dog, with two kids basically tucked under the dog, on our way from Queens to Brooklyn. We must've looked hilarious.

I would get to their house and Gretchen and I would make grilled cheese in her little Easy-Bake Oven. It was always fun.

As I got older, I'd still spend the weekend at their house. Aunt Jean was moving up the ladder. She was becoming a registered nurse. They had moved from Brooklyn to East Twenty-Third and Second Avenue in Manhattan, into a big building called The Plaza. Uncle Johnnie had gone from working at an A&P to becoming a corrections officer. As a matter of fact, my Aunt Jean was working so much and never really put a lot of effort into cooking. For our meals, she would send us across the street to McDonald's. Yes, breakfast, lunch, and sometimes dinner. Needless to say, I enjoyed this very much. For a kid my age, I was living a fantasy. And my cool-ass Uncle Johnnie took me to my first professional basketball game. I think it was the Knicks against the Nets. I really enjoyed hanging out with them, and the older I got, the more I appreciated their relationship. They're a mixed couple who got together in the '60s. In fact, they got together in high school. I'd learn later on that my Uncle Johnnie and my father knew each other. When my father was dating my mother, Uncle Johnnie was dating Aunt Jean. They would wait together on my grandmother's couch for the girls to come downstairs. Uncle Johnnie and I wouldn't talk about Mutulu much, and he also never stopped calling him Jeral, but he asked about him from time to time. I thought it was just in a general, how's your father, how's your parents type thing. But they actually did know each other and had their own history. So few family members on my mother's side acknowledged him that it was comforting to have someone ask about my father, from love. As I write this, they have been married more than fifty years. I admire them as a family and as people.

For a long time after my mother took me back from my father, it's fair to say that I had a little 'tude. I honestly missed my father, Afeni, Pac, Sekyiwa and his world. I missed the Lesanes, my cousins. I liked my father's friends. One day, when I was around eight, I marched out and told my mother that I was going to back to live with my father. I don't know what in particular set me off, but it was definitely a "fuck this shit over here" moment. I stomped out and told my mom that I was leaving. And she said, "You want to go back and live with those people who feed you seeds? What did they make you eat last time when you got sick over there? Lemon and orange peels? And using Vitamin E as lotion?" She thought all that shit was weird, but she let me go back—*if* I left *everything* she'd bought me in *her* house. She had me fucked up right there, because she bought me nearly everything of any use. I was, like, "Um, Mommy, can I take my clothes?" "Yeah, you can get a couple sets of clothes," she said. "But no toys, no books." I ended up leaving. My mother will be quick to kick a nigga out. But let her tell it, I returned within a week and a half.

One weekend when I was with my father, we went into the office. I was around eleven, and I heard the people outside playing music. I knew it was *my* music: hip hop. My father saw me light up and said, "You like that, don't you?" I already knew hip hop was my thing. Over in Queens, there was a growing group of artists that would come to make their mark on the craft: Run-DMC, Eric B. & Rakim, Chuck D from Public Enemy . . . I could go on. I would go to parks and check out the competition while I worked on my rhymes and my delivery. I would listen to the music they were making with wonder, delight, enthusiasm. I could mostly rhyme, and I was teaching myself how to write. Music has patterns, so you start to recognize those patterns and then build on them in your own way. I was learning the rudimentary skills that would, eventually, become songwriting. I was learning that shit in the streets, by watching my generation create. I was soaking up game and building my skills. I learned how to pop and lock. I couldn't break and do all the acrobatic moves, but I had—shit, I *have*—hella rhythm. I was learning how to keep the audience entertained. My parents didn't encourage it—but they didn't *discourage* it, either.

The truth is it wouldn't have mattered, because they couldn't have stopped me anyway! Let me tell it: It was mine, from my people.

Junior high meant a ton of new adjustments for me. My mom and I were able to move out of the projects in Redfern, but don't get it twisted: It was still a humble, hardworking life. We literally moved from one project to another, into the Rochdale Village Projects in Southside Jamaica, closer to where my grandmother lived. Still, it was definitely a move up. Queens was bustling with people on the grind, and my generation was creating a cultural shift in our urban centers; hip hop was vibrant and alive while the government was completely disinvested in the very communities the music spoke to. My mother, like most people in her generation, was not impressed with hip hop's potential. To be fair, it wasn't for her, anyway; it was for us, by us. But music was my magic, so I would come to her, genuinely enthralled with a piece of music I just knew would excite her—usually it would be a disco or soul record. *Mommy, listen to this!* And she'd just be like, *Yes, Maurice*. Deadpan. We did share one moment though. When we moved into Rochdale, my mom was so happy. She put on the 8th Wonder of the World, Stevie Wonder's *Songs in the Key of Life* and danced around the apartment for hours in sheer joy, with no furniture, just the record player on the floor.

I took band that year. The music teacher assigned me the baritone horn. Do you know how big that instrument is? I would lug that enormous shit all through Queens. I was happy to be in the brass section, though, and it didn't matter too much to me at the time how ridiculous it was to assign a kid my size an instrument so damn big. At the same time, I was thinking about my look, which in the late '70s was essentially my statement to the world: my shell-toe Adidas and a gold nameplate I'd wanted for as long as I could remember. Meanwhile, my mom was focused on things that were more tangible for her: my education, my safety, my future.

When I was in sixth grade, living in Rochdale Village, my father took me and Pac clothes shopping at the beginning of the school year. I was eleven and Pac must've been seven. It was a weekend with my dad, and we went shopping at some clothing store in Harlem. I was excited, because I knew my pops would hook me up with whatever I really wanted to get. My mom, on the other hand, was more practical, less trendy. I was also glad to be going with Pac so I could help him pick out some cool stuff like me. It was a nice day and it felt good being with just the guys. We had to cross a busy Harlem street together to get to the store. My father said, "Mutulu, look out for your brother. Grab your brother's hand, hold your brother's hand." I quickly grabbed Pac's hand tight, because there was such a seriousness when my Pops asked me to.

We hurried across the street together and when we got into the store, I saw the very shoe that I wanted—low top, blue suede Pumas with the gray stripe. My father asked for my size and asked for Pac's. The guy came back, but they only had my size. And Pac was pissed. Little dude was stomping around the store. "I want the ones you got! I want the ones you got!" I said, "I know, but they just don't have them. They're out." The guy saw Pac was upset and offered up a shell-toe Adidas shoe as an option. And actually, the Adidas was a newer style than the Puma. This is around 1978. I tried to convince him, "Naw, Pac, this is the new, new shit." But being younger, he just wasn't familiar. He still wanted that Puma like me. Honestly, I couldn't blame him, it looked real good on my foot. The suede was smooth and soft and they were pretty fresh. But he ended up getting the Adidas, because that was the next best option.

We went to the counter to pay, and my father pulled out a big ol' knot of money. He could barely hold it in one hand. I was impressed because I had never actually seen that much money at one time. We got the shoes and left, and I made sure to hold Pac's hand this time, just like my father had told me. I was going to try to never forget it. It may sound corny, but it meant something. It meant I'm supposed to look out for my brother all around. I was the big brother. Between making sure he had the right kicks and holding his hand across a busy street, that crystallized in my head in that moment. I was always supposed to look out for my little brother.

Now, those very same shoes caused me a little problem as soon as I started school. I was in the bathroom, and a kid complimented my new sneakers. He stared at 'em for too long and in a way that made it uncomfortable. I began to realize that this wasn't just a compliment.

He was sizing me up. He was bigger than me. I'm thinking, great, dude's gonna try to rob me for my brand-new sneakers. And then a switch flipped in me and I went into fight mode. I started making a scene, in a way to make myself bigger to show him I would meet him at his size. I threw the soap container against the wall and started kicking the bathroom door. I was like, "Okay, nigga, okay." Now, I wouldn't say that word in my mother's home, but I *would* use it at school. I started getting loud, hoping to attract attention. I guess dude figured out it wasn't gonna be an easy lick, so he stopped and went on his way. IS 72 in Queens on New York Boulevard was notorious for being hard as fuck, and I didn't get robbed that day! It was a fucking great day.

I was twelve years old when hip hop was really born for me. I was listening to "King Tim III (Personality Jock)." This record was just before Sugar Hill and Flash and the Furious 5. We're talking the early days. I'd actually heard *about* the song before I ever heard the song on the radio. When I finally did, I was so happy to get to know the record that I'd been hearing about. Now, imagine this: It's the age of the boom box. Up to this point, I'd been hearing rap in the streets, either people performing or, more frequently, playing early raps on their boom boxes. I'm not talking about professional recordings. I'm talking about people playing tapes that they would record in the club, of the DJs mixing the disco breaks with vocals. People would literally bring their boom box to the club and record the DJ and then play these recordings in the streets, on the bus, blasting from their cars.

I was too young to go to the club, so I heard the early formulations of hip hop—this rudimentary and developing art of mixing, which would later become the backbone of hip hop production—as a young kid in a very public and ultimately communal setting. When I heard "King Tim III," I was elated. I was finally up on the new shit. And truth is, I was in on the thing before it *was* a thing, and the reason I was so happy was that this professionally produced record on the radio confirmed that *my* thing was gonna be *the* thing. And what a thing it would become!

Hip hop music was so new, so rare at this time, that I had to work to get my hands on rap. Literally, I was on the constant hunt for someone who had a tape so I could get a dub of it, which was a difficult thing to negotiate at the time. People didn't just hand over their recordings or dub their shit for you unless you were legit friends. So I would try to go to places where I could hear rap to make my own tapes. I learned that hip hop shows were being held in parks and school playgrounds. Up in the Bronx, they were tapping into electric poles to get power for the sound systems. When I heard that there was going to be a hip hop show in my neighborhood on the basketball courts at 150th Street, I was amped. There was no way I was not going to be there. I was hearing about it from everybody in the neighborhood, and I knew everybody else was going. So I was like, *Shiiiiit, I'll be damned if I'm not gonna be there. That's my shit!*

My moms, on the other hand, didn't give a fuck. I thought, *My moms is not into hip hop at all so she's not going to be aware of it, so it'd be cool if I just went. How would she even know?* I didn't bother asking her. The problem was, the party was so turnt up that it fucked up traffic in the whole neighborhood *and* brought a whole bunch of different people to the neighborhood, which nobody could ignore. Day of, I just went. It felt good to be at a real, authentic hip hop show in the park, hearing live scratching through the subwoofers and speakers on both sides of the park. It was like ear candy. Mind you, I knew I wasn't supposed to be there. I knew I didn't ask for permission. But whatever happened after this, I knew I'd made it there. I felt so happy, and so cool. Most of the people were older than me, but there were also people younger than me. It really was the whole neighborhood—except for my responsible-ass mother.

So I'm chilling at the park, listening to the music, kicking it with my homies, checking out the girls. I was happy that no fights or no beef jumped off where they would have to shut it down. It seemed like everyone was cool. And through the bass and through the scratches, I hear a familiar frequency. And that frequency was saying: "Mauriiice!" I'm standing with the homies thinking to myself, *Is that my mom?* I'm hoping that I didn't hear what I thought I heard. But here it comes again: "Mauriiiice!" *Oh shit, that is her. Of course, she knows I love this shit. She knows I'm gonna be here. The whole neighborhood is here.* But I stayed quiet. I figured there were so many people she would never find me, and I could just ignore it until she went back home.

But again: "Mauriiiice!" She would not stop. She wouldn't even stop and look a little. She would just repetitively yell, "Mauriiiiice!"

Julio said, "Yo, that's your moms, yo. Ain't that your moms?" There was fast approaching an imminent embarrassment. To what degree was up to me. I turned back and looked and saw my mother's broad shoulders and curly perm heading straight for the park. I recognized her no-bullshit walk. I knew that stride. I knew I was in trouble. So what I decided to do was limit the damage and go to her before she got fully in the park and everybody heard her. I didn't even say goodbye to my homies. I just said, "Oh, shit," and ran. I was running towards her, and I saw her arms straight down and her two fists balled up, and when she saw me her eyes popped open and with a deep growl in her voice, she said, "Get over here!"

I swear I thought she was going to hit me in front of everybody, but she didn't. My mother said, "Who do you think you are?" And I was not about to respond. We turned around and headed back home, which was like four blocks away. I was in trouble, of course, for not letting my mother know where I was. I do not recall the extent of that particular punishment, but it was likely me being grounded. I was young, and I was chasing hip hop. To be pinned down at the house was the most painful thing imaginable.

I thought I was holding my own in Queens, but later in junior high, my mother decided to send me to school back down in North Carolina. Along with my grandmother and Reverend Holmes, my new grandfather, my Aunt Mona and Uncle Harold moved down there, and my Uncle Joey was there for a little bit, too. My Aunt Mona was a few years older than me and had also spent her formative years in Queens, so she also grew up in the hip hop era. She was very pretty, but a little hardcore. I always thought that she was too pretty to be that hardcore, to be honest with you. She and I both had a love for music. She would come up to me randomly, trying to sing these classic R&B and love songs, like "Always and Forever." I listened to her because she was my older aunt, and I had a love for music, too. I got her in that way.

She was getting into rapping, but I was still on the breakdance tip. Neither one of us liked being down South and going to school down South. We were always looking for something to do to fill the void. One day, she and her friends were going to the county fair. Without much going on in North Carolina, that sounded like a fun thing to do. Everybody I knew was going anyway, but I knew Grandmother wasn't going to let me go by myself. About four of Aunt Mona's girlfriends came by, they scooped us up and we went to the fair. I remember her friends being real cool and not minding hanging out with a little dude. When we got to the fair, I was so happy and excited: I hadn't heard music and concert sounds for quite a while. I started doing my thing as soon as we got close to the music. I just started dancing. I didn't care who was watching, I was feeling it too good. Mona's friends started watching me. "Ah, look at him! He's good! He's so cute." And that really gassed my head up. I started dancing a little harder. Now I had a little audience. I danced long enough to where I didn't get too tired to make a mistake. When I stopped, they started clapping. And in typical Mona fashion, she was like, "Yeah, yeah, that's my nephew." But her tone didn't exactly make it sound like a compliment.

We went out together again. She had been into rapping for a while now and was going to try her hand at a live performance. Even though I was younger, she knew I was into all that shit, and pretty good. This time, we were going to a day party at a club on Fort Bragg Army Base. I thought this was cool, because I might have a chance to get on the mic myself, maybe even rock the show with my auntie. And I hadn't really been able to hang out at any of the clubs on Fort Bragg yet. I mean, I was in junior high, but still.

Down there, it wasn't that hard for her to get a show. First of all, she was from New York and second, she was cute. It wasn't that big of a crowd that day, but it was decent. People were chilling, walking around with drinks, the vibe was good. Then it came time for Mona to get on stage. I had never really heard her rap and do a full song, but I was hopeful that she was going to kill it. She got on stage and when the music started, she started to rap.

She sounded . . . okay. But she wasn't getting the response from the audience that she wanted. She didn't wait too long before she started letting the audience have it. "What's the matter with y'all? Get on your feet! Why you ain't dancing? You must not be used to this real shit." Things took a turn fast. I felt bad for her, and I was ready to go. I don't remember staying long after, but that experience taught me a lot. It taught me about performing live, preparation, likability, and showmanship. No audience is going to like you berating them, and they'll always outnumber you, so your best bet is to get them on your side.

The other one in the house was Harold, and our job was to help Grandmother. In the summers though, I had my cousin Jermaine, Uncle Joey's son. He and I would work the land together and we got tight; he was like a little brother to me. Besides all the work in the field, Grandmother still had land that needed to be cleared. That meant us chopping wood. I was cutting down big-ass trees with a two-man saw at thirteen. We had to cut down wood to clear the land, and we used the wood for the fireplace for heat in the wintertime. There were so many chores that I didn't have a lot of fun time. I had a few friends—Derek and Greg across the street—but not many. One of the ways that I made friends was by playing basketball. I had already asked my grandmother if I could join this basketball tournament. I busted my ass all week with the goal of being able to go on Saturday. Tryouts were on the weekends, so I knew I had a good shot. Saturday came and I made sure to do my chores in the house first. Then I hit her: "Grandmother, can I go try out for this basketball tournament?" All she said was, "No. Go out there and cut some wood." And of course,

I started pleading my case: "Grandmother, you said I could go. I did all my chores. I did everything." And she said, "Boy, did you hear what I said?" I stomped out the house, mad as fuck, slamming the screen door on my way out. Then she said, "Boy, keep on slamming my doors, hear?"

I go off stomping into the woods, where Harold was already cutting wood. I bust through the bushes and small trees, mad as fuck. He could tell. Because I was already angry, I guess he chose to fuck with me. He was about to start the chainsaw and I just stood there while he started it. It was taking a few pulls, so I drifted off for a second in my anger. When he finally got it and the engine started, it startled me. Seeing that I was startled, he started racing the chainsaw engine and walking towards me slowly, with the chainsaw pointed right to my stomach. I guess he was trying to play the madman, coming at me with the chainsaw, with a crazy look on his face. I don't know if he was trying to be funny or just terrify me, but I was mad as fuck and showed no reaction. Frankly, I was tired of his shit, and I was tired of my grandmother's shit.

So, Harold kept racing the engine and approaching me with the chainsaw. I still didn't move. He got close enough to where the chainsaw caught on to the hoodie that I was wearing, and it just rolled up my face. I felt it hit my forehead, and I fell back to the ground. Everything went silent and still. Next thing you know, I hear Harold's voice, "Oh, shit, Maury, I'm sorry." I could see out of one eye, but I knew there was blood in my other eye. I guess I was in shock; I don't remember feeling any pain. Harold just kept apologizing, but I don't think he was actually sorry; I think he was just scared about what would happen and what I'd say when the rest of the family found out. Harold picked me up and carried me to the back of the house. He went and got Grandmother and she grabbed some towels and rags to make a compress. She put it on my eye and told me to hold it there. Then she got her coat and keys and we rushed to the hospital.

One of the blessings for me was that my grandmother was a nurse and she knew what to do. When we got to the hospital and they walked me in, I bypassed the waiting room and they brought me straight to the back. I'll never forget the reaction of the people in the waiting area. They recoiled. There were gasps, a few children's screams, a couple of *oh my gods.* I couldn't see them all, but people where actually moving, backing up away from me. They took me to the back, cleaned me up from all the blood, and they had me lying on the hospital bed for quite a while. I had received a few shots for pain, so it didn't hurt as much anymore, and I had to go to the restroom pretty bad. Unfortunately, that also gave me the opportunity to look in the bathroom mirror. Apparently, the chainsaw had cut me a bit on my upper lip, right on my left eyelid, and the top of my eyebrow. It was all opened up. My face was literally hanging down, like the incredible melting man, and I had a big gash on my forehead.

When the doctors finally got there they discovered there was a piece of bone chipped from my brow. They stitched me up and I ended up with thirteen stitches in my face. I would be a real Scarface. I didn't stay overnight, but they gave me this huge, huge patch for my eye and told me to use cocoa butter for the scar. But before I was discharged, the doctor told me how lucky I was. How fortunate I was. I mean, how thin are your eyelids? That's how close I was to losing my eye. I had stitches right on my eyelid. After he told me how lucky I was, he told me to be careful and sent me home. *Sure, dude, I'll try not to let my weirdo uncle torture me.*

I got a few days off, less than a week, but I had to prepare myself for going back to school with this big crazy-looking injury. I remember thinking, *That's it. No more girls for me. Not while I'm walking around looking like Black Frankenstein.* To my surprise, it had the complete opposite effect: People were compassionate. Girls had pity on me and wanted to help me, take care of me. I did appreciate it, especially being in a place where I didn't want to be. I didn't get to play basketball that year, but I did get to keep my eye.

CHAPTER 6

HIP HOP YOU DON'T STOP

After finishing my two-year stint in North Carolina for seventh and eighth grade, I came back to New York for ninth grade. I was excited that my mom decided to bring me back home to start high school in New York. And in Manhattan, no less! My mother used my aunt's address on East Twenty-Third Street so that I could go to IS 104, which had students of all nationalities, ethnicities, and backgrounds. I didn't see my pops much that year. And, yeah, I totally got why. Even so, I loved that time of my life. I loved going to school in Manhattan, even though the commute was a hump. I loved being in the city. I felt grown, at thirteen years old, and I loved being responsible for myself. By the time I got out of the subway in Manhattan, I was surrounded by everyone, from all walks of life, from all backgrounds, speaking different languages. Queens is diverse demographically, but I felt like Manhattan seemed more diverse in thought and style. Queens had the hustle, Manhattan had the bustle.

In Queens, I would get my Jamaican beef patties with coco bread before school. My spot was at the corner of Jamaica Avenue and Sutphin Boulevard, right next to the Q40 bus stop. Beef patties are delicious, heaven-sent meals for a young boy. They have this orangey, golden, crispy, flakey crust on the outside, and then you have the Jamaican ground beef with all the Jamaican spices on the inside. They have chicken ones and veggie ones, too, and sometimes people place them in the middle of some nice warm, hot coco bread made with coconut so it's light and fluffy, almost like brioche. I mean, the beef patty by itself is exquisite, but the coco bread makes it portable, so all the flaky parts of the crust stay in the bread as you eat it. I would get it with a Kola Champagne, a Jamaican soda. The smell of those Jamaican patties cooking was like a pied piper. Even if I wasn't hungry, if I smelled one, I wanted one. But sometimes, the line was too long and the bus was there. On those days, I'd get a fresh, hot bagel from my spot in Manhattan, on the corner of First and Twenty-Eighth. As soon as you hit the block, you could smell them baking. It just hit you in the face. There'd be a long line, but I could always get my order in: either a plain or onion bagel, with butter and cream cheese.

This would turn out to be my favorite year of high school: I had been waiting to get back to New York. I'd always considered New York my home, no matter how long I was in North Carolina. I guess because I was so open and happy to be there, I acquired a lot of friends quickly. My first friend was Monique. She was the daughter of Pat, who was friends with my mom and Aunt Jean. They sent me to school there with a mandate to look out for her, and I took being her "bodyguard" seriously. Then there was Leo, who brought me back into my hip hop game. We traded mixtapes that he brought from Uptown and the Bronx. Freya was my girlfriend. Full of pubescent hormones, you'd better believe we humped in every corner of that school. And then there was my Puerto Rican crew: Jolie, Jessica, and Georgie. The four of us had a couple of classes together, so we became tight, always sitting in the back of the classroom. Jolie and Jessica were beautiful, and Georgie was hilarious. He would look at me and say "Yo!" while putting his hands on his knee and then dramatically stretching his arms out. As in, "knee-grow." And I'd say, "Whatchu want?" and then I'd pretend to spit. As in, Spic. We would fuck with each other, laughing the whole time.

But my main man was Perone. He was one of the first people I met when I got to the school. We met on the basketball court, like a lot of young Black boys do. Perone was tall, even in the ninth grade, at almost six feet, brown-skinned with curly hair. His hair was like a

Latino person's hair. It made sense, as I would later find out he was half Cuban. He was pretty good at basketball, one of the best in the school if not *the* best. I had a solid game myself, so we made a pretty good duo. From the first day we played together, we were inseparable.

He and I ended up becoming very popular in school. We chased girls together. We ended up playing together on the school basketball team. He lived in Harlem on 129th and Convent Avenue. We were so tight, he would come to Queens to spend the weekend with me, and I would go to Harlem and hang out with him. We ultimately started a rap duo together, my first rap group called the High Power Two. Rap was more my thing than his, but everybody loved the music and culture at the time, so he was game to try to rap with me. There was an upcoming school talent show, and I felt it was time for me to test my skills. I felt I was ready, and it would be my first time on stage. P and I chose a piece of music and started working on our routine for the show. I can't remember the track we chose, but we did write original rhymes. It was two verses, and we each wrote our own, held together with a hook that I wrote. Even at that point, I was aware of showmanship, stage presence, and the basics of songwriting.

First, we had to pick our outfits, which was very important. We were gonna wear sharkskin slacks and a mock neck, which was very popular at the time. I wore gray on gray, and I think Perone wore blue sharkskins and a black mock neck. For footwear, I was rocking shell-toe Adidas—you know Queens—and Perone was wearing Bally's loafers.

Our stage entry was supposed to be a little choreographed. They were gonna give us both our own microphones and we were going to enter the stage from opposite ends, then meet in the middle, face the audience, and start the song. Real simple, fucking Perone. The day of the show, I'm like, "Yo, P, you ready?" He goes, "Hell yeah, I'm ready." Perfect. So he gets to the other side of the stage, we each have our microphones, the music is cued, and we're about to go. I looked at him from across the stage and he gave me the sign like he was good to go. The music came on and we began our approach to center stage.

We'd also coordinated a little walk that we were supposed to do as we approached. The music dropped and I'm *excited.* I know my shit and I can't wait to get out there. I'm following the routine, I'm doing the walk, I'm excited, smiling, looking at Perone.

We're almost at center stage and Perone just folded like a cheap suit. I think he might've gotten one or two words out on the approach, but then he turned around and fucking booked it offstage. I froze. I couldn't believe he left me stranded out there. I wasn't an experienced enough performer at the time to know what to do. I was frozen for a minute and then managed to say, "Welp, sorry, y'all," and walked offstage. When I got to him backstage, I gave him the business. I talked all kinds of shit to him: "Dude, you made us look stupid out there. What the fuck?" But he didn't get it. He didn't understand why I was so upset. "Come on, Mo, fuck that shit." What I learned is that I was taking it way more serious than he was—and not everybody can do it. Me and Perone were still cool, though, even though I was *quite* pissed. Turns out just entering the talent show raised my stock at school.

Another good thing about that school: I had greater access to the emerging hip hop scene. After school, I would literally see kids dancing on cars, just because. We just loved hip hop *that much.* And when I would spend those weekends over at Perone's house, I learned that his neighborhood was another bastion of hip hop. LA Sunshine from the group the Treacherous Three lived in his building. Besides the group coming to his building to visit Sunshine, we ended up playing with their DJ, DJ Easy Lee, at the basketball court in his neighborhood. For a young hip hoppa, I was literally meeting my idols.

Perone and I would also kick it in the summertime. Once he got his girlfriend's car—and his girlfriend had some money, so it was a white Jaguar—and drove it all the way to Queens to kick it with me. He swooped me up and blew my mind. I'm like, "Nigga, did you steal this? I mean, P, you're gonna get in trouble. Did you steal this car? My mom's literally working for 911, my pops is hot as hell on the streets, and my uncle Joey is an addict who's robbing banks. So the last thing

I need is a hot car pulled up to my house." He assured me that it was all legit.

So I hopped in and we burnt up like a tank of gas. We went all the way Uptown, came back, rolled around Queens. And of course, I wanted people in my neighborhood to see me in this car. The best way to do that is to hit up the Bully—Rockaway Boulevard. I told P to pull up in front of the liquor store, the main liquor store in the middle of everything. I hop out, I go inside, and when I came out the store, I hear somebody calling me. And they sounded *angry*. "Maurice! Ay, Maurice!" I listened a little closer. That angry man was my Uncle Joey. He was on the other side of the Bully and saw us when we pulled up. "Maurice! Get over here!" I was just happy to see him, because he was still my favorite uncle. He asked, "What'chu doin' in the car? Where'd you get that car?" I told him it was my homeboy Perone's car. But Uncle Joey was pissed off, and he wasn't easily convinced. He thought for sure I'd stolen it. So I had to call P over and introduce him to my uncle, so that we could assure him that the car was, indeed, legit. Although once he believed that it was Perone's, he had a few questions for him: "What are you, a pimp?" We all laughed at that. It felt good knowing Uncle Joey was trying to make sure that I wasn't getting into trouble.

Now, it wasn't just Perone I was hanging with. The Reverse Oreo was this guy Breeze, me, and Julio—I was the chocolate in the middle. The three of us were notoriously tight, but Breeze and I had that hip hop connection. We eventually became a breakdance duo. We didn't really have a name; it was just Mogie and Breeze. I have long arms, so my specialty was poppin' and wavin' and moves up top. We both had good footwork and our sliding was top-notch. Breeze had this one move as a crowd-pleaser where I would pop over to him, touch him, and he would vibrate like a beeper.

We would listen to hip hop and dance in his grandmother Nana's basement, which was right up the street from me, on the next block. We put together a couple of short, rudimentary routines. And every summer, there would be block-party days. There would be several on the same day, and a few later on during the week. It was very seldom our block, but blocks all around us would have block parties. It was cool because we would know a few people on each block. And me and Breeze would hit it. Whatever dance battle was in sight, we would pull up. We would let dudes get their little shit off, and then me and Breeze would bust in at the same time with our little routine. I'm very proud to say that we didn't suck. We would be rockin' from late afternoon 'til, like, midnight, ending up far as fuck out of our own neighborhood. Our clothes would be drenched, T-shirts would be lost, sneakers all scuffed up, but we were having the time of our lives.

Breeze also had a cousin named Big Breeze who lived out on Long Island, and Big Breeze was an actual, real-live DJ. He would DJ at various parties throughout Long Island. He used to drive a big blue van with a concert speaker in that motherfucker. Because I was such a hip hop head and all into my rappin', I *loved* hanging out with Big Breeze. He would invite me to come kick it with him in Long Island, when he would DJ at Wyandanch Day in Wyandanch Park. We called it Wine Dance, and it was an annual festival in the park that was cool because it was a very family-oriented thing. All of Breeze's sisters, and sometimes his mom, would come, and they'd let me tag along. Me and Breeze would get to ride around with Big Breeze in his van all around Long Island, bumping Big Breeze's current, fresh mixes. It was hip hop heaven. Big Breeze knew all the rappers on the island, including Rakim; one of Breeze's sisters, Rhonda, actually dated Rakim. There would always be a buzz on the block when The R came through. He was a real quiet brother, but his presence was felt. Breeze and I also rapped together, but as a duo we were better dancers than rappers.

Me, Julio, and Breeze loved each other hard, like brothers. We would have our different arguments and make up. And the next day we'd get into another argument. Breeze and Julio became particularly tight. They ended up spending more time together, especially because they went to a different high school than I did. Plus I was gone for stretches of time, either visiting down South or with my dear old dad on weekends and holidays. One day, Julio and Breeze got into a particularly bad fight. The argument started at Nana's house and then overflowed out into the street. I had just come from down the block, so I didn't really know what they were arguing about. But both of them were arguing, right in the middle of the street, getting into each other's face. They both were literally turning red.

Next thing I know, Breeze turned around and rushed back inside. While I had a moment, I tried to calm Ju (pronounced "who") down and ask him what the fucking deal was. I got no clear answer. All I got was, "Naw, fuck that, Mo. Fuck that. Fuck Breeze. I don't know who the fuck he thinks he is. Maybe them weights got to his head." Next thing you know, Breeze comes rushing back outside, yelling, "What'd you say?" And then he pulled a little chrome revolver and pointed it right at Ju's forehead. I was shocked as fuck, 'cause I didn't even see it or see where it came from. I didn't even know that Breeze had a gun.

I quickly ran behind Breeze and grabbed both of his arms. "Breeze, don't do it. You're gonna regret it. That's your brother, nigga!" I yelled while I tried to push his arms down. Breeze was a Leo like me, so I kinda understood his temper. I was honestly scared of him cocking the gun. If he cocked it, I knew we were in trouble. Luckily, he never did. I got him to put the gun down, and everybody kind of calmed down because of the shock of the gun just being there. Julio stomped off mad. I couldn't blame him. To this day, I don't know what they were arguing about.

We also fought together. One night, Julio asked me to go to the Bully with him. I didn't think anything of it and figured me and Ju would have time to catch up while we walked. It was kind of cold, so everyone was wearing bombers, Timberlands, and hoodies. We hit the Boulevard and go into this Chinese restaurant. Now in this type of 'hood Chinese restaurant, there was no furniture. There was just a counter separated from the rest of the empty restaurant by a plexiglass wall. You just walk in and order through a window in the plexiglass. We both ordered our usual—three fried chicken wings and fried rice with extra duck sauce. That was street survival food that I loved and was looking forward to, because it was hot and delicious while it was cold outside. Right when the guy was putting both of our orders through the window, *boom!* Niggas kick in the door. There were like seven or eight of them. Me and Julio turned around fast as fuck. *Oh, shit!*

Julio and Breeze went to John Adams High School and would get into shit there that would follow them back to the neighborhood. And I, unknowingly, walked my ass right up into it. What I would later find out is that Ju had a beef with these dudes in particular. Now they had us trapped. "What's up now? What's up now, nigga? What's up now?" they taunted. That's about all that got out before fists started flying. They started socking us up, fucking us up against the counter.

The Chinese dude was yelling, "Get out of the store! Get out my store! I'll call the police!" I'm fighting and I get a couple good blows in and then they double-tripled up on me. Same thing with Ju. He'd get a good couple of blows in and they'd double-triple team him. They fucked around and got Ju on the floor. And that was bad for him, because Ju was at least six feet even back then, so it was harder for him to get back up. One of the dudes kicked him in the eye with a Timberland. Then they all started going at him with their feet. I got real scared for him at that point, and I just charged the dudes like a bowling ball charging towards pins.

I knocked them off him and went directly to help Julio. I didn't bother trying to fight anymore, I just started picking him up and put his arm over my shoulder. While I was doing that, I got a glance at his face. His eye was swollen shut, real bad, with the skin stretched all the way out. The dudes were like, "You all right now? You still talking?" Of course, I gave them no answer. I just carried Ju out of the restaurant. We were fucked up bad; we were leaking. Apparently, Ju's leg was messed up, too. His swollen eye started turning purple. I'm trying to get Ju back to our block as soon as possible, and with our height difference, it wasn't easy. But I got into a rhythm as I carried him, and I'm thinking that we're good. Next thing I know, I'm hearing footsteps coming up fast behind us. Then I heard someone scream, and I felt an excruciating pain in the back of my head. Dude busted me in the head with an Old English bottle! I had a flash of pain and anger, but I couldn't do shit because I had to get Ju back to the block. He couldn't defend himself any longer. I eventually got him to Nana's, yelling for Breeze and Ran Chan the whole way. Once I got him to Nana's, everybody was freaking out. I hit up all the homies' houses like I was Paul Revere, yelling in the middle of the street in between. Like, "Yo, they jumped Ju over on the Bully!" It was a big deal because Ju was one of the most beloved dudes in the neighborhood.

Once I got the word out enough, I went home to change. I put on my fucked-up sneakers, my old jeans, and hoodie. Fight clothes. My mom didn't get off work until like eleven, so she didn't know what was going on. After I got dressed, we all posse'd up in the middle of the block. There were probably like eight or nine of us, but the homie named Rob was the only one with a car at the time. Rob had a cream-colored Pinto station wagon with wood panels. We all piled in, scrunched up, until it started riding low in the back. There were so many of us, we couldn't even close the back of the station wagon. Once we got in, we smashed up to the Boulevard. We pulled up and hopped out and was like, *Where the fuck y'all at now?*

No exaggeration, there was nobody out on the Boulevard. I guess the people knew there was a big fight out there and wanted to stay out of the way of guys coming for get-back. We started pacing up and down the block, looking in every store. We eventually see some of the guys on the next block over, on Inwood Street. Ran was our OG and he approached them and was like, "Yo, you guys jumped my man Mogie and Ju? Oh yeah? Word? Well, we need a fair one, 'cause Mogie don't fuck with nobody." And the guy who I was going to fight was their main knucklehead, let's call him Benson. For whatever reason, I could just tell that this dude didn't like me. I could tell that he didn't really like our entire clique. We weren't no super gangsta niggas, but it was well-known that we had a lot of love for each other, and we were tight, which gave us a whole different type of power.

We eventually just started fighting. I was tired as fuck from already getting jumped earlier, but my adrenaline and anger kept me in the fight. I busted him in the head, he punched me in the stomach. We were grabbing, pulling, kicking. It was like that as we fought all the way down the block and around the corner. I was starting to get tired again, but I knew I couldn't give up, and my OGs had my back. We were both tired at this point, honestly, and it was visible. And while I was weak, one of Benson's boys tried to get in a cheap shot on me. The next thing you know, here comes Breeze taking off his shirt. "Yeah? Now you fight me." And then Breeze and that kid started getting into it. Breeze was a known brawler in the neighborhood. I remember, there was a moment where I was still fighting and Breeze was fighting and I could see all of our guys had our back. I did a little better than I thought. The Benson kid was apparently fucked up. Breeze beat the shit out of his tall, lanky homeboy. It looked like the Reverse Oreo got a win, but it was really a win for the whole block—because, by the way, Benson and his boys were notorious assholes.

This taught me a lot about loyalty and friendship. Sure, we got jumped and that was the price we paid, but riding for the ones you love was well worth that price. I could always count on them and they could always count on me. It was a bonus that nobody in the neighborhood liked them niggas anyway, so it also felt like I was on the right side even if it left me with a couple scrapes and bruises.

CHAPTER 7

SHIT GETS REAL

As a young teen eager to grow into a man, and particularly as Mutulu's child, there wasn't a lot of reason to question or think critically about why it was important to prioritize my Blackness in my experience as a young man. It was just part of who I was. And then, as I got older, I started having experiences that made me think more critically about how I lived out loud in my skin as a young Black man, experiences that reinforced the lessons my father had taught me.

From time to time, my crew would go up a few blocks, through Sutphin Boulevard, in the hopes of finding some girls to talk to. While Tony, Rob, Breeze, and I were driving down Sutphin one day, a city bus was pulling up to the curb, to the bus stop. It was a little ahead of us, so we could see it slowly coming to a stop. The bus hadn't fully stopped when we saw that it was rolling over a small child. The little boy was clearly dead, his skull cracked open. I realized the small, little white things around his head were brain matter. I had never seen someone's brains before.

We immediately started freaking out. We kept driving until we could make a left and, luckily, immediately upon making the turn there was a police car stopped in the middle of the street. We pulled up right next to them, rolled down our window, and started losing our shit. The cops probably didn't understand what we were saying at first, because we were all talking at the same time. But it was clear there was a problem that required their immediate intervention. We started yelling, "Yo! Yo! A kid got run over by a bus. It's crazy! His head is all busted open. They need some help. It's right around the corner." After going on for ten or fifteen seconds, we paused to see what the cop was going to say. And he says, calm as can be, zero fucking sense of urgency, "I know. I know." And slowly rolled up his window on us. It *infuriated* me, and it pissed off everybody else in the car, too. As we pulled away slowly, we were losing our shit for another reason: being pissed off at the fucking cops. In what world do the cops not care about a dying child? Because the people telling them about it happen to be a car full of Black teens?

That incident made me flash back to my childhood rolling with my father, putting up FUCK THE PIGS posters, which the little ones, like my little sister Sekyiwa, would draw. I always remember that pig had a little police hat on top of his head, but that was the main thing that I took away at the time: the visual of the cute little police pig. Now I understood what those posters meant, and it was crystal clear. The most infuriating thing was just witnessing their total lack of empathy. There was no concern, no asking us any questions. In fact, they looked annoyed that we were even talking to them at all. We're thinking, *So you know what happened and you're just sitting around the corner without a care in the world.* It also made me reflect on what my mother would always say: "Maurice, you think they care about you? They will kill you." Seeing that lack of empathy, I was really starting to get it. We weren't human to them. We weren't worthy of their concern. But how could you be charged with looking over a neighborhood if you don't give a fuck about the people who live in it? In that way, their lack of empathy wasn't just a lack of interest. It seemed openly hostile to me. Because, in my mind, if you don't care about the people you're supposed to be there for, then why *are* you there? To watch us? To find an opportunity to punish us? That apathy was malicious. I saw that as clearly as the pigs on the posters.

I began to understand the urgency of my father's point of view. It wasn't just about being Black, it was also about taking care of us, our health, and our welfare in the face of a system that didn't understand that we are equals. If liberation meant taking care of our own, then there was no question my father's commitment to achieve it by any means necessary was just logical. I was proud of my father's resolve—but I was also starting to worry about him.

It was shit like that that really connected me to my father and his mission. A big part of my mom's concerns at that time was my safety, and her worries over my father's political activities. By 1981, my father had really solidified his relationships with the radical left. He had raised money for ambulances to support the anti-colonial revolution in then-Rhodesia. He had traveled to Central America — Nicaragua for sure, and also El Salvador—where he became familiar with the guerrilla tactics there. From the '70s and into the '80s, he had built strong relationships with members of the Weather Underground. Keep in mind, this was a period of global upheaval and change. While the U.S. had left the quagmire of the Vietnam War, it was also asserting itself aggressively—and, ultimately, illegally—into neo-colonial, tyrannical, and counterrevolutionary efforts around the world. My father and his comrades supported liberation. Whether it was in Africa, Central America, Palestine, Northern Ireland, or Black folks in the U.S., they believed in and supported the struggle for self-determination at all costs. Period.

I wouldn't say my mother disagreed, necessarily. It just didn't matter to her. She was focused on my daily existence, survival, and ability to thrive. Her primary concern was my safety, and those concerns were real, just from the perspective of me being a young Black boy in New York City. My generation was the latchkey kids. We spent lots of time on our own, making moves around the city. My mom was a 911 dispatcher at 1 Police Plaza in downtown Manhattan. She didn't work *for* the police—she was a civil servant—but she did work *with* the police every day. "For" versus "with" was a distinction that was often lost on my siblings and the other women in my father's life, like Afeni and Makini. But my mom didn't turn a blind eye towards the police. She knew exactly what they were capable of, in a very real way. And she knew exactly how the police would see a group of young Black boys running around town on their own. To the police, we were full-grown men, perceived through a lens of criminal bias. We were thugs unless proven otherwise. Especially in lower Manhattan, where we were the other—out of place.

And. That's a word I cannot emphasize enough: *and*. And she was aware of the company my father kept, and the things he was fighting for. She knew my father was a target. We saw well-dressed men, in suits, going through our garbage all the time. Feds. And as I got older and started to look more and more like my pops, that fear came into crystal-clear focus for her. "Maurice," she'd tell me, "they will kill you. They will shoot you dead in the street. I know how they are. They will kill you." My mom was terrified of me becoming collateral damage in my father's political struggle.

I wasn't unaware of my mom's concerns, but as a teenage boy I didn't always have a grasp of when things were not entirely within my control. I was still in my freshman year in Manhattan around 1980 when I was asleep on the floor at my cousin's house and the news came on, a local report about an expropriation. You would call it a bank robbery. They were looking for my pops. I was half asleep, and because I was looking more and more like him every day, I wasn't sure if it was me or my dad in the photo at first. I hadn't seen that picture of him before. He was really young and it looked like someone had caught him candidly, off guard. It definitely wasn't from the scene of this particular incident. His chest was all swole up, his nostrils were flared, and he had a short hairdo. You know how the police do: They find the craziest looking picture.

My father had been on the feds' radar since he was a sixteen-year-old member of RAM and, of course, being a member of the provisional government of the RNA and a key figure in the Black Liberation Army didn't make him any less of a target. The RNA and RAM scared the feds and they, law enforcement, and particularly the FBI that Hoover built, saw full civil rights for Black folks as a scary threat to the American way of life. But the BLA? The Black

Liberation Army? An armed and trained anti-capitalist, anti-imperialist, anti-racist, anti-sexist organization that functioned in a decentralized way to support the abolition of systems of oppression? An organization committed to using any means necessary to support their revolutionary goals? Yeah, that scared the shit out of them.

It turns out, what I was seeing was the news of what I would come to know as an expropriation. Going back to the early 1970s, when my dad was at Lincoln Detox, it was becoming increasingly difficult to function as a member of the RNA or the BPP or the Young Lords or really any leftist radical organization because of the police and FBI's continued increasing harassment of its members through a covert and illegal program called COINTELPRO (Counterintelligence Program, sometimes stylized CoIntelPro). COINTELPRO is a very real program set up by the FBI with the help of local law enforcement. The whole purpose was to place undercover operatives within Black civil rights and progressive organizations, and those operatives were not just reporting back information—they were agitators, intentionally causing strife that would lead to in-fighting in these groups, encouraging and pushing members into illegal activities, and causing fights between organizations that had built coalitions. The goal was to destroy the advancement of civil rights and all progressive movements. And to be clear, their methods for their "intelligence gathering program"—which is how they justify the program's existence—were entirely illegal. COINTELPRO had existed since the late '50s—a systematic program to surveil, infiltrate, and discredit organizations they deemed a threat to the U.S. That sanitary description does not do justice to the brutality of it—COINTELPRO destroyed families, turned brothers against brothers against sisters and their sisters, leaving the kids of those families fucked. They imprisoned, falsely charged, publicly humiliated, and even assassinated folks, using confusion, misdirection, lies, and tricks to turn people against each other. By 1978, my father and Afeni were both directors of the National Task Force for COINTELPRO Litigation and Research. But make no mistake, the devastation had long been underway. And for this reason, for about a decade leading up to this, many members of the BPP and RNA joined the BLA because it was decentralized and allowed them to function living underground, less in direct confrontation with police and the FBI. My father was not living underground at that time yet, but he did join the BLA.

It turns out, expropriations were how they funded their organization and efforts. You would call them bank robberies and sometimes the targets were large corporations. The BLA used the funds to support independence wars in Africa, and to purchase medical equipment and weapons in support of anti-imperialist liberation movements in the US and worldwide. They also worked with other anti-imperialist organizations and used the funds to provide direct services to the community.

To be honest, I'm not 100 percent sure which expropriation I was seeing on the news that day. By this time, my father and his comrades had been implicated in about a dozen expropriations. Also, by this time, he was implicated in the liberation of Assata Shakur, my father's sister, who had been a Black Panther and then a leader of the Black Liberation Army and had been held on charges fabricated by an informant. She had also previously addressed the United Nations about the ongoing oppression and systematic abuse of Black people in the United States—something that really pissed the government off. She had been held in a federal facility after representing herself against a slew of charges stemming from a shootout with New Jersey state troopers in which she and Sundiata Acoli were injured and a trooper and Zayd Shakur were killed. She had also been implicated in a number of expropriations going back to 1971 and most of the charges were eventually thrown out, but as the case waxed on and charges kept being added whenever others were thrown out, it looked grim that the government was ever going to let her go. So, they were planning to liberate her. Eventually, in November of 1979, they did, without a single shot fired. My father was one of those implicated, and eventually convicted as the mastermind, in her liberation. But at that time when I saw him on the news, I was too young to remember if they were talking about Mutulu still being pursued in her liberation, or in connection with another expropriation, or both.

This is because the times I got to spend with his side of the family were few and far between, by this time. Mutulu was not underground quite yet, but he was more and more occupied with revolutionary activities than his acupuncture practice and clinic at BAAANA. One of the last times I can recall being with them before he went underground, was leading up to my little sister Nzingha's birth. I remember being dressed up, wearing my little kufi. I was able to spend time with my other little sister, Sekyiwa. Since her infancy, I had not had a lot of time with her. She was around five by this time, just a really cute age for a big brother in his early teens to spend time with his little sister. I remember things being festive, us eating our favorite foods, getting to play together for the first time in a long time. Everybody was excited, waiting for Nzingha to come.

It was a special occasion, and we had some special times at BAAANA in those days, different people on different floors, doing different things, all related to the overall health and wellness of the community. It was a clinic, sure, but it was so much more than that. It was also a center for political, social, and family life, and I was learning more about my father's side of the family, which was beginning to grow and expand real quick. There was of course my brother Tupac, my sister Sekyiwa, and my sister Nzingha on the way. I also learned that Moto, whose house I'd stayed at a few years earlier, also had a child by my father, and that I had a brother named Ayize who was a year older than Sekyiwa. Turns out that Moto and Afeni didn't get along, nor were they compatible with my father's whole blended family thing. My father also had another son in Queens, Tyrone, two years younger than me, but none of us would come to know him until we were adults.

I was beginning to see and understand the significance of these other women in his life. My mother would have no part of this blended family lifestyle; I could spend time my father, but she wasn't about to be a part of this communal life. And while Moto wasn't too keen on the communal living, either, Afeni remained at BAAANA and raised her kids around this growing family. What crystalized my father's desire to live a communal life in harmony with his children and their mothers, for me at least, was the mother of my new little sister on the way: Makini, whom I had met once before at Mutulu's house. She would be embraced in BAAANA, and actually had a leadership position there. Afeni was there with Tupac and Sekyiwa. My father always wanted all of us to be together. In fact, Makini would later tell us that he cried all the time for my little brother in Queens, whose mother raised him apart from us. Makini would eventually have another child, Chinua, my youngest brother. The idea of this family all living, working, and playing together, sharing communally with others who aren't blood but who are for sure family is beautiful . . . in principle.

The thing is, the reality was that the stakes were so, so much higher for my family than I could imagine. The communal idea of family by choice seemed amazing, but there was so much collateral damage when my father was eventually forced underground. In the spring of 1982, the Joint Terrorism Task Force raided BAAANA with tanks, cutting off the electricity and entering the building with battering rams and guns with laser scopes. With children inside. My father had tried to live in the open, with his children, but prior to the raid he was forced underground in 1981. Later, when the government brought charges against my father, it was under RICO (Racketeer Influenced and Corrupt Organizations Act). RICO allows the feds to charge and convict based on a conspiracy, to act without direct evidence of involvement in actual criminal acts, provided there are corroborating "witnesses." There has to be, at the core, a criminal conspiracy to fund an illegal organization. The basis that was required to charge my father with being a criminal mastermind under RICO was that he funded this exact organization (which, remember, was a holistic health clinic treating all manner of illnesses with a combination of acupuncture, Western medicine, and diet) . . . and a children's camp in Mississippi.

By this time, I was in the tenth grade and had transferred to Thomas Edison High School in Queens, the same school my father went to. My father's sister, Aunt Sharon, lived in South Jamaica, right on my way home from Edison. I would stop by her house after school sometimes and she would cook for me. She would make her famously delicious oxtails and I would get to spend time with my cousin Nicole. Sharon would tell me how much I was looking like my father. We would ask each other for news of my dad, but honestly, neither one of us really knew much or saw him much those days.

Still, I was getting older, and my father wanted to see me. Because of my school's proximity to Jamaica Avenue, where the movie theater was, we met there. We hung out, just father and son, saw a movie and got some pizza together after. It was pretty unremarkable at the time, but it would be over forty years before I would see him in person again, free in this world. My father had expanded his coalition of radical progressives, and they were—allegedly—actively involved in the expropriation of funds through bank and armored truck robberies, the proceeds of which were going to support liberation movements in Africa and the U.S. Allegedly, mind you. In 1981, one of these capers went wrong, two cops and a security guard were killed in a shoot-out, several people associated with my father were captured on the scene in upstate New York, and my father—who was not captured at the time and who was never connected to the shoot-out forensically—was accused of masterminding the whole thing. He was also wanted for a string of other expropriations and for his role in the liberation of Assata Shakur. He went underground the fall of that year. It's not like they circulated a memo, I just started to see him less and less and eventually not at all. I remember having this *New York Times* newspaper clipping that said "Terrorists," literally as the title of the article, right above his name, Mutulu Shakur. It hurt, man. I knew how much good my pops had done for the community, how much he cared, how respected he was, how much he loved. And they reduced him to one word: *terrorist*. I was officially scared for my father. Through various people in the movement, he sent my mother word that he was alive. But when he went underground, I didn't have any direct contact with him, for my own safety. In July of 1982, he was put on the FBI's Ten Most Wanted list.

CHAPTER 8

FROM A BOY TO A MAN

I was fourteen, so I wasn't too young to understand what was going on, but I was probably too young to fully appreciate all of the ways this would and could impact our lives. It's interesting, looking back, the things that a person can normalize. Nobody ever talked about it directly, so I had to piece it together myself. The first time I really figured it out was when I saw wanted posters with my dad's face on them in the post office. I pointed them out to my mom, and she shook me, hard, as if to tell me not to draw attention to myself. She wasn't mad, she was scared. I knew then that it was serious.

I was already used to seeing well-dressed men in suits going through the trash at my mom's house in Queens. It was a pretty regular occurrence. Being watched, and knowing that my loved ones and I were being watched, was normal, too. At the same time, I knew that my loved ones were watching over me, because I knew that my father loved me. He knew that being in regular contact would put all of us in danger, so he mostly stayed away—aside from one time, when he popped up on me in the street to give me some cash—and that also meant I didn't get to see my siblings. Damn, I missed them. But I couldn't have contact with them unless my mother hooked it up. She never did, for my own safety.

It got worse: I was sent back South for my eleventh-grade year because, clearly, things with my dad were getting too hot in NYC, and my mom wanted to keep me safe. Honestly, even as all that was going on, I was still a teenager, which meant I was caught up in my own life and more concerned how this move would affect my social life. But I was a fish out of water again, and what pissed me off more than anything was that the move took me away from the center of hip hop. I hated the entire situation, and I *really* hated finishing high school in the South. I was a city kid, and Fayetteville was just not New York. Even though I'd loved it as a child, the South just didn't have my flavor. There were no parks with kids rhyming and battling. I could pop and lock my ass off, but it didn't matter if nobody down there was in the culture. Plus, I was living with my grandmother, and she was *strict*. It was school, church, and working the land—mowing, pulling weeds, picking vegetables. She wouldn't even let me play a sport, and Southern high schools revolve around sports. I did manage to become vice president of the drama club, something my grandmother found amusingly useless for my future. Still, whenever we put on a play, she was there in the front row in her fur and her hat.

More than anything, the crushing boredom of the South affected me the most. I know the assumption would be that the biggest culture shock would have to be racism. *Of course* there was racism in the South—and in New York, for that matter. But the life my grandmother confined me to in the South and my natural instinct for self-preservation limited the direct confrontations I had, personally. Outside of school, my life was pretty segregated, and I think that's still pretty normal for the South. My social life was church, which was not integrated, and my family. The friends in close proximity to me in my neighborhood were Black. Ramsey Street, a few blocks in downtown Fayetteville, was where I would get my hair cut. It was all Black.

My school was pretty much fifty-fifty. Now, I had my Uncle Johnny as a reference point, and that's a big difference for young kids. Interracial familial relationships give a person a different point of view. Also, there had been white folks at Lincoln Detox and at BAAANA who were in close collaboration with my dad. It made it pretty easy for me to see, *Oh, those are the ones I'm not trying to fuck with,* or, *Oh, these ones are down as fuck.* I would ride my bike to the little general store close by and from time to time, as cars passed, I'd hear them yell, "Nigger!" I would most definitely see white folks treating people fucked up, calling men "boy" or addressing people in fucked-up ways. At the same time, I had white friends at school, mostly girls, but I didn't see them outside of school or drama club. Make no mistake: I knew racism existed and I saw it there. But and however, I had also come back to the South with a firm sense of love for my Blackness, so I just didn't give any air or attention to it. I was too busy being miserable and bored to care that these white folks lived in a system in which they believed themselves better. That struck me as ridiculous. Absurd, really.

So I was safe, sure. But I was also miserable. Still, as long as I had my box, my little radio/tape cassette player, I could sink myself into music. There was an R&B/Soul station, which I loved for itself just generally, and they also had a little hip hop show on some nights and over the weekend. When I was out in the field, I would think up rhymes. Then I would write them out and perform to myself, practicing my flow, diction, delivery. When I was shelling peas, I would memorize my rhymes. Once I had mastered the rhyme, I would perform it for myself on the back patio. That was my stage, with an audience of my imagination, preparing for my return to New York.

All of the academic support I would have gotten to go on to college had I stayed in NYC—including financial support for SATs and applications, let alone financial aid once I got into college—was simply not there for me in the South. As clear as my mother's own vision was about going to a good school so I could go to college to build a better life, that was simply not attainable in the South. My safety was my mom's priority in moving me to the South, and my path towards a college education came second. I mean, this kind of opportunity is the whole reason my grandmother left the South for New York in the first place. It felt backwards, being there as a teen. Even with my grandmother there, I felt like I was on my own when it came to school. I really had to figure everything out for myself.

The way the family dynamic was at the time, with my grandmother having to care for me when I really should've been with my mother and father, made me feel like I owed her something. Because she had already been so helpful to me and my mother, I'd be damned if I was going to need her or my mom's help once I graduated. At the same time, my father's voice was in my head: "You're my little soldier." He meant it in the context of the Black Liberation Army, but I was young and still learning, so I took it way more literally. I decided that I would enlist in the U.S. Army. I didn't know it at the time, but I learned later that many of the men who were leaders in the movement for Black Liberation, people I looked up to from the foundations of Afrocentrism, including a lot of Black Panthers and members of the RNA, also spent time in the military. I learned that although they disagreed with the government's continued imperialism around the world, they learned valuable skills from military training. That made a lot of sense to me.

I knew who I was and why I was going—to earn my own college money, to make sure I wasn't a weight on my mother or grandmother, to learn certain skills that I felt my father would have wanted me to learn. It's one thing to know how to fight in the street amongst untrained people with weapons. It's another thing entirely to train to fight as a team against other people who are trained to fight. And the U.S. military had the best weapons. My path was clear, as were my values, so I didn't feel worried about being brainwashed by the military or anything like that.

I did my basic training at Fort Dix, New Jersey, which wasn't too far from Queens. Basic training is exactly that: basic. It's where they teach you the fundamentals of how to handle weapons, how to shoot, how to set up a mine, how to throw a hand grenade. Besides my M16A2, I was issued an M-203 grenade launcher—it would make a deep sound, a *boooosh*, when I fired it. I always loved that sound. You run exercises as part of PT (physical training) and they teach you how to march and work in a group under supervision. They run drills and really break things down so that you understand how to follow orders and follow a chain of command.

I never knew what the Army knew about my father, if anything. I enlisted right after high school, and under my mother's maiden name, Harding. It was never an intentional effort to conceal my father; when I was with him, I enrolled in school as Shakur, and when I was with my mother I enrolled in school as Harding. I don't suspect there was a terribly thorough background check on teens who enlist, aside from whether they had a juvenile record. If anyone knew that my father was on the FBI's Most Wanted list, there was no hint of it from my superiors. And if anyone higher in the chain of command knew, it never became an issue, nor has that been revealed to me, to this day.

I mostly hung out with two other young recruits I met there, Lenny and Ronald. Lenny was funny as fuck. I mean, honestly, just the visual of him was hilarious. He had sleepy eyes and was short, maybe five foot. His helmet was always way too big, and when he would turn his head to talk to you, his helmet would rattle around like a bobblehead. The three of us found that funny as fuck. And it was important to find people who would help you find the lightness in things, the joy and the humor. We pushed it, sometimes, but we never really got in trouble. Drill Sergeant Shell was entertained by us, I think, always cutting up. He was cool as fuck, wore these glasses like Malcolm X, and he'd always laugh and tell us to go do push-ups so it looked like we were doing something.

There's a lot of physical work that goes into breaking a person down in the military, psychologically. I assume they do it so they can build you back up into a useful soldier who follows instructions without asking questions. But coming from my grandmother's house, I figured there was no physical work they could put me through that would compare to what I did on the land down South. And I was right. Guys around me were having full-on breakdowns, crying from the physical and mental exhaustion. I was just chillin', cutting it up with Lenny and Ronald after we finished PT. Women were posted for basic training there, too, but they kept us separated. We'd still find ways to flirt with each other, of course, catching glimpses of each other, waving and passing notes back and forth whenever we could. I even had a girlfriend there, a Latina girl from Harlem, but we broke up after I got placed in engineering, which meant that I'd do my training at Fort Belvoir in Virginia. She got angry that we'd be posted to different places, and the idea of a long-distance relationship seemed premature. Still—it was a fun few months.

So, I was off to Virginia—but before I went anywhere, I had leave for three weeks, which meant it was back to New York to see my people. Though I was young, it wasn't lost on me, the journey I was about to embark upon. I was seventeen, no kids that I knew of, and my mama's only child. The cold, hard truth about it was that I could lose my life. When I first enlisted, we weren't at war. But this is the United States: A war could pop off at any time. Knowing that my near future was not within my immediate control, I had certain things I had to do, people I had to see on this leave.

Just getting home, I was walking towards Nana's to check on Breeze and Julio and saw my boy Ju pulling up across the street with some dudes. They damn near pulled up to a screeching halt and I started to walk over, but they all pulled their fucking heat out on me. I put my hands up in the air real quick and said, "Whoa, whoa, whoa!" I wasn't that scared because Ju was still my brotha, but he looked like he was in pain. He waved his boys down—"Nah, that's my man"—but grimaced getting out of the car. "Ah, yo, Mo, help me get to Nana's," he said. "I got shot." *Oh, shit!* I helped him get out of the car while the rest of the dudes peeled away, I'm assuming to go find the guys who shot him. He put his arm around me and we limped across the street to Nana's, down to the basement where Breeze lived. Eventually, I found out that he got shot in the foot—I saw a hole in his fucking shoe. Luckiest Puerto Rican I ever met, getting shot in the damn foot. Eventually, one of his girls came to pick him up and take him somewhere else. And that was my welcome back to Southside.

By that time, it was 1986 and shit had *changed*. New York was in its full-blown crack era. Everybody those days was driving around in crack cars. They had access to these rental cars—in an informal economy everybody plays their part and has their hustle; Southside is right next to JFK and all those rental car businesses—and they would just drive them around and do all their dirt and then never return them. They literally called them crack cars. The hustle level was way higher than what I had seen in my childhood with my uncle and heroin. This was different, way grimier. People were more desperate, and crack was everywhere. There were more crack addicts than the old-school dope fiends in the days of heroin.

I got to kick it with another group of my homies while I was home. Wanting to make my leave memorable before my bon voyage to begin my specialized training, my friends Big O, Tobago, and Cash took me to the legendary Club Paradise up on Jamaica Avenue. We got into the club and everything was *smooth*. In them days, all you could smell was whooz in the air. Whooz were cigarettes, half emptied of tobacco. They'd push tobacco out the end, put powder in there (for those unclear, that would be cocaine), shake it up, remove part or all of the filter, replace it with a carb (which is a small piece cardboard), and smoke it. It smelled sweet—like tobacco and sweet flowers. That's all you could smell in the air. There were *a lot* of drugs in the room. It was so much that I was actually kind of paranoid, because my system was so clean at the time from going through basic training.

That wore off quick once I saw this girl I wanted to dance with. My homies were big guys, football-playing niggas. I was the smallest out of all of them. Plus, they all knew my first love was dancing. For whatever reason, this girl was kind of by herself, and I had no fear. I went up to her and just started dancing, and my homies kind of encircled us. We were just getting our boogey on and they were chillin', watching us. And then we started noticing how everyone else in the club was backing away from our little group. I started hearing little whispers, but I couldn't quite hear what they were saying. My man Cash started tapping me to try to give me a heads-up. "Yo," he was saying, "yo. She's Fat Cat's." But I was dancing and having way too much fun for whatever he was saying to register.

Next thing I knew, another group of guys approached our little group. They got so close that we just had to stop dancing, which I found *quite* annoying. Cash said, "Yo, she with Fat Cat." *Now* I was getting the picture. And it answered a lot of questions. Fat Cat was a notorious, homegrown South Jamaica, Queens, gangsta. He was just standing there looking at me. I don't remember him even saying much. But he gave me a nod, nodded to the homies, and it was clear we weren't on no bullshit. I think he could see I was just a young hip hop kid having fun. But he was with a few people, and one of them was this kid with a Kangol. It was a young LL Cool J. We didn't have a battle, exactly, but we had a little mini-cypher. I knew who he was, and I knew he was a talented rapper. He was the young gun out there.

At that point in my life I had absolutely no fear. I honestly think I just started rapping 'cause I liked the track that was on in the background. It was clear that it wasn't adversarial. I did my shit, and then LL kicked a little something. And then I kicked another little something. We ended our encounter peacefully, with pounds and nods of affirmation. I was fully confident in my rap skills at that point. I'd had enough practice and had been doing it long enough that I was ready to go. The encounter could've ended up very differently with other personalities involved. Thank God it ended peacefully.

I wanted to make the most of my time before I had to report to Virginia for training, so I made sure to visit all my people. One day, as I was leaving Manhattan to go to Queens, I saw a poster in the subway supporting my dad's freedom. I remember it distinctly—it was yellow with black writing. I ripped the poster off the subway wall, and when I got home I told my mom what I'd found. That was how I discovered that my father had been captured. The feds had tracked him down to Los Angeles; FBI agents and members of the FBI–New York City Police joint terrorism unit had staked out a corner where they expected him to meet with someone. When he arrived, they arrested him. Turns out, though, one of the NYPD officers that was part of the task force was a bank robber himself. No lie!

It had been five years that my pops was living underground. Honestly, more than anything I felt about him being captured, I was just so relieved that he was alive. Given everything he was accused of, there was a lot of talk saying that he wouldn't be taken alive, and that scared the shit out of me. I loved my pops, and I just wanted him *alive.* It may be fucked up to say that him getting caught gave me a feeling of comfort, but it did—because it meant that I didn't have to keep wondering what would happen to him. They were odd circumstances, unique and emotionally strained, but I found out most of my family felt the same way. Of course, we'd all rather he were free. But more than free, we needed him alive.

Since I'd finished up school for those two years in North Carolina, I had been completely disconnected from my father and my siblings who, as far as I knew, were with their mothers. We had no interaction, for our own safety. It may have been safer, but the feeling of absence, and the longing to see my brothers, sisters, and father was intense and profoundly sad and lonely. It was always something that I tried to bury deep beneath an affable and sunny exterior. But now I didn't have to anymore. I decided to visit my dear old dad.

I had some idea what it was like to visit someone who was being detained, but visiting someone who is in federal custody—someone who has already been denied bail and who, if found guilty, will certainly be sentenced to a maximum or super-max facility—involves a whole different level of security. There were forms, metal detectors, pat-downs. Eventually, I'd get used to it, and it just became part of visiting my pops. But that first time got me.

I remember being so happy waiting for him to come out. Whatever the circumstances, I was just excited to see him. I was anxious, too: Did they beat him up? Did they do something to him? But when he finally came out, he had this big smile on his face. He didn't look worried at all, just pleased to see me. I just stared at him, because I hadn't laid eyes on him in years. He had some of his African jewelry still on; I had no idea how he got to keep that. I saw he was just starting his dreads, which was surprising to me. I had never seen him with dreads, never imagined him with them. I thought, *I wonder how that's gonna turn out.* I didn't think he had the right hair for them. I had no idea I'd see those dreads grow over the next thirty-plus years.

Pops asked about my mom first, then me. I told him I'd joined the military and that I was on leave. I really wanted to know his opinion about me joining the military, because I knew that he wasn't so fond of the government. I had a feeling he wasn't going to trip, but I wanted to see if I was right. I did have a little anxiety. I had my rebuttal prepared, but I didn't want to use it. He hadn't been there these past few years, and I really didn't want to have to say *that* to him. At the same time, I often had flashbacks of seeing that duffel bag full of Army rifles. In the end, he wasn't alarmed at all. He actually seemed kind of pleased. If being a soldier was like being in school, the US Army's one of the best schools. I remember him saying, "Oh, yeah? That's good. You're gonna learn some things in there." And he mentioned that my Uncle Geronimo, his comrade, a high-ranking member of the BPP and Tupac's godfather, had been in the Army. I felt relief, a confirmation that my gut was right. I felt encouraged that I was on the right path. We didn't get into the politics, much less the fact that one of the "criminal enterprises" that he was charged with financing under the RICO statute was in fact a youth camp in Mississippi where they were training youth in a number of areas, including arming themselves. I would find that out later.

He started telling me, *contact your family, contact Afeni, contact your brother, contact your sister, contact Makini*. He gave me a long list of family I was supposed to call. If he was worried, he didn't show it. I don't remember the exact moment we said goodbye, but I remember standing down the street after I left, looking back at the cold white stone of the Metropolitan Correctional Center building, and then seeing across the street the blue and white insignia of the NYPD.

Now, this is some surreal shit right here, some shit you couldn't make up if you tried: My father was captured in California and then transferred to New York, where he would be tried by Rudy Giuliani, who was the federal prosecutor for the Southern District of New York at the time. My father was being held at MCC. My mom worked at 1 Police Plaza across the street, in the 911 dispatch. I would go visit my pops and then literally walk across the street to see my mom at her job, in a building that was just crawling with police. Nobody ever said anything. I moved through both spaces in a way that might only be possible in a big city. Like I said, you can't make this shit up! And that's how I spent my leave: visiting my loved ones, just like every other soldier on leave does. My three-week leave felt like it passed in a New York minute, packed as it was with all the things that make my life full . . . and uniquely mine.

What I realized after that visit was the impact of being on the run, of living underground. The absence, the repercussions from all those clues I saw as a child—the newspaper articles, news reports, wanted posters, the duffel bag of rifles. It's one thing to have a discussion about the means through which my father sought justice and liberation—and we can disagree philosophically on the merits of seeking revolution by any means necessary. It's another thing entirely for the state to misuse its endless resources to destroy your family and drive you underground. COINTELPRO terrorized my family, and no part of it was ever legal. It's totally fair for us to disagree about the merits of my father's actions and the extent to which he may be in some part responsible for our separation. But that conversation is bullshit unless you first consider the government's actions harassing, falsely arresting, discrediting, and undermining the very social fabric that held my family together, through the use of double-agent informants, and that drove my father and others in our family underground in the first place.

I've always taken into account the generation my father grew up in as a young man. He lived through the assassinations of King, two Kennedys, and Malcolm, not to mention all the comrades he lost. The generations of today, I think, would have a hard time understanding what that felt like. The psychological warfare waged upon them in those days. The priority they put on catching Mutulu in particular. It all came full circle, him sitting there in a federal prison, facing sixty years. At the time, I was kind of numb and in reflection about the rest of the family. I wondered how they were doing through all this. I thought about my siblings—about Tupac, Sekyiwa, Nzingha—and about Afeni and Makini. I was worried they could be arrested, too. I missed them, and worried if I'd ever be able to see them again.

Once I arrived at Fort Belvoir, I started my training in engineering. I learned electrical engineering, mainly—both running generators and running wires to light structures in the field. The next move was where we'd be stationed for duty. They called out all the names and the duty stations to which we were assigned. When they called out my name, they said Fort Ord. Everyone erupted in cheers. To be honest, I didn't really know what they were cheering for or why, but everyone sounded happy, so I figured it was something good. Fort Ord was on Monterey Bay on the coast in California. I had no real concept of California, and even less of an idea of what West Coast cities were like. I had no idea what Monterey had in store for me. Looking back, I miss those youthful days—having that kind of open-minded, innocent optimism for the future.

When I got to Fort Ord, I couldn't believe it. There were palm trees and beaches, man! Shit, California looked like a picture book. It was almost unreal. Fort Ord is—was, up to the day it closed—considered one of the best posts in the Army because of its proximity to the beach and the California weather. I started to understand why as soon as I got there. Monterey is right on the water and hella scenic, one of the most beautiful coastal cities in California. It's got pristine, sandy beaches, and all these unique cliffs and rock formations. There were no extreme weather situations; it was never too cold and it was never too hot. Pretty much just sunny and pleasant all the time. It proved to be an interesting contrast, all the rough and rugged training within such a serene, oceanside setting.

Monterey was surrounded by farming communities, too, but they were different than the farms I knew from the South. I got to know Mexicans and Mexican Americans for the first time. That was new. People would take their lowriders out and cruise on the main drag in Salinas, a town close to Fort Ord. I had never seen that particular kind of car culture before. In the South, people cared for their cars, sure, and some people kept their cars pristine or built hot rods as a pastime. But this was on another level. It was, it is, art. It was the beginning of something that I was seeing was distinctly Californian: old cars, not just restored, but customized and upgraded, with elaborate systems installed in them. I could definitely appreciate the dedication.

Then we got deployed to Panama in the United States' invasion of Panama. The U.S. was deposing, or about to depose, Manuel Noriega, the Panamanian dictator. The U.S. had originally put him there, and he had a long relationship with U.S. intelligence agencies, even going to school at our own little dictator school, School of the Americas. I guess the relationship was complicated, because things soured and the U.S. stopped looking the other way at his human rights abuses, weapons trading, money laundering, and drug trafficking. We were sent in to get him out and the codename was, quite ironically, Operation Just Cause.

My time in Panama preceded him eventually being removed, when Noriega had just survived an attempted coup that he blamed on the U.S.—which, you know, sure—and we were deployed as a military response to him strengthening ties with Cuba, Nicaragua, and Libya. By the time the U.S. removed him from power, in early 1990, I had already finished my tour. I was there as part of the contingency plan in preparation for the invasion of Panama.

In Panama, I put my engineering training to use, and I actually enjoyed my time there. Sergeant Antoine Smalls, who was in my company, just happened to be from Panama, and showed me around. I fucking loved the country. It was my first real experience with Black people outside of the U.S., and that blew my mind. Up to and beyond the '80s, very rarely did movies and popular culture or even history books, if we're being real real, show Black folks, even in countries where there's a Black population. And I hadn't been out of the country much at that point. This was different. And this is where my father's uncompromising efforts to center Blackness in my life really made me take Panama in, in a special way. Naturally, they were all speaking Spanish, so it was different, but there was also so much that was familiar. Like, Panama was the first time I'd ever seen fried chicken, I mean on the bone, at a McDonald's. Obviously, both of those things were familiar—but together? That was new. I was with the people.

Sergeant Smalls had a car and would drive me around town. We had a blast. I was used to Puerto Rican Afro-Latinos, but I had never seen Latinos who were dark like me—or even darker than me—speaking Spanish. Panama was also the first time I experienced Carnaval. Carnaval is an experience for every sense: street dancing, music, parades, big floats, elaborately dressed dancers and parade courts, and long hours of partying. It's bright, lively, loud, and full of every color. There are food and drink booths, live music, and vendors everywhere selling anything you can imagine. It's not just a parade, it's parades *plural*, with fireworks. People gather in the streets and in their homes to eat, drink, and party for days, every day, until the sun comes up. The aroma of roasting chickens and all kinds of Panamanian delights mingle in the air, overpowering the sulfuric smell of fireworks and the musk of wet people soaked with water spraying from the floats. Beyond the parade, music emanates from houses and from massive speaker systems set up in car trunks. People visited and danced on their front porches, greeting all passersby with big waves and smiles. Each float had brass and drum bands—*murgas*—with them. The dancing and singing was infectious. Parading Carnaval queens and princesses wear tiaras and glittering over-the-top costumes covered in beads and gems. Long multicolored plumes fan out behind them to the sides and above their heads. There are also dancers in traditional dress, skirts and blouses, layered with ruffles in every color. The men accompany them wearing long-sleeved embroidered white shirts over black pants. There are also these guys running around in scary handmade devil masks in red and black. I had never seen anything like it.

Sergeant Smalls also took me to his family home, where I got to eat homemade Panamanian food. I don't know what everything was, I just know it was *good*. Panama was also the first time I heard reggaeton, and I loved what I was hearing. This infusion of hip hop and Caribbean music was growing and would eventually cross over into the American music scene decades later. The Panamanian people felt like *my* people. Luckily, my division didn't see too much action. A car did get blown up on the base, but mostly our presence there was just a show of physical might, and we returned to Monterey unharmed.

CHAPTER 9

IT FEELS GOOD

Once I got back from Panama, it was about three months until my ETS (Expiration Term of Service) date. Exiting the Army, I had some decisions to make. I knew that I was not going to re-enlist. I also knew I wasn't going to go back to live anywhere where I would feel my grandmother's controlling pressure. When I enlisted, I had also left behind my psychopath Uncle Harold, who had since been arrested when he messed with a little white boy and would eventually die in prison. This time, though, I was more influenced by optimism for what was ahead for me than what I wanted to leave behind.

My friends, Darnell "Blade" Brown and Roland Brooks were about to get out, too, and were headed back East. But my girlfriend from back home and her family, by chance, had moved to the Bay Area because her mother had been transferred by IBM. I had met Tiwan on leave when I went home to visit my mother in like 1987, before I had been deployed to Panama. I met her through her cousin Nicole, who lived on my block, 146th Street. Tiwan was a cute, light brown–skinned girl with a short Anita Baker haircut. She eventually just wore a high-top fade. She was a very pretty girl, so she could pull off a boy's haircut. So, Tiwan, her mother Vera, and brother Michael had moved to Oakland a few months before I got out of the military.

I decided that I liked California enough to stay. You can't beat those beaches and that weather. Plus, my pops had been captured in

California, and by that time it looked like he would be serving his time there. While I was stationed in Monterey, we would often drive up to the Bay Area, to San Francisco and Oakland to go to the clubs and take in the city life. I liked Oakland, and I saw opportunity there. I just had to take advantage of it.

Tiwan and her mother had a place off Fruitvale Boulevard, and when I got out, I went to Oakland and stayed with them until I got an apartment. It didn't take me long to find a place because I had a little savings. Actually, the building where I ended up getting my apartment was the same building where Tiwan's mother's friend Andrea lived. Andrea was older but a cool, hip lady. Besides being Vera's friend, she became real close with me and Tiwan. She had a youthful spirit and helped me get a job where she was working at the time, the American Automobile Association (AAA). She knew a lot of people there, and I just followed her directions about what to do. I got out of the Army on August 4th and had a full-time job—with benefits—by the end of the month. Thank you, Andrea. I liked working at AAA, too. I liked having a job, first of all, so soon after getting out. And I worked in an office, taking calls, doing data entry, and dispatching tow trucks to people in distress. I started making friends pretty quick—my man Hawk and Ron and my homegirl Mesha. We kept each other entertained and kept each other laughing throughout the workday.

While I was getting settled into Oakland, Mutulu told me he was going to be sent to Lompoc, California, for the first portion of his prison time, which meant that he'd be close enough for me to visit him. We talked a lot during this period, getting reacquainted. He told me that during our years apart I had gained another brother: Chinua. Makini gave birth to Chin towards the beginning of Mutulu going underground. Mutulu told me Chin had Down syndrome and that Makini was raising him and Nzingha in Texas. I was elated about having another brother.

Another good thing about being with Tiwan was that she was from around the way, Queens. I would come to find out that her mother, Vera, also knew my father from the neighborhood back in the day. Like I said: It was my pops's business to know everyone. And as I came across people who knew my dear old dad, I felt there was a certain amount of trust I could have in them. Once I got my apartment, Tiwan came to stay with me. It was a small, small place, a studio. But it was in a nice building and in a great location, right by Lake Merritt. Tiwan and I got along well. She was solid, especially for someone her age, two or three years younger than me. We would go visit Mutulu together and make a trip of it. Andrea worked her magic and got her a job at AAA, too.

At the end of the day, adjusting to Oakland wasn't difficult. I'm a city kid, and Oakland, although slower than the grind of Queens, was still very much a city. I lived by Lake Merritt, a manmade lake in the middle of Oakland, which was really beautiful. There were always paddle boats out on the lake and people barbecuing and having parties and family reunions in different parts of the park. There was a fairy-themed amusement park, too. And the type of city Oakland was (and is) appealed to me. Oakland is proud to be the home of the Black Panthers; people are connected to the community in a real grassroots way, and it's liberal. New York is liberal, too, sure, but Oakland has radical roots that the people are *proud* of. It felt good to be Mutulu's son around the type of people who were on the same wavelength as him. I would often and casually meet the children of revolutionaries whose parents had made the same sacrifice, people who wrote for revolutionary publications, people who would show me where all the old Panther offices were. People who knew who my father was, who knew the history of the Black radical left and the sacrifices he had made.

One thing *was* hard to adjust to: earthquakes. I'd experienced a little tremor when I was at Fort Ord, and even that was disorienting. But an *earthquake* earthquake? My first one was huge: Loma Prieta. I was in the car—my funky little GTI with my MOE NYC plates—driving through downtown, coming home from work. I was in between lights, and I was slowing down, but all of a sudden it felt like someone pushed me or hit me from behind. But when I looked behind me, nobody was there. Then I got to the next light, and it's blinking. I didn't understand what was going on, but I got to my house and the garage door didn't work—I realized the electricity was out. I went upstairs to my apartment and when I opened the door I saw that the VCR was on the floor, pictures had fallen off the wall, little stuff around the apartment had fallen over. What the fuck was going on? As I was looking around, my Aunt Jean and cousin Gretchen called me, asking if I was okay. They told me there had been an earthquake, a terrible earthquake. When the electricity came back and I was able to turn on the TV, I found out that buildings and bridges had just collapsed. Part of the Bay Bridge had fallen onto the lower level. I had just been on that bridge the night before. That was a big way to get introduced to earthquakes, for sure.

Eventually, I enrolled at Laney College. I was interested in media communications—it was the closest thing to my thing, and my thing was still hip hop. And though I was working and had a good job, I still wanted to fulfill my ambition as a rapper and recording artist. As a kid learning the craft in Queens, I'd spent years refining my writing skills and cutting my teeth on the streets. I knew what I wanted to accomplish creatively, and that I had the skills to take the next step and record. I just had to find my way into a community of musicians. And that's exactly what I did. I started inquiring about the music scene, studios, where to record, prices. I put myself in the studio immediately to record with the money I'd saved in the Army. I set out on a mission to record a demo. I booked sessions and found my way to producers and musicians.

Through this process, I ended up being featured on a song by an artist named Iranetta. I had met a producer by the name of Eric Baker, later known as Kenya. Eric produced the Iranetta song, and had some more tracks that I could hear. I jumped on the opportunity. We recorded at Joe Capers's studio in the Oakland Hills. Bay Area notables recorded there as well, all the time: Tony! Toni! Toné!, a young MC Hammer, Digital Underground, Too $hort, and Dawn Robinson of En Vogue all recorded at his studio. He had a fully professional studio at his home, which was not common at the time because of the equipment and technology needed, especially back then.

My relationship with Eric was a blessing. He was the brother of Elijah Baker, the bassist and a founding member of Tony! Toni! Toné!, an established group with a solid hit under their belts on their debut album. Now they were working on their sophomore album, though I didn't know that at the time. All I knew was that Eric was my friend and a producer, and he said he was going to help me get my demo made. In one of our sessions, while working on a track that I got from Eric, in strolls Elijah, Tim, and Raphael, three of the four original members of Tony! Toni! Toné! I can't remember if Dwayne was there or not. I was well aware of the group and their success. Their single "Little Walter," a funky little R&B record with a funny video featuring Sinbad, had hit #1 on the Hot Black Singles Chart, the U.S. soul chart. All the members in the group were related. They came from a church band background in East Oakland. Raphael was the lead singer and Dwayne and Raphael were the lead producers. Tim played drums and Elijah played bass. I felt fortunate that there was more than one of them at my studio session. Their music wasn't fully in my lane, but the musician part of me respected their talent. And them actually having a deal and being professional musicians made meeting them even more enticing. I was in the booth when they walked in, so I couldn't get a clear view of everybody, but I saw Eric talking to this nigga that looked just like him.

I wasn't nervous meeting them, because I knew my shit. I tried to always go to the studio prepared, because I wasn't about wasting no money. I came out of the booth when they got there and met them briefly. *Oh, shit! It's really them!* I tried to keep my excitement in check, because you gotta play it cool, but I had all those butterflies going on inside. I went back in the booth to finish laying my song. They listened for a while, then left, and Eric and I finished the session, and I went home. Within the next day or two, Eric called me and said, "Yo, the Tonies wanna see if you'll rap on this song. Raphael got a track for you." *Word? Hell yeah!* I was happy and extremely flattered, because they became interested in me from watching me doing my own music. It was super validating for a young artist.

Eric gave me Raphael's phone number and address. It turns out Raphael was still living in East Oakland, I think on East Ninety-Fourth. So, I showed up at his house on time, bright-eyed and bushy-tailed, ready see if this was going to be my shot. I honestly thought it *was* my shot, but I had no idea where this opportunity would lead. When I got to Ray's house, he was cool, a little shorter than me, soft-spoken, but talented as shit. He told me what was up. He had the track already with some vocals, a skeleton, and wanted to see if I could do something over it. It was called, "Feels Good." When he played it, I just knew it was a hit. They were planning on this being a single. They had also been talking about having MC Hammer do the same part. I didn't really know who MC Hammer was at the time, nor did I care. It wasn't personal. Remember, I'm from New York and, back then, radio—particularly urban radio—was way more regional. Being new to the city, I had limited exposure to West Coast artists.

I told Ray that I loved the track and that it would be a hit, before I even got on it. He gave me a copy to take it home so I could listen and get familiar with it. "Put something together and let's see what it sounds like." There was only an eight-bar space I was supposed to write for. Not a lot of room to flex my skills. To make it more difficult, this group was not your average group. They weren't a rap group; they were an R&B group. It wasn't gonna work to put the hard edge on it like I would've liked. But I did recognize that this was a big opportunity. So I wrote them eight bars—specifically for them. When I got a solid eight bars that I thought were ready, I hit up Raphael. Let's do it! They booked a studio session at the world-famous studio The Plant, in Sausalito.

The Plant is legendary—Prince, Sly and the Family Stone, Metallica, Rick James, the Grateful Dead, Bob Marley, Fleetwood Mac, Linda Ronstadt, Jimmy Cliff, Chaka Khan, Carlos Santana . . . the list of people who have recorded there is practically endless. Our session was at night, but even walking in, in the dark, I could feel the hugeness of the studio. It was the biggest studio I had been in, up to that point. And I wasn't even familiar with the full history of it then. It was dark, with high ceilings, wood—a lot of wood. The biggest mixing board I had ever seen until then. The lighting was low and they had those velour curtains hanging down. It felt rich. It felt like money.

They gave me my headphones and in that moment it felt like God was talking to me. *You want your shot? Here ya go. Good luck.* I was doing what I loved, and I knew I was good at it. Most importantly, it was where I knew I belonged. I never felt like it was this huge or unreal thing. It just felt right, and that I was there to do what I do. I have to say, I killed it. That verse was and is memorable.

We eventually recorded a video for the single in Los Angeles. It was a big production by most standards, but especially for my first music video. I knew it was going to be a performance video and I was gonna rap, not necessarily act. We shot it on a soundstage on a lot. When I walked in, the soundstage was set up like a stage at a concert. It was all lit up, and a lot of the band and cast were already there. A couple of grips came up to me, anxious to show me the stage trick that they had planned for my entrance. They were studio geeks, guys who just love what they do. They walked me back, upstage, and took me under. They were like, "Dude, you're gonna be coming from beneath the stage! You're gonna be coming out the freaking floor!" They were so hyped about it. Then they showed me the hydraulic lift that was set up to push me up through the bottom of the stage so that I could appear for my part. They had a bunch of tech tricks, like part of the stage floor was glass, and they shot from both sides of it. They had a couple of Fly Girls from *In Living Color* amongst the dancers. I had to admit—yeah, it was fucking cool.

The only thing was the wardrobe. Now, I don't know if you're familiar with Tony! Toni! Toné! and their wardrobe at the time, but they had their own style, okay? And being that I was a young feature artist and not part of the band, my style was a little different.

Remember, I'm a native New Yorker. I'm thinking Adidas and Lees. And then here comes Raphael talking about, "We want you to wear this." I love my dude, but he had a chain mail shirt in his hands, like something Isaac Hayes would wear. I can see it to this day. I said, "What else y'all got in wardrobe, man? Cuz I'm not gonna wear that." How I'm gonna be Mocedes the Mellow when y'all got me coming out in a muscle-bound chain-mail shirt? We found an applejack hat, and I was cool with that cuz we rock all kinds of hats out in the East. Then I found an electric-blue blazer, probably the only thing in wardrobe that I'd wear. I wore my own black shirt underneath, and my own jeans. It was whimsical, and not traditionally hip hop. But it worked.

After recording my part for "Feels Good," I was still working, waiting for something to happen. I met a couple of friends at AAA that kind of introduced me to The Town—my man Ron and my man Hawk. They were both Oakland born and raised, and good, decent dudes. We were the Three Musketeers at the job. Ron was a little extra, a hustla from West Oakland. He and several members of his family were still connected to them streets. And my boy Hawk was from East Oakland, right near Eastmont Mall. They introduced me to Mac G, who lived not too far from me around Lake Merritt. I had these three guys, plus my man Shorty B, who played bass for Too $hort and The Dangerous Crew. These few guys helped break me in and put me up on game in Oakland and the surrounding areas.

Actually, working for AAA had a benefit beyond just the paycheck. It helped me learn streets, freeways, and neighborhoods from Oakland all the way past Rodeo, basically the East Bay. On our time off, me, Ron, and Hawk would shoot to the City—San Francisco—because the City was the best place to go to party and have a relaxed time. I learned, eventually, that while hip hop thrived in the culture of Oakland, it was sketchy in the clubs. In Oakland, shit was likely to pop off when rap was played in the club because there were lots of issues between the players in the region. These friendships were crucial because they helped me get the lay of the land both literally and culturally. I was with the people.

CHAPTER 10

REUNITE ON THE GRIND

I'd been living in Oakland for about a year. In the fall of 1989, I got a letter from Afeni telling me that she was living with Pac and Sekyiwa right across the Bay, in Marin City. I never thought about how she got my address. Like I said, I lived a life where I knew I was being watched, both by the government and by my family, and by loved ones who wanted me to be okay even if they couldn't be with me. She included her phone number in the card, and I called immediately. It had been about eight years since I'd seen them and, honestly, those were crucial years—me and Pac's teen years, and Set's childhood. Pac was now eighteen and Set was fourteen. I had missed so much and I missed them so much. Afeni asked me to come over for Thanksgiving.

It was my first time seeing them in a long time, and I was concerned about what they would think of me. I wanted them to be proud of me. I wanted to make a good impression. I wanted to appear like a self-sufficient older brother. I washed the GTI and got a fresh fit. When I got there, I was surprised to see that they weren't living in a regular apartment complex. It looked like a housing development—low-income housing, the projects. I was later told it was called The Jungle. It was the first sign that things were not going as well for them as I had hoped and I had a little anxiety for their well-being.

When I arrived, Afeni was outside smoking, waiting for me. Set met us at the door to hug me, and Pac wasn't far behind. It was just us at dinner. Afeni always could cook, but I don't remember the food. I just remember we were talking so much. We had a lot of catching up to do. I mentioned recording "Feels Good," and Pac was really excited because Tony! Toni! Toné! was big. The song wasn't out yet, but the whole family was excited and hopeful. They were especially impressed that I'd recorded at The Plant.

After we finished eating, me and Pac went outside to shoot the shit. As he checked out the car, I told him what I had been up to, that I had a job and was working, that I'd been recording. In the middle of the conversation, I stopped and said we should go somewhere or do something, so we went to the store and I bought us a six-pack of beer. I didn't know what else to do. I was trying to bond with him on some grown level. I think we smoked a joint, too. But I didn't need to worry; we fell right into our sibling relationship, as if no time had passed. I remember Pac smiling a lot. I remember everyone smiling that day. We were all so damn hopeful that the future would be filled with more good days like this one.

But I also realized that Pac and Sekyiwa weren't having the easiest time. They had a small two-bedroom apartment with not a lot of furniture. There were no frills. It was just the basics, bare bones—a small TV and a kitchen table. At one point, Set or Afeni mentioned that they had come out to California after spending some time in Baltimore. It seems things got rough for them out there, in terms of their living situation, and that brought them West. I can only imagine how bad things were in Baltimore if this apartment in Marin City was a step up. I also found out Pac had spent some time as a teen in Atlanta, too, without Afeni and Sekyiwa. Life was not stable for them, that much was clear to me. Sure, I hated being separated from my father, but the life my mother provided for me was stable, even if I didn't like some of the sacrifices we had to make for that stability. Things were different for Afeni as a mother caring for children while also living the life of an activist and organizer. Mutulu being locked up had considerable consequences for Afeni, both as the mother of his children and also in the sense that it was part of a larger, more systematic effort to destroy a movement that was ultimately the social fabric that held her world together. For all the dedication to equality and respect for the matriarchs, ignoring the harsh reality of the material responsibility of caring for children when the men have been locked up, is simply foul. Not acknowledging this, along with the compounding struggles of Black women to maintain a household in general, would be obtuse. This life had clearly taken a toll on Afeni and what she could provide for her children as a single mother. Their living situation was frankly one of abject poverty. Make no mistake, there was no lack of love. There was, however, shabby furniture and clothes. And even though she pulled off a Thanksgiving meal, I suspected there were hungry days, too.

I knew it was up to me and Pac to get them out of there, and I was for sure gonna do my part. Even before we reconnected, I suspected Pac was rapping. There were times I just felt it—times I would think about him, imagine what he was up to, and hip hop was always in my mind's eye for Pac. The odd thing is, I really don't know why. When we were little, we were definitely surrounded by music, but it was our parents' music—soul music, for the most part, and African drum circles. Hip hop was this spark of a thing that was out there for *us*, not our parents' generation. Somehow, I just knew that Pac had found our generation's music, just like I had, that he had to be rapping, just like I was. And I was right.

Pac had been working on his craft. In Marin, he'd started working with artists, some of whom he met through the streets and some through poetry workshops he'd been doing with Leila Steinberg, an art and music professional in the community who was mentoring and developing young talent. He told me all about this rap group that he had been working with, Strictly Dope, with Ray Luv and DJ Diz. At one point, Leila introduced Ray and Pac to Atron Gregory, a music manager who would eventually take Pac on as a client.

Marin was only a thirty-minute drive to Oakland, so in an effort to reconnect with my siblings, I invited them over. Set came to spend the night in Oakland with me and Tiwan. We didn't have much room, but Tiwan was cool and I was happy to do it. Tiwan and Set made quick friends on some girl shit, and it felt good to see my sister happy. Pac also started to come over to my apartment, sometimes with different friends. He would come to see me at my job at AAA, and I'd introduce him to my coworkers. We would do brother stuff. He'd get dropped off at my house and tell me everything that was going on. Or I would give him haircuts and we would smoke and talk. We had our little routines.

We had a lot to catch up on, and even though we had been separated, we had so much in common. We'd talk about music, who we were listening to, who we liked, where we saw ourselves going. We also talked about who we wanted to record with, specific records and breakbeats and samples. We talked about politics and culture, what was going on in the world and, really crucial for us both, what was going on with our people. We caught up on the years we'd spent apart. I'd had rough experiences, being down South, and Pac and Set didn't have it any better. Afeni had struggled with addiction. Pac had gone to a school for the arts in Baltimore, but their home life had required them to grow up quickly. Even though their mother was there, they were on their own in many ways. They came out to California because Fe had allies there from her Panther days, but even that wasn't enough to put her in a position where Pac didn't feel the need to step up as the man of the house at an early age. Turns out we both had experienced filling that role way too young.

A little later on, Pac made an audition video for Atron, and that led to him joining Digital Underground. I was happy for him. He started going on the road with them. It felt like things were happening for him, and he deserved all of it. Now, a lot of people like to say that Pac joined the group as a dancer. That's not true, and even Shock G, the leader of the group, made that clear every time he talked about those early days. When Pac joined the group, he joined the group. He did everything. He was a roadie, he carried equipment, he backed them up on stage and, yeah, sure, he danced. But he was more than that. He was a true member of the group, putting in the work in the hopes of getting on a record.

While Tupac was on the road, "Feels Good" hit the radio. It was like the third or fourth single from the album, so it was being worked nationally, and it was a hit, a major hit. I knew Pac was proud of me because the guys from Digital would later tell me that whenever the song came on he'd be like, "That's my brother! That's my brother!" And they'd fuck with Pac, especially Money B. "That's not your brother! Where's he at then?"

When Pac came off the road, he came by my apartment as usual. I gave him a haircut, and then we headed to Berkeley to see Shock and Mon (Money B) and the guys from Digital. Except we didn't have any weed that day, and you know we can't have that! But Pac had a pocket full of money. Honestly, it looked strange, because Pac was a little "bummy," at least as I saw it at the time. He had an old leather trench coat that Shock G had given him, but it had holes in it, and the lining was ripped. It was a particular look from that Bay Area bohemian style mixed with hip hop that my NYC head couldn't fully wrap around.

After we picked up the bud, we stopped at a liquor store on East Fourteenth Street to get some blunts. It was pouring rain, so we got a bottle of E&J brandy, too, Erk & Jerk as we used to call it. We just rolled a blunt and talked. He was excited about how things were going with Digital. I'll never forget, at one point he looked over at me and said, "Mo, everybody is gonna know my name. Everybody!"

"Feels Good" climbed the charts quickly in the spring and summer of 1990. It was number one on the R&B chart and top ten on the Billboard Hot 100 list, so it wasn't just big in the Bay. My family was hearing the record out East, too. It was a such a big hit that Tony! Toni! Toné! was on the bill for KMEL Summer Jam and I performed with them that year. It was at Shoreline Amphitheatre in Mountain View, and while Summer Jam would become a national festival, it started in the Bay and at this point there was still a hometown pride in it. Tony! Toni! Toné! was on the bill and Digital was there, cuz backstage with all the artists was the place to be. It was dope. Both me and my brother were at what was the biggest festival of the day, in a professional capacity, and I took the stage at the biggest venue I'd been at yet . . . within months of my first professional recording. It was a sweet spot in our early careers.

I was making a name for myself with the success of "Feels Good," and getting to know different people in the Oakland rap scene. Erroll, who had been managing me since I recorded with Tony! Toni! Toné!, was also deepening my connections. He wanted me to record this song with Spice 1, who was bubbling on the scene with a local hit, "187 Proof." Turns out we were both going to do a feature with this up-and-coming group, The Coup. Boots Riley, the group's front man, had asked me to be on the record and when I met up with him, we clicked. Boots was a little, light-skinned dude with a big Afro and long, Elvis Presley sideburns. He had his own funky style that I could dig. The Coup was a revolutionary group and Boots's father was a civil rights attorney. We shared common views on politics in the community and after kicking it for a couple of days, we recorded "Dope Lika Pound or a Key" at his house.

At the same time, Pac was recording more with Digital, landing some features, and Shock and Digital got an opportunity to record some music on the soundtrack for the movie *Nothing But Trouble*. They ended up using "Same Song"—one of Pac's features—but the great thing for Pac was that all of Digital got to appear in the movie. The film starred Dan Akroyd, Chevy Chase, and Demi Moore; it was Dan Akroyd's directorial debut. Dan actually appeared in the video for "Same Song," too, as a Scottish bagpipe artist. Pac was dressed as a pharaoh, brought into frame in a sedan chair carried by six guys, three on each side, to deliver his verse. Shock always had an irreverent sense of humor, and I love that he brought that out in my baby brother. Now, Shock was also serious, a musician to the core who played piano with the best and produced music to an exacting quality that he could and would only measure against himself.

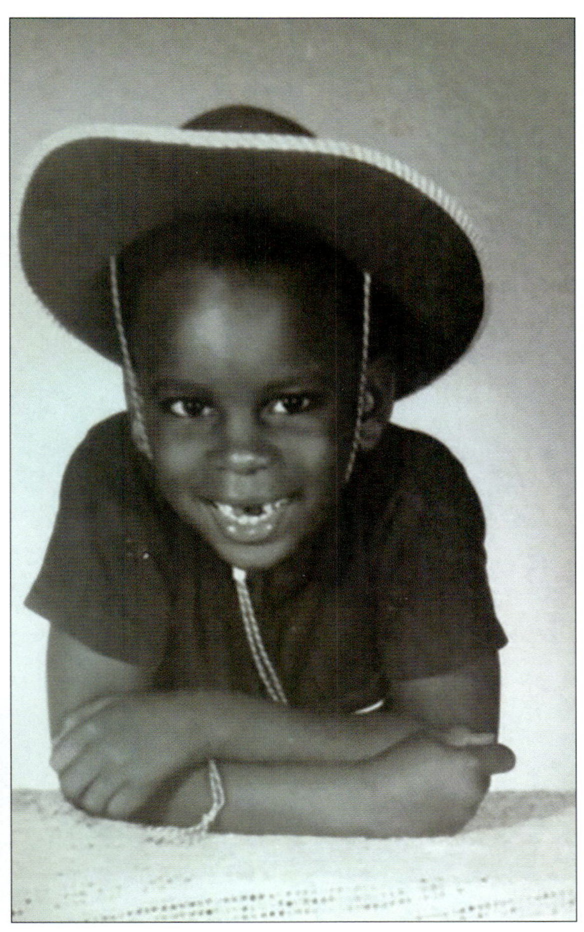

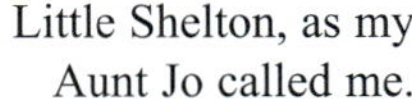

Little Shelton, as my
Aunt Jo called me.

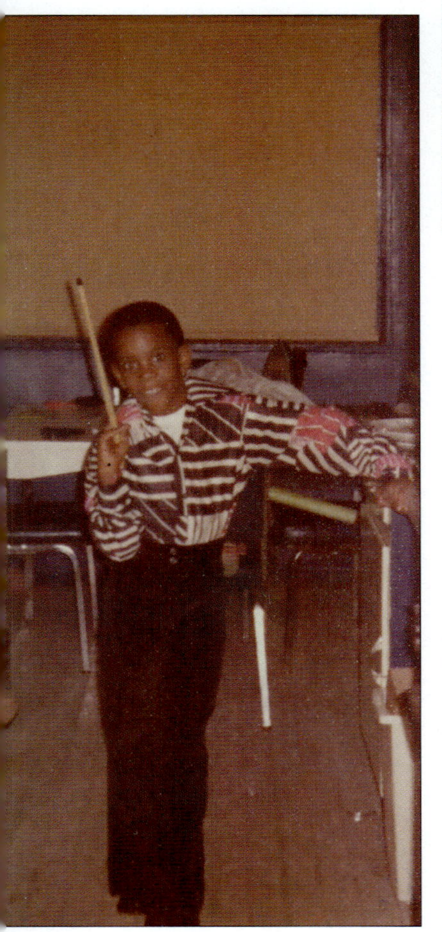

A really good Christmas.
© *Sharan Golston*

My mother, the beautiful Sharan Harding.

Aunt Jean and Uncle John the best of peop

Uncle Joey and my cousin Jermain in Jamaica, Queens.

Takeover by Lincoln Hospital workers from Detox program at 25 Worth Street NYC Hospital Corp, Main Office on 9/24/75. Mutulu Shakur (center) with Mickey Meléndez, a prominent Young Lord (left), and lawyer Stanley Cohen (with beard).

Mutulu at Lincoln Detox.

My loving and very lovable siblings, Sekyiwa, Nzingha and Chinua.
© *Anita Hearn Shakur*

Pac hugging Chinua, with me and Mouse, at Malcolm X Grassroots Movement event (February, 19
From left (bottom) Ayana Sunni-Ali, Ifetayo Tyehimba, Tupac Shakur, Chinua Shakur, Dana "Mousen
Smith, Ayo (above) Boatema Sonyika, Asantewa Sunni-Ali and Tashiya Umoja-Mkanga, and me.
© *Anita Hearn Shakur*

Big 'Tulu at USP Lompoc (circa 1990).

The beginning: from the "Feels Good" video shoot.
Courtesy of Motown Records under license from Universal Music Enterprises

e Legend.
Maurice Shakur

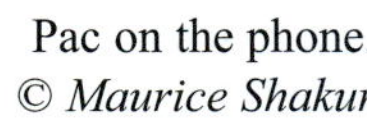
Pac on the phone.
© *Maurice Shakur*

Me on my Day One cell phone.
© *Maurice Shakur*

Poetic Justice road trip,
Tupac and Mouse Man
standing on Pac's trailer.

rk Ahead: Pac, me,
l Mike Cooley in Hollywood.

Mouse, Serg, and me.

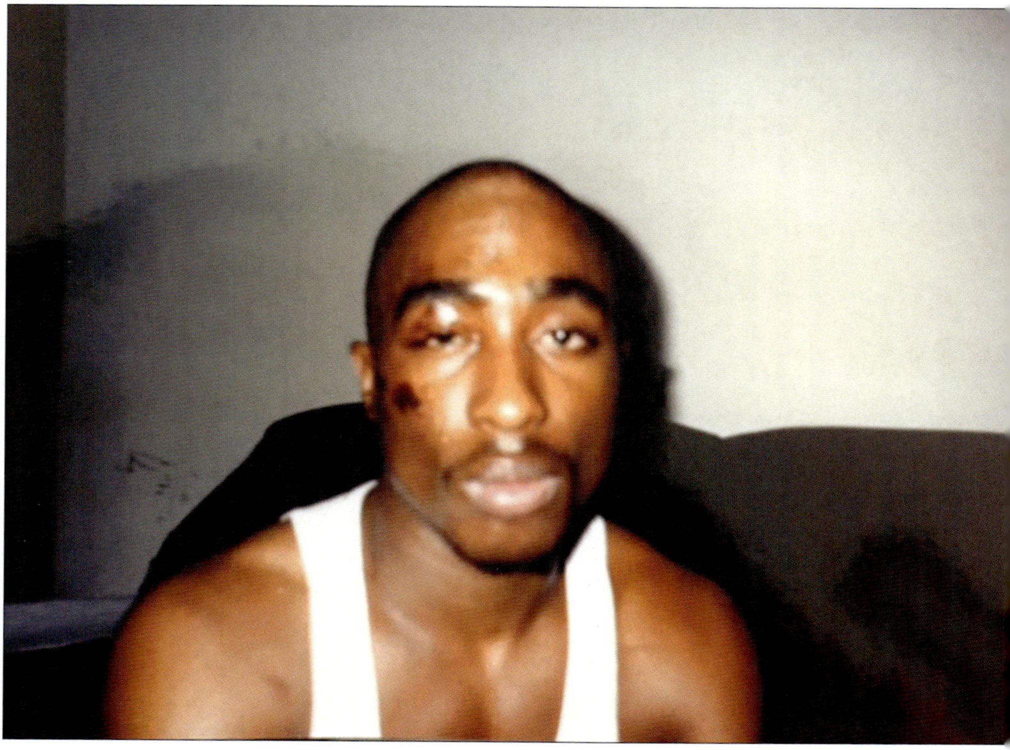

Aftermath of OPD assault.
© Maurice Shakur

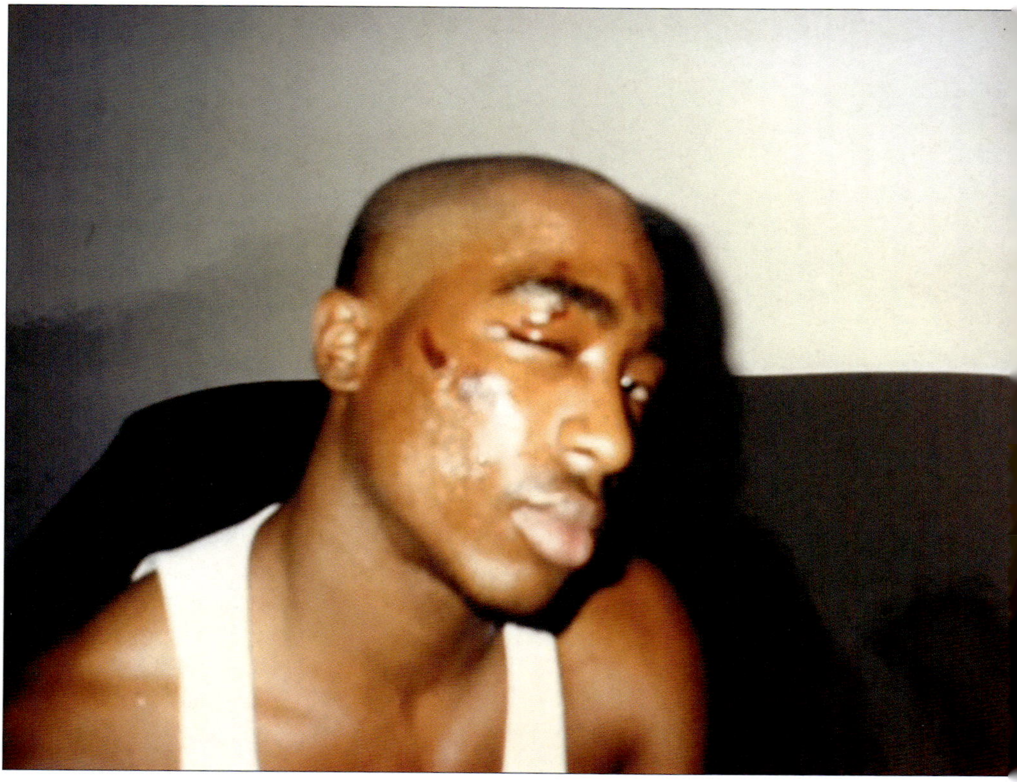

Mutulu introducing THUG LIFE
at USP Lompoc.

UG LIFE waiting to perform
USP Lompoc
ont row: Pac and Y?N-Vee
cond row: Me (center) and Serg (right).

THUG LIFE in Harlem (155th St & St. Nicolas Ave) NY, 1994.
From left to right: Me, Macadoshis, Tupac, Rated R and Big Syke.
© *T. Eric Monroe*

Brotherly Love: Me and Pac in NYC visiting Pac's old elementary school, 1994, Big Syke and Macadoshis behind.
© T. Eric Monroe

Tupac and Cheyenne "The Pea" chillin' in the Bu (Malibu, CA, summer of 1996).
© *Maurice Shakur*

Me, Mutulu, and Los Angeles Mayor Karen Bass in Hollywood (January 8, 2023).
© *Tracy Danielle Robinson*

Grandmother (GG) and Cheyenne (2017).
© *Maurice Shakur*

Hollywood Walk of Fame: Me and Sekyiwa dedicating Tupac's star (June 7, 2023).
© *Stefany Baclaan*

I'm just saying the video really did encapsulate Shock, Money B, and Digital—serious about the music and irreverent about life. The cameo they did in the film was short, but Pac was in a key shot and got to shine. Honestly, the record did better than the film, but that really didn't matter to us. Pac filmed that over the summer while my record was charting. We both ended up on the radio at the same time! It was just insane. We felt like we were taking over the world. What Pac had said to me—that everybody would know his name—was coming true.

We were starting to meet all kinds of people from different parts of the Bay. Pac was still in Digital, but we started recording together, too. I always knew he was special, and I felt like the work I was putting into recording as a solo artist would be better focused on the two of us together. Around this time, Mike Cooley and Man Man, who Pac had known from before, started playing a larger role in his career. They were from Richmond, but Pac met them when he was still living in Marin. Mike Cooley started working as his road manager, and Man Man started working as his manager. We really needed their type of business structure; Atron owned TNT Records, which was the label under Tommy Boy that Digital was signed to. Atron and Man Man worked closely together, and eventually Atron would be part of Pac's management, too.

At one point, Shock was approached about an acting role in an upcoming urban film, *Juice*. He thought Money B should try out for the role, but Mon ended up telling Pac he should go for it. A couple of weeks later, Pac called me and told me that he got the part! He told me I should come out to New York while they're filming. It wasn't even a consideration: We were linking up again as brothers, just like when we were little ones in New York. I was gonna hold my little brother down and we were gonna run around the city, work and play, as young men. For a creative, every experience is an opportunity to meet new people, to create, collaborate, inspire, and be inspired. Shock had a friend he knew out in Queens, Stretch, who was also signed to Tommy Boy, and he wanted us to link up. Stretch would end up being pretty key in our musical sphere of collaborators. We also met Treach, from Naughty By Nature on set.

People are always surprised about Pac's acting background, but I have no idea why. As kids, and even when we were separated, Pac and I both enjoyed theater all through high school. I'd been the vice president of my drama club in North Carolina, and Pac had performed in NYC and was in theater at the Baltimore School for the Arts. We loved theater, especially August Wilson. I also loved *Porgy and Bess*, especially "Ain't Necessarily So" and "Summertime." Pac had performed in *A Raisin in the Sun* at the Apollo; I'd played the Great Caribeno in a production with the North Carolina Opera. We loved *West Side Story*, we loved *Carmen Jones* and Dorothy Dandridge's performance. I knew of *Les Mis*, but Pac really brought it to light for me. Later, he would play the entire album on long road trips back and forth to LA and we'd sing along. It would become a theme for us, an anthem. This shouldn't be any surprise. We were experiencing all of these concepts in our lives and grappling with how to synthesize them into our music: incarceration, an unfair and biased criminal justice system, poverty, classism. Victor Hugo was for real an influence on us.

From the time we all met on the set of *Juice*, Treach, Stretch, Pac, and I became pretty close. Stretch was a big dude, about six-four, three hundred pounds, dark-skinned, with a real deep voice. Anytime we were shooting a video, Stretch and Maj, Stretch's brother, would come and hang out and make an appearance. We would also go to New York to record and hang out with Stretch and his crew, Live Squad. We all got along, but more important than that, we made each other feel stronger, like our crew was deeper. A lot of times, Pac would go by himself to New York and hang out with them alone. That's how safe he felt with Live Squad. In fact, Pac and Stretch would clown around so much, Stretch knocked Pac's front tooth out just playing around. We were in the car and Pac was joking around and smacking Stretch. They're just laughing, and Stretch was trying to block the smacks by holding up his arms, *Come on, man*, and Pac caught an elbow in his mouth. Knocked Pac's tooth straight out! I thought Pac would be mad, but instead he was play mad. He called him every Black, stupid, motherfucker in the book, just laughing. That's how close they were.

Pac had already known Treach from when Digital toured with Queen Latifah, and Treach was part of Flavor Unit. Pac and Treach got close, and the two of them became notorious for getting in fights. People tried to give Latifah a lot of bullshit because she was a woman. And if anybody said anything out of line, the first ones flying offstage to whoop somebody's ass were Pac and Treach. City to city, same thing, several times.

We all thought Treach was a dope artist, so we were supporting him and he was supporting us. In fact, Pac went on a campaign to try to get Treach and his group a record deal. He was promoting Naughty By Nature to anybody willing to listen. When we would come to the East Coast, we would link up with Treach and go to New Jersey, to his neighborhood. They called it Naughtyville. I had very little familiarity with New Jersey back then. One time in particular, Treach had just bought a brand-new gold Mercedes and he wanted us to come with him back to Jersey to show it off. So of course we went. When we pulled up, I kinda got why they called it Naughtyville. It wasn't exactly a cul-de-sac, but it seemed like everyone lived around each other. Vinny was there, KG, their DJ, was in another house. Latifah lived near them. All of their group members lived very close to each other. It was like a middle-class neighborhood, with sizable houses. And they treated us like kings. We laughed and smoked, cracking jokes on each other all afternoon. That trip was really what bonded our friendship. Treach ended up getting a deal for Naughty By Nature, and we were all happy when Naughty came out with a monster single, what would become a hip hop classic, "O.P.P."

Even with Pac a part of Digital, we were on the smash to get him a solo deal. We knew we needed to have one before *Juice* came out—he had a big role and we were set on piecing the work together in a way that all the parts amplified each other. We wanted to maximize his presence. And our creative sphere was just growing and growing. Pac and I were living together in Oakland by that time, and I was hanging out with all of them in Shock's studio in Berkeley, getting to know the dudes. The first time on stage with them, in San Francisco, I started to feel like I was part of the clique. It was a hometown thing, and that meant our people, like three thousand of them, got to see us perform with Digital. Doing that first show with them is how Digital got to know and see me as a professional performer for the first time. And I got to see the process, the way that Humpty came out in real life. We killed it and had a ball that night. Well—until we got home after and found that somebody had robbed the house while we were at the show.

We worked constantly, but it was what we loved, so the hustle never bothered us one bit. We each had our own ideas and creative concepts, and we were always balancing them out with the ideas and concepts of the circles of people we were working with. Say, for example, one of us had written a new rhyme, but there was no accompanying music yet. Somebody else would be like, this track would work good with that rhyme, that flow. The song would then take shape in a new direction, but with the same foundation. Shit like that would happen all the time. Or the reverse: a great piece of music, but not yet a track, that we'd write to. Even when the music comes first, it's always the collaboration that turns it into an actual song.

Many of the people we were working with in the Bay were parts of new circles that we were getting to know. People forget, we were New Yorkers coming of age as musicians in California. So when Pac or I or both of us went on the road, we always built real connections with artists who were coming out of New York and New Jersey. Plus, Pac had his friends from Baltimore. The two who were really around the most were Jada and Mouseman.

I think Mouse was Tupac's first music collaborator. I mean, it's possible he wrote or recorded as a shorty in New York, but I really think Mouse was his first creative partner. When Afeni, Pac, and Set were living in Baltimore, Pac became best friends with Mouseman, who got his name because he was a little dude that was real fast. He ran track. His uncle was respected in the streets, which gave Mouse a certain amount of clout, and he looked out for Pac, Set, and Fe. In spite of Pac having multiple creative outlets from being in the Baltimore School for the Arts and working with Mouseman, he still had a dismal home life. Or perhaps it was precisely because he had a dismal home life that he really needed multiple creative outlets. The family was really struggling at this time. These were the early days of Afeni's struggles with addiction, and Pac would reflect on how poor they were and the raggedy clothes they had compared to Mouse, his good buddy.

Nevertheless, they were homies, and they stayed homies. Pac and Mouse would collaborate on songs and record them a cappella, being too young and not having access to a producer who could make the music with them. They would even go to the local radio stations and perform these songs, getting on the radio a time or two. So when we really began pulling things together for Pac's first professional music project, Mouseman was one of the first people he called. Pac and Man Man literally went to Baltimore and asked him to join the team. Mouse said yes, of course, and he became another ingredient in our gumbo. Immediately, Pac's juices were flowing, and he had an idea to put me and Mouse together. The three of us eventually lived together in Pac's apartment on MacArthur. We were moving as a unit and did almost everything together. As I got to know Mouse myself, I began to like him, too. He could rap, he could write songs, and he was funny as shit. It all worked.

By the summer of 1991, it was Pac's turn to perform at KMEL Summer Jam. This time, Digital was on the bill and Pac was performing with them and I was backstage with all the artists. Pac, in his young wisdom, used the opportunity to build relationships. He got some weed and said, "Yo, Mo, come on. We're gonna go to everyone's room and bless 'em." When we got to the venue, we started doing just that. A young Redman, who was early in his career, was in the first room we went to. I don't think Pac knew him already, but, being with

Digital, Pac was becoming popular enough that Redman knew who he was. We got to the room and there were hugs and handshakes. They were both happy to meet each other and then Pac said, "Let me bless y'all with some love from California," and pulled out the weed. Red was like, "Hell yeah, Pac." We watched Red and his boys marvel over the weed—mind you at this point, nobody had weed like California. Red was real appreciative. We didn't stay long and went to the next room, Super Cat's. Cat was also familiar with who Pac was, and was happy to start smoking right away. We soon left and were just catching people in the hallway. I was having a good time being the assistant to the Ambassador of the Bay Area, my baby brother.

Around this time, we put together a duo with me and Mouse, with me recording as Wycked. This was while we were still putting together a demo to get Pac a solo deal. These recordings would end up being used on other projects down the line, but we never ended up releasing a project together in that formation. Meanwhile, Jada was in LA starting her career as an actress, but she would drive up to see Pac whenever she could. By the fall of 1991, she had started on *A Different World* and she would come up with Cree Summer. Jada was always a steady fixture, and a precious part of Pac's life.

By this time, I had broken up with Tiwan and moved in with my brother. We were living right there off MacArthur Boulevard—a stretch of the boulevard since named Tupac Shakur Way in 2023. We were on the rise, but we were still broke. Pac would be all around town, running his errands. I had quit working at AAA by that point, and in our down time, me and Mouse would chill at the house, waiting for Pac to get back. I remember one day in October, we heard a car drive up and an angry door slam. Next thing we know, Pac busts in the house cursing, mad, yelling. And when he turned around and I caught a good look at his face, his shit was fucked up. Me and Mouse asked, "Yo, what the fuck happened? You got in a fight? You got jumped? What the fuck?" He said, "OPD. Mothafuckas jumped on me while I was trying to cash my check." And we were like, "Oakland Police? Are you for real?" He's like, "You see my mothafuckin' face, right?" Mouse asked him, so what happened? And Pac starts telling the story.

As he's talking, we're taking in how bad the cops fucked my baby brother and started looking for peroxide, gauze, alcohol, things to clean him up. I also started looking for the camera. We used to keep little disposable cameras around to catch some of the moments. By the time Pac had basically finished telling the story, I had found a camera. I yelled, "Let me get some pictures." Pac was about to take off his clothes and change, but before he did, he let me take a few shots. I made sure to get all the wounds, gashes, and deep, bloody red scrapes. He wasn't still bleeding, but he was swollen and the wounds were this awful, deep, bloody red. They scraped his skin completely off his face in places. I was just looking at exposed, bloody, face flesh. I tried to get in close to the biggest one. I shot from a couple of different angles. And I was like, yeah, we're definitely going to need these pictures. I couldn't believe this shit.

Apparently, when he crossed the street to go to the bank to cash his check, he jaywalked, and the cops jacked him up on the sidewalk. They started asking for his identification. And when they heard his name, they decided to make fun of it. One of them said, "Tupac? Your mom named you that?" In one contemptuous sentence, he managed to disrespect both my brother *and* his mother. His mother, the same woman who successfully defended herself as a member of the Panther 21, who was among the leadership of the Harlem chapter of the Black Panthers. And here he was, confronted by OPD in the birthplace of the Black Panthers, and that pig had his mother's name in his mouth. It pissed Pac off, triggered him something fierce, that they mentioned his mother.

So Pac, being Pac, proceeded to curse them out. And they, being the police, proceeded to grab him, throw him down, and scrape his face on the sidewalk. They eventually cuffed him and took him to jail. Needless to say, we were all pissed the fuck off. Pac and Shock and the rest of Digital held a press conference with a local Bay Area news channel, and it was *on* with them mothafuckas. Pac was going to sue, and we all felt he had a good case. He had everybody's support—our crew, Digital, the community, I mean, basically anyone who saw his face and what they did.

On top of the assault, Pac was also heated that they took him to jail. I don't remember how long they held him, and I know it wasn't long, but it didn't matter. They'd beaten him and taken him to jail. From our side, we were frustrated that we didn't know what was going on for those few hours. There was no communication. Between them beating him, taking him to jail, and releasing him, there was zero communication. He eventually called Atron, who came and got him out, but we had been in the dark. We had no idea where he was, and to see him come home in this condition was so deeply unsettling and infuriating.

Pac had now entered the statistics of thousands of young Black males who were unjustly beaten by the police. I was real pissed off because, just when we're about to catch momentum and a good stride, the fucking police had to fuck with us. I was pissed off because Pac was doing nothing wrong, just going to cash his first check from his first film. This should've been a happy occasion. Instead, they'd damaged his film career by so completely messing up his face. He was on his way to being a fucking movie star, for Christ's sake. He already was, to us.

I was also relieved that it wasn't worse. They could've killed him. I understood that so clearly as a brother, as a Black man, as the child of a New Afrikan. This was the same police department that the Black Panthers took their stand against back when they were first formed. I understood that so *painfully* clearly, and while my heart burned with anger, in the pit of my stomach I felt relief that he, at least, lived so that he could sue their asses. As much as things had changed from our parents' generation to ours, some shit stays the same. I didn't know it at the time, but it was the start of what would become the Tupac Shakur legend. He did sue the police and won, and lived to tell about it.

Ironically, prior to this incident, we had shot the video for Pac's first single, "Trapped." In several scenes in the video, an OPD police car is featured as these cops are chasing him. "Trapped" is about being trapped in the system—through society, poverty, and law enforcement. I'm in a scene in the video with some other guys attacking the cops that are beating on Pac. "Trapped" was released as the first single on *2Pacalypse Now*, three weeks before OPD beat him. Talk about life imitating art.

Keep in mind, six months before this, the world had seen the video of the LA cops beating Rodney King. The whole world pretended to be shocked; we knew this was nothing new. This was our experience as young Black men. Between the time the world was horrified by that video and when the album came out, Pac reminded us not to forget Rodney King on a song called "Soulja's Story." He was talking about retribution, about holding the cops accountable when the system won't. It's an imaginary world, of course, where we, as citizens, can fight back against the state-backed violence of cops as equals. Imagine that.

2Pacalypse was released the same day that he announced his ten-million-dollar lawsuit against OPD. It was never about the money, although in truth they should've paid more than the $42,000 that he settled for. It was about publicly holding the police accountable and making the world see that police brutality is not a glitch in the system, it's actually a feature in the system's functionality. For Pete's sake, the cops in Rodney King's case admitted that they beat him, because taking someone down in a choke hold isn't legal anymore. And this cop talked about it like it was just regular to beat someone as the only way to subdue and make an arrest. At the same time, part of the egregiousness of my brother's case was that they put him in an illegal choke hold. Seems we get beat either way.

As Pac's career started to grow, he started feeling the power of his success. At this point he had already been beaten up by the Oakland PD, and had just finished shooting *Juice*. So when news started spreading around the city that MC Hammer had bought, purchased, and paid for a helicopter for the OPD to fight crime, of course we had an opinion about it. The whole damn hood had an opinion about it.

We shared our outrage amongst each other, but we hadn't had the chance to run into MC Hammer yet. So when Pac would do certain interviews at the time and speak on it to other people, word eventually got back to MC Hammer.

We didn't actually run into Hammer, but we got word that his brother wanted to talk to Pac. We ended up meeting backstage at some event in Oakland. Pac was very anxious to relay to Hammer's brother how he felt about the situation. He wanted to do it right, and articulate why we felt the way we did. When we finally met up, I didn't realize how tall the guy was. Big, tall dude, but he seemed cool. Pac, of course, wasn't intimidated by this brother's height in the slightest. But he didn't exactly make a measured argument; he totally unleashed his anger about the situation: "Bruh, how the fuck y'all gonna buy a helicopter for OPD? They beat my ass, they beating and killing niggas in the street." Pac was passionate, yelling and getting in his face about the situation. Hammer's brother was saying something to the effect of, "Nah, it ain't like that. We need the good ones to look out for our communities, too." People say the same shit now. Nonetheless, his argument was *not* going over well with Pac. For better or for worse, it kinda deaded the issue, which was good, because there were a lot of people who thought it was gonna blow up into a real thing. We all knew that it would've been bad for the city, and Hammer or Pac or both was gonna lose money. Nobody wanted that.

We would find out later that Hammer didn't actually buy OPD a helicopter. And a few years later Pac would be on the same label, Death Row. They would develop a cool creative bond, so much so that Pac wrote a song for Hammer to perform. "Unconditional Love" was, in my opinion, one of Pac's best songs, but Hammer never ended up recording it. Pac wrote him a hit and he knew it. But it was coming from a really vulnerable place and Hammer couldn't record it. They were just two different types of dudes, coming from different places, but they came to genuinely respect each other.

CHAPTER 11

SMASH FOR THE DREAM

All of this was going on while we were still racing to record a demo for Pac's solo deal. It was all hands on deck. Shock started pairing Pac up with producers to record, like DJ Daryl, Chopmaster J, Deon "Big D The Impossible" Evans, and Fuze, to name a few. Ray Luv was recording with him; so was I. We were surrounding ourselves with intensely creative and talented people, many of whom aren't fully appreciated to this day. In the end, only two songs made it onto his demo, and "Papa'z Song" was one of them—making me the only other rapper on that demo. Now, it's true that Tom Whalley signed Tupac to Interscope after hearing the demo. But there's an important detail that often gets left out of this story: At the time, Jimmy Iovine and Ted Field owned Interscope, and Ted was the finance behind the deal. But it was his *daughter*, Danielle Field, who heard the demo and told her father that he had to sign Pac. It wasn't some big music exec with an open mind and a good ear—though for sure we needed those guys on our side, too. It was a young girl who first heard Pac and knew he was going to be important. That's the real crux of my brother's genius: his ability to touch people, no matter who they are.

As soon as we got that green light, we accelerated our schedule and started recording in Richmond, at Starlight Sound Studio. I mean, the deal was done in August, and *2Pacalypse Now* would be released in November, so we were smashing through it. But that was nothing new for us!

That fall, Treach came to town with Naughty By Nature who, of course, we knew from *Juice*. They had "O.P.P.," which was a huge record, and he was our boy. Earlier that day, we were kicking it with Ecstasy from Whodini. Originally, it was a big group of us, but somehow everybody got scattered, so it was just the four of us together that night: me, Pac, Treach, and Ecstasy. I think we might have been south of Market, where there were tons of clubs and warehouses with big parties. So we were in this club, and the four of us got on the stage and were doing "O.P.P." It was epic, a dream come true. Ecstasy had the hat on, that famous Zorro hat, and the crowd went bananas. The city was *packed* that night. It was fall in San Francisco, when there are actually warm evenings. The traffic was bananas. It felt like we shut down the city.

Five months after *2Pacalyps*e was released, while we're still promoting the album and singles were still being worked, within weeks of each other two events would continue to blur the lines between life and our art. First, a young man in Texas would be pulled over by the police, and he would then shoot and kill the cop who pulled him over. Because he was listening to *2Pacalypse* at the time, Pac and the record would be dragged into a case about our lyrics, our art being responsible for violence instead of what we were really doing: describing the violence that already existed in our world. That shit got us banned from performing in Texas. Then, a couple of weeks later, the cops that beat Rodney King would be acquitted and the world exploded, especially LA.

I was in Oakland and Pac just happened to be in Los Angeles on business. Everyone was waiting on the verdict, but we were so busy that we weren't keeping up with it minute by minute. But then it came down. I, and everybody else I knew, was glued to the TV, watching the beginnings of what would become known as the Rodney King Riots. Then Pac called me and I could hear the sheer joy in his voice, the happiness, the relief. Actually, he was kinda laughing.

"Mo, you seeing this shit?"

I'm like, "Hell yeah, I'm seeing this shit. Where is you at? Where the fuck is you at?"

"I'm good. I'm with Jinx. We're in the hood. We're in the heart of it," he said. "We strapped. It's all love."

Sir Jinx is a legendary West Coast producer and Dr. Dre's cousin. He and Pac were ridin' around, and they would stop and talk and riot along with people Jinx knew from the hood. I told Pac, "Yo, don't get caught up in no bullshit out there! Get your ass home!"

Rodney King represented us. And the fact there was finally some retribution, even if it was in the form of riots, felt appropriate in some way. Honestly, I felt good, too. I wasn't rioting—although I could've in Oakland—but I understood where they were coming from and I supported everyone that was. I was of an age where I understood the anger and frustration. The creative side of me, the part that needs to understand where people are coming from, just knew this was a legitimate response, even if it may not have been the most productive. Sometimes the act of expressing that anger and making yourself felt is the entire point.

Between *Juice* and *2Pacalypse*, Pac was growing in popularity, but we still did regular shit. One of the very regular things we did was go to the record store and buy music from all the local artists on a weekly basis. We were still new to Oakland, and Pac wanted to hear all the artists in the area. One of these times, we came across E-40 and the Sick Wid It clique. We quickly fell in love with their music and felt the 40 was one of the most unique talents in the game who hadn't really been discovered yet. The Bay, after all, is not that big. We met and became quick friends, showing up at each other's video shoots.

Speaking of regular shit to do. One day me, Pac, and Mouse were going into Lucky's grocery store on Lakeshore to get groceries, just like anybody else. Pac made the trip specifically because he had plans to cook something—lobster tails in red wine sauce. These two girls spot Pac as we're walking through the parking lot and start losing their shit. They both start jumping up and down. "That's Tupac! That's Tupac! That's Tupac!" The older girl grabs the younger girl's hair and keeps jumping up and down with the younger girl's hair still in her hands, shaking her up and down like a rag doll. The three of us were so shocked at her actions. We hurried over to them and the three of us were like, "Stop, stop! No, stop! What are you doing?" We tried to take her hands out of the girl's hair. The older girl was in tears. The younger girl was just in shock, stunned from being jerked up and down, stunned from Pac putting his hands in her hair . . . all of it. Pac was like, "Nah, don't do that. You're gonna hurt her." And the girl was like, "I just love you. I just love you, Tupac. I just love you." He said, "I love you, too," and she asked for an autograph. It was one of the first *whoa!* moments for us, about how some people could act when Pac was around. It definitely wouldn't be the last.

Even so, popularity doesn't pay the bills. We were still basically broke, and we were still living together in a one-bedroom off MacArthur Blvd. We were on the come up, but we also had friends coming up who were ahead of us, some of whom would come over to our house. One of the first ones I remember coming by to visit was Queen Latifah. Now, we had visited Latifah in her city, but this was her first time coming to check on us. Though Treach had Naughty By Nature, he was still part of Latifah's crew, Flavor Unit. With Pac and Treach's relationship, we were all becoming kind of close. I remember when Latifah and her friend stepped through the door, she looked around and had a look on her face like she smelled something bad. All I can remember is her snapping her head around, with that look on her face, like she'd just stepped into a junkyard.

Sure, me, Pac, and later Mouse were not the most cleanliest mothafuckas. It was a testosterone-filled bachelor pad. But we were three grown men living in a one-bedroom with a regular-sized living room space, kitchen, and breakfast nook, pretty basic. We had a small couch on the other side of the living room, and the infamous futon. Man, if that futon had eyes, the stories it could tell. It served as a bed. It served as a couch. It served as a location for sexual activity.

It served as a hiding place for guns and drugs, and it might've had a bullet hole or two. That futon went through two rounds of guys; first me, Pac, and Mouse, and then Yak, Katari, and Malc. The one bathroom would actually look exhausted, with wet washrags hanging off the sink, shoes and socks on the floor, full hamper. You ever seen a bathroom look exhausted before? And the bedroom looked like an urban clothing store blew up inside it. Just shirts, jackets, T-shirts, bags, shoes, shoes in the box, shoes out of the box.

La and her friend didn't stay long, as you might have guessed, but Pac was real happy that she came by at all. They arranged to meet somewhere else in town later, and I could tell La wanted to get the hell out of there.

We were still technically at the beginning of our careers. Mouse and I never actually got paid in the beginning, because there was no money to pay us. We were in it for our love for Pac, our love for music and, truthfully, at this point in everyone's career, it's all an investment. You piece together money from a show to pay the rent, it's paycheck to paycheck. Whatever Pac was getting, which wasn't that much, he was spending on the crew.

But eventually we started booking more shows. Luke Campbell, Uncle Luke of 2 Live Crew, had a handful of clubs down in Florida that he was running. When Pac got booked for one of his clubs, they booked us for all of them, and there were about four. Luke even had a famous strip club at the time, called the Rolex Club. None of us had ever been to the Rolex yet, but we were looking forward to it. We started with the first club, then the second club. We started getting a feel for the people in Miami and south Florida. Things were different there than in the Bay and other cities where we had toured. They allowed table dances at the time, where a topless woman would come right up to your table and dance there instead of being on the stage. Some of the clubs we did on this Miami Loop Tour were partially nude. We were breaking all kinds of rules.

At this time, mind you, we had the Young Thugz on tour with us, and they were between fourteen and sixteen. It was Katari (K-Dog),

Aunt Glo's son; Malcolm (Big Malc), Aunt Glo's friend's son; and Yaki (Young Hollywood), Sekou and Yaasmyn's son. The Young Thugz were essentially our cousins, and they came out for varying periods of time, like over the summer or if they were having issues at home.

One of the most memorable things on this tour was when Luke took us to the back to the VIP room at the Rolex Club. Luke's guys were being real cool to us, because they wanted to impress us. We were all laid back in the chairs in the VIP getting drinks, and this dude with a deep Southern accent comes up to us. He's with this pretty chocolate sista with a humongous booty. He introduced her to all of us and then he said, "Go ahead. Show 'em." She smiled and proceeded to turn around, enthusiastically pulling her thong down, bending over, and spreading her ass cheeks. Now I did notice before he said it, but the guy she came in with very helpfully pointed out, "Her booty hole bigger than her pussy." We were like, "Damn, oh shit!" I think all of us were more fascinated than turned on, because it *was*. Everybody started busting out laughing. The Young Thugz—who, remember, were teenagers—were pushing each other's heads towards her booty. It was pretty hilarious. They're good and nasty down there.

After that, we were excited about getting to go to the Rolex Club with Luke. It was everything we expected. Pac and I had been to Magic City in Atlanta several times, but the Rolex was on another level. Luke introduced us to a few girls, but didn't have to: They were attracted to Pac like bees to honey. During these shows, we met Brother Marquis, who would end up being a dear friend to the clique. We connected because we were both going through a similar thing, being banned in the USA. Marquis was part of 2 Live Crew. Their album, *As Nasty As They Wanna Be*, was declared obscene and they were actually arrested in Florida. They had M16s on the beach in their video. You'd never see that in a video anymore. But the guns weren't even the problem: It was the sexual content. Eventually, they were found not guilty on the obscenity charges. But that shit was fucked up. None of us liked that they were trying to tell us what to do.

A few months later, we would get another visit from Jada and Cree. The thing with Pac is, when something or someone was special, he kept it quiet. His friendship with Jada was one of those special things—they had a deep emotional, intellectual, and creative connection and a profound love for each other. Pac had really hopped on acting after *Juice*, and began to do several TV shows, one of which was *A Different World*. Pac had a friendship with Jada from way back, at the Baltimore School for the Arts. And of course, Pac wanted to be on her show. So, Jada and Cree found time in their schedules to drive up. I was real happy to see the both of them, because I didn't get to meet up with them when he was shooting these episodes and because we were still too broke for all of us to travel with him all the time.

There's a real big difference between the culture and business of music and that of television and film. The studio is a collaborative space—writing, composing, recording is most often groups of people working and creating together. Then when you perform as a musician, you have a backline. That's the production that makes the show possible—from sound engineers, technicians, lighting, effects, pyrotechnicians, some of which can be provided by the house. Then there's the musicians, your collaborators, your band, vocalists, dancers, all the things that make a show. As you grow and command higher performance fees, the budget to support the backline also increases. But any way you look at it, it's pretty rare that the artist is showing up by themselves to sell out a show. Plus, in our case, we were working and recording as a group. We rolled deep, which is not particularly unusual for musicians.

It doesn't matter whether it's film or TV, it's a completely different vibe. The crew is the production. The crew is determined by the producers. As an actor, you're mostly expected on set by yourself, or maybe with an assistant. And if you're in a guest role, you're likely by yourself unless you're of a certain caliber. Travel for your personal team isn't a given unless it's negotiated. Pac wasn't there yet, so we couldn't travel with him all the time, and definitely not deep like how we rolled. Truthfully, even if we could afford it, it's not exactly welcome to show up on set with a mob.

We started recording *Strictly 4 My N.I.G.G.A.Z.* in 1992, mostly in the Bay and some of it in Los Angeles. For most artists, the sophomore album is make it or break it. Your first album is like a bet the label makes, and in most cases, labels hedge that bet by limiting their investment. There's less studio time, at least on the label's dime, and the studios are smaller. Many artists, like Pac did, record the majority of their debut album on their own dime before they even have a deal. The musical talent is there, but you're tasked with being more creative and resourceful—to do more with less. Now, with the sophomore album, there were more resources to support the creative vision. Along with more resources, though, came higher expectations from the label. And the way we were working, we didn't need any external pressure to push forward. Pac had a clear vision of the many, many things he wanted to say, from day one. We probably, maybe, just had too much to say all at once!

Even though his debut and sophomore were Pac's solo albums, I was right there with him. I was involved in the albums both creatively and, increasingly, on the business side. Part of this was because of the speed at which we were working. Pac had this bottomless drive to create, and there were only a handful of people who could really keep up with him. He had management, always, even if those teams changed and the people were shuffled around. But I had, like, fifteen jobs. I was the only one of the crew who could handle both the creative and the business. To be clear, Pac absolutely could, too, but there are only so many hours in a day. I was often the one liaising with the label on the creative choices, something that suited my analytical mind well. I could see, participate in, and build strategy for reaching our audience. But as a creative, I was also able to speak for the work in an authentic way. Mostly, the A&R (Artists and Reperatoire) at Interscope trusted Pac's decisions, even if they didn't always understand them. They knew, musically, that we were blending funk and soul, and that our records were arranged and engineered in a truly masterful way, flawless.

Our sound was, like the genre of rap itself, a sampling of our unique sonic experiences. That's really the crux of rap, as an art. Musically, Pac and I experienced parallel childhoods, even when we were separated. We were exposed to soul and funk, appreciating the distinct ways we could blend them. Pac also had an appreciation for folk music, from the radicals and hippie overlap of our parents' generation. We were also, like the pioneers in hip hop before us, influenced by disco—a lot of the breaks in disco are used in hip hop, and new recording and musical technology was pioneered in the genre. Plus we both appreciated the fullness of large productions, like in musical theater or an epic piece of classical music or a big pop production or a film score. We also—and this is where rap really excels—knew how to tell a story. I'm not sure that the label always understood our stories, and that's okay. That was for our people, anyway, and we really were bringing together some of the best in the business: Live Squad, Ice-T, Ice Cube, Treach, Apache, Dave Hollister, Digital Underground, and I were all on the album. Stretch, Big D, Jam Master Jay, Bobcat, Laylaw, Shock . . . the production was on point.

It didn't surprise any of us that people wanted to be a part of Pac's sophomore album so bad. After all, Pac was a movie star before he had this record deal, so he was quite popular, to say the least. He had what most people would call magnetism, the whole package; he was a guy's guy and a girl's dreamboat. I may have my own charm and charisma—or so I've been told—but Pac's was over the top. People were just drawn to him. Beyond that, we had a lot of freedom with the new album, and a new, bigger budget. That excited people, and artists wanted to get down and make art. On the flip side, we were exposing the label and the industry to all that new talent. There was opportunity on all sides—get on a record and shine, show the suits what you can do. We were creating our own community of musicians.

While we were working on the album, I met a new friend of Pac's over the phone. Left Eye had just gotten her deal with an up-and-coming group TLC, though they didn't have a single out yet. The first time I answered her call, she asked for Pac and told me to tell him that Lisa called. This wasn't a new phenomenon: Pac, most of all of us, would get calls from different women, all the time. I just took the message and wasn't really paying much attention. But this Lisa woman kept calling. If I didn't catch her call, Mouse would. And then I would hear Pac call her back and they'd have these deep creative, political, interesting conversations for like an hour. They talked about a lot of music, too. I know they wanted to collaborate at some point, but they didn't end up doing anything together that would be released. They weren't often in the same place for long.

The fame was sweet, of course, going from young little Black dudes who nobody knew to getting recognized by fans. It's a sweet, natural high, especially to be received in a positive way—old, young, women, men, just loving what we were doing and what we were about. Random girls would ask for Pac's autograph and then be like, "Wait, we want yours too." Needless to say, it did a lot for our self-esteem. But where we really felt we were making it was among our peers, and the musicians who we came up on and were fans of. When we were in LA, we'd hang out with Ice-T in his studio at his house in the hills and with Eddie Griffin and Chris Tucker at the Comedy Store. We would also hang out with Warren G, Nate Dogg, Kurupt, and Snoop in Long Beach. They would all become lifelong friends; Warren and Nate, in particular, would come to collaborate on several records. Nate and I became particularly cool because we had both served in the Army, which is rare among rappers. It felt rewarding, like we belonged. It was fast, but so was our work pace, so it simply felt like it was meant to be. Like we were stepping into a path that was there for us all along.

Strictly is, of course, where we first used the N.I.G.G.A.Z. backronym: Never Ignorant Getting Goals Accomplished. We would build on that concept later, throughout both Pac's and my musical careers. Pac already blended numbers into words and phrases, even in how he stylized his name as 2Pac. We probably weren't the first to do that—I suspect it's something we got from the streets—but we certainly popularized it in a big way. We were wordsmiths, after all.

We made portmanteaus, and Pac loved an acronym. And we really, really loved backronyms. We were unapologetically Black, and Pac—and all of us in this creative sphere—loved taking something that had a negative connotation in dominant culture and flipping it on its head. It was our way of subverting the mainstream culture and pointing to the ridiculous hypocrisy at the root of the very ideas that disempowered us. We would use a lot of acronyms and backronyms in that way. Ironically, our parents and their generation never really got it. For all their very direct confrontation in trying to subvert the system, they never completely understood what we were doing and never thought that what we were doing was in any way as important or impactful as what they did or had tried to do to empower the people. But that's okay—they didn't need to get it. We knew who it was for, and those people knew exactly what we were saying. *Strictly* was strictly for our people. And it resonated with a generation.

Many older folks and outsiders, they were looking at us, particularly Pac, and saying, "Y'all are the sons of revolutionaries and you're calling yourself a nigga?" Let me take it back first. We had *always* planned on a cohesive movement that would be crystallized through a group, with corresponding recordings. This was us taking our gift for this particular creative expression and using it to both build community and reach people, touch people, maybe even change a mind or two. I know a lot of people, especially now, believe this was just a natural extension of what our parents were doing. Well, yes and no. We had our own experiences and our own ideas about how to connect with people. Our parents were serious, direct. We were serious, but we wanted to change minds by touching souls.

Corresponding with *2Pacylypse Now*, our first collective was the Underground Railroad, which conformed ideologically more to the inspirations that our elders found acceptable, on its face. There were a broad group of artists in the collective, and we supported each other's work but didn't record a project under the banner or make a deal for the collective, even if Pac did have business cards printed up. We needed the mutual support, honestly, and that was, in truth, the real meaning behind the name. We were just feeling like, we're coming from the bottom up, we're coming from the underground. Nobody really knew us, and we were just starting out. So what our elders may have assumed was our inspiration was so much more on the nose than what we actually meant, because even in our use of Underground Railroad as a group name, we still meant it as a metaphor with multiple meanings.

Underground Railroad was the first of several formations of the unified group concept, from which we were trying to create opportunities for lots of people. However, and at the same time, we had a different set of life experiences, in no small part due to the consequences of the fallout from our parents' actions. There were many moments when that truth led to conflicts with our elders. And this is the genesis of 50 N.I.G.G.A.Z. Though we were having a taste of success, we were often reminded that we were just some little niggas working for somebody else. This was a conflict within the industry that was a duplication or even an amplification of our lives as young Black men. This was also underscored by the abandonment Pac and I had experienced, even as we lived it in parallel but different lives as a result of the failure of the movement to support our parents. Neither one of us felt like this community of revolutionaries came and supported our mothers when they were left alone to raise us. And Pac, rightfully, took them to task for this fact any time they tried to admonish us. Cuz if you ain't looking out for the kids, who are you to judge? We embraced where we were getting love, attention, and guidance: the streets.

As a lot of artists do, we improved, built on, and updated the concepts for the album as we worked on it. Around the time we started recording the material for what would become *Strictly*, we changed from Underground Railroad and started 50 N.I.G.G.A.Z.—as in, one good one in each state can create a movement that can accomplish anything. Because it was a new concept, not many people knew of it. But we were still determined to represent. A few of us—Pac, Mouseman, Man Man, Mike Cooley, and I—even got the tattoo, 50

N.I.G.G.A.Z., which is a design Pac made up. Pac, Mouse, and I got ours together at this tattoo shop on the west end of Sunset. It was a random night, but we were just excited about the concept and maybe a little bored at the same time. Pac was like, let's get a few drinks and go get this tat. I had never really been a tattoo guy. Pac already had at least one, but I didn't have any yet. To be honest, I was questioning if getting a tattoo was really necessary. I've never been a joiner. Even in the military, I saw myself as an individual. At the same time, it would be another bonding experience with my little brother. So, yeah, we got a few bottles and drank right there outside and inside the tattoo shop. Pac got his in the lower center of his chest, right below his sternum. Mouse and I got ours on our arms. It was a chill white dude who tattooed us, and I do believe he knew who Pac was, though he played it cool. We spent a lot of time trying to pick the gun, going through books of images for the gun and fonts for the 50. Pac ended up picking the biggest gun he could find, the AK. I'll say: I was uncertain at the time, but I'm glad I have that memory now, and the ink to remind me of that night every time I see it.

CHAPTER 12

THE BIRTH OF T.H.U.G. L.I.F.E.

About six months later, I had been away for a few days on business and when I got back to Oakland, Pac started telling me about this dream he had about T.H.U.G. L.I.F.E. He was all excited, talking fast, hyped up. He wasn't specific about the dream itself, just the concept: "This T.H.U.G. L.I.F.E. shit is gonna be the movement. I can see it! We gonna be on this T.H.U.G. L.I.F.E. shit now." I was with it, we just needed to figure out how to do it. It's one thing to have a great concept, it's another to actually put it out into the world, y'know?

We started recording T.H.U.G. L.I.F.E. guided by the notion that the concept would exist as a group, a set of albums, and a movement. We started with the music and the group, because we were creatives and our approach to how we could impact culture, politically and socially, was always going to lead naturally with our strength. It's where we could own our space authentically. After that, we would expand into the broader T.H.U.G. L.I.F.E. concept. We began introducing the thug concept—often simply spittin' the literal word "thug" in a song—because it was a T.H.U.G. L.I.F.E. song, a T.H.U.G. L.I.F.E. recording, and was specifically intended to provide foundation for the T.H.U.G. L.I.F.E. movement we were developing.

And that's how we found ourselves developing T.H.U.G. L.I.F.E. as both an album and a movement. First, as I had mentioned, we started with Underground Railroad—something centered on bringing our people through to the other side. From the outside, I could see how people could think that naming a group Underground Railroad could sound like Racial uplift. But that's only if you take it literally, with the sole frame of reference being the historical significance of the Underground Railroad. We meant it metaphorically, as in, we would be bringing in artists from the underground into the mainstream—a conduit for the type of creativity that is not always commercially viable but is crucial for the art form to live, breathe, and push boundaries. We never had much chance to record under that banner because we started broadening the vision of the impact culture could have to move people. What could we organize? How could we mobilize around the messages delivered through music in a more expansive way? That morphed into 50 N.I.G.G.A.Z. I think the reason we moved so quickly from 50 N.I.G.G.A.Z. to T.H.U.G. L.I.F.E. is that it was clear early on that we were going to build on that in a more inclusive way.

During that same period, we started going down to Los Angeles a lot, so much that the Hallmark Hotel on Sunset and La Brea and Echo Sounds became like second homes. But we never lost our connection to the Bay, and we had those Bay artists come down a lot to hang with everyone whenever we were doing shows in LA like at The Mayan or the Glam Slam. And Pac would always try to take advantage of the opportunity and get them on a record or two at Echo Sounds while they were in town. Stretch and Maj would come in from New York to work on the album, as well. We really liked recording at Echo Sounds because it was intimate, right on Los Feliz in Atwater Village in the northeastern part of the city. There were two big recording rooms, and a small parking lot that doubled as a basketball court.

A producer who we began to work closely with, and who we would end up working with throughout our lives, was Johnny J. Johnny J was a Mexican guy who was adopted and raised by a Black family, and he was Big Syke's good friend. He was willing to help us with the T.H.U.G. L.I.F.E. project and it turns out he was more than able to deliver. He was an extraordinarily talented producer. In fact, besides Pac and myself, he was the only one in our crew that had been on a big record before working with Pac—"Knockin' Boots" by a rapper named Candyman. Johnny had a fast and efficient work pace. He could keep up with Pac, and that's another reason why they worked so well together for so long.

While we were playing around in LA, Pac also got to spend time with Yolanda, aka Yo-Yo. Yo-Yo was a dope up-and-coming female rapper whom Ice Cube was mentoring. Pac had met her years before, but they started to get closer around this time and started a relationship. It was real cool to kick it with her, and sometimes her sister. Yo-Yo is real warm, and it was very easy to like her. She was also a solid, known rapper in the game! She became so close to us that she embraced our little sister, Sekyiwa, into her new organization, the IBWC—Intelligent Black Woman's Coalition. Pac and I thought it was super cool that Yo-Yo was connecting with our little sister like that.

We continued recording T.H.U.G. L.I.F.E.–inspired songs in hopes of one day putting out a T.H.U.G. L.I.F.E. album. While we would be doing shows from the *Strictly* album, we started yelling and talking about T.H.U.G. L.I.F.E. to start the buzz about the group and build the momentum. It caught on immediately, but still didn't have any clear direction. During this period, Mutulu, in the federal facility in Lompoc, would call to check on his sons because he knew we were out there in the life. And of course we wanted Mutulu, his wisdom, and his guidance, involved in T.H.U.G. L.I.F.E. When he would call, Pac would be all excited, telling him about the concept. But off the face, Mutulu wasn't feeling it. He said it was too negative, and that we had to make it *mean* something. We were young Black men, and that was like putting a target on our backs. Mutulu would ask, "What does T.H.U.G. L.I.F.E. mean? Does that mean you're gonna hit an old lady over the head and take her pocketbook?"

What the fuck? We knew that's not what we meant, and I suspected my father knew as much. But he was pushing us to refine it for pretty much the same reason we felt we had to ride for it. Sure, we explored the origin of the word "thug" from the Thuggees in India. And, of course, there were through-lines across the cultural divide. But you don't reach a broad audience with a history lesson, especially one that's kinda esoteric and doesn't speak immediately to their own experiences. Plus, we were turning thug on its head. The same way our elders questioned us for calling ourselves niggas, we were embracing the real ones who were there for us when, as hard as this truth is, our parents could not be, whatever the circumstances. We needed to focus on how abandoning kids fucks further generations. The abandoned, the unloved, they're the ones that turn into the monsters that everyone fears. The Hate U Give Little Infants Fucks Everybody. T.H.U.G. LI.F.E. We loved backronyms, and Pac wasn't ever gonna let people forget about the young ones, the kids, because many of us felt abandoned.

The reason we had to ride for it was that at the same time we were developing the THUG LIFE concept, and maybe in no small part because of it, Bill Clinton was running for president and talking about what would eventually become the crime bill. He announced his candidacy in late 1991 with a commitment to move Democrats away from being "soft on crime." Crime was a focal point of his candidacy, and he announced what would become policy in the summer of 1992. And after he became president, he and Congress defined and debated policy all the way until they passed the crime bill in the summer 1994. I'm giving you this timeline for a real reason—the *entire* time we were recording, up until we eventually released the album in September of 1994, we were up against "anti-crime" public sentiment that we just saw as anti-Black and anti-poor.

We had seen the devastation of gang injunctions and the disinvestment in community resources. We knew this was a thinly veiled way to criminalize Black and brown men and create a carceral state. So we were singularly focused on the young, Black male, who we thought, and who proved to be, the most vulnerable to this legislation, this policy, this mindset that was taking ahold of society. And we watched in horror as "respectable Negroes" stood right there nodding and agreeing with this bullshit. We knew what they wouldn't accept; there is no amount of respectability for Black folks that convinces the system to allow us in. So fuck it—we were unapologetically Black, and we weren't gonna play their game. We were gonna make an album for the niggas who knew how to play *around* that game.

You know that whole corporate "work hard, play hard" shit? They ain't got shit on us. We knew how to have a good time, and we definitely partied. But don't get it twisted: Believe it or not, our minds were always on the people. We knew the value of a party record and an anthem, and I'm not just talking about the commercial value. I'm talking about the need to let loose and come together in plain joy, to see a club erupt in dance, chanting out the hook. We needed to feed people's minds and souls—and we needed to feed ours, too. And sometimes, some rare times, we could do it all with a single record. That song was "Niggaz in the Pen." It's just me, Pac, and Mouse on that track. It didn't make it onto the album and to this day has never been released. Nonetheless, every time we performed that song the audience would erupt on the hook. *This is for my niggaz in the pen, I'll see you when you get out, if not when I get in.*

Around this time, the machine that was the business of Tupac Shakur needed some help. Now that my father had been captured, tried, and was starting to serve his sentence, we had a lot more communication with him. Living underground had separated him from us for five years; ironically, him being captured brought us together. I know that's counterintuitive, but now that he didn't have to be underground, we could communicate more frequently, talk on the phone and strengthen our bond, now as men. He was someone we listened to, whose opinion we cared about. That may be unique for young men in their twenties, but it's who we were.

Pac reached out to Watani Tyehimba to join his management team, because we needed someone we could depend on with some life experience, since pretty much everyone on our team was around our age: Young. Watani was from Los Angeles and knew my father from having been active in the civil rights and Black nationalist movements of the '70s. Mutulu enthusiastically supported him for the position because Watani had known my father and held him down out in Los Angeles when my father was living underground. Watani had subsequently been living in Atlanta; in fact, that's who Pac stayed with when he lived there as a teen. As we moved through the business, we came into contact with all types of new people. We were young, making a mark in an unfamiliar business known for its lack of transparency and tendency towards exploitation. Mutulu wanted someone to protect us. Watani was a man we could trust, and he was my father's trusted right hand until my dad passed away in 2023.

Plus, remember and also, we weren't from California, much less Los Angeles. We were starting to spend time in LA and we needed someone to be our eyes and ears with the real ones on the streets. We wanted to engage with, collaborate with, create with our folks. LA is funny like that—Hollywood is its own thing and Los Angeles, LA LA, is not the same thing. Watani eventually introduced us to his nephew Serg, who would introduce us to the hood politics of LA and help us navigate that terrain. It was important that we built relationships with real LA niggas to create fair and equitable opportunities for the young Black male in the communities we lived and worked in. That was always deliberate.

At the same time, being in the pen gave Mutulu access to the brothers in the federal system. That could make the THUG LIFE movement hood-official because there are always deep connections between the streets and the pen and a particular respect for those in the Feds. We started showing up at our shows, thirty to forty deep—no exaggeration. We started seeing our influence and power across state lines. We had our core family in the Bay Area, our base. We had Stretch and the Live Squad and his team in New York. We had Treach out in New Jersey. We had cousins in Detroit. We had Atlanta. We had Milwaukee. Even though we couldn't perform in Texas anymore, we sold a lot of our records in Texas. I think we were selling more records in Texas than in California at that time, precisely because the fans didn't have access to our shows; instead they bought more records. It's funny how the system holding us back in one area actually propelled us in another. And I do mean the system.

The reason we were banned in Texas is worth revisiting, so I'm gonna pause on it for a moment here. I mentioned earlier that, in the spring of 1992, a young man in Texas was in a police chase and, when the cop pulled him over, he shot and killed the cop. He was young, nineteen years old, Black, with only an eighth-grade education, and a history of interactions with the police. He was exactly the type of young Black man we were talking about, whose individual stories spoke to the deep chasms in this country's social fabric when it comes to race and class. He was also listening to *2Pacalypse Now* during the chase. There's a song on that album called "Soulja's Story" about a character, a young man, who has fallen through the cracks in our social system. Poverty led to his feeling of desperation, and he has an encounter with the police where he kills a cop. It's fictional. The fact that the real life young man was listening to Pac talk about a fictional man killing a cop, however, got used in a number of duplicitous and insincere ways in this kid's trial.

On the one hand, his defense used the record, the album, and Tupac's artistry to say that he was influenced by our music and not responsible for his actions. I say "our music" because we intended to continue "Soulja's Story" on *Thug Life vol. 1*, due to the label asking that Pac dial back addressing these exact issues in his solo work. However, "Soulja's Story" didn't even make it onto *Thug Life vol. 1*, because we were asked to re-record material that referenced killing cops. This was in no small part because at the same time the criminal defense was saying he was influenced by the record, the widow of the cop sued the label civilly, and the president of the label personally, for some bullshit about being reckless in distributing the material. Mind you, her legal team was financed by an organization that was headed by Oliver North, who while at the National Security Council headed up a number of missions designed to undermine practically every international movement that our parents stood by, including illegally selling weapons to Iran in order to illegally fund a counterrevolution in Nicaragua in the Iran-Contra scandal. So you see why it's easy for us to feel like we had an intergenerational target on our backs. It was a fuck bag, and it was really painful for us to confront in any meaningful way. We were banned from performing in Texas, and of course we were profoundly disturbed by the case. On the one hand, if the criminal court accepted that the music made him do it, it could save this kid's life. They were seeking the death penalty, and we for sure didn't want the government putting a nineteen-year-old Black kid to death. But that argument would make us somehow complicit in this man's death, simply for making art about the violence that we saw in the world. It would also let society off the hook for the very conditions that led this kid to such a tragic place.

In the end, the court did find him responsible, independent of the music's influence. Truthfully, his life was illustrative of what we were talking about through that fictional character; it wasn't the song that led to these circumstances, but the conditions of his life, which is what we cautioned the world about in our music in the first place. But that meant he got the death penalty. And even with the state of Texas getting their pound of flesh, the civil suit continued. The family was arguing the exact opposite position that they used to take his life: They argued that the music *was* responsible, to get into the label's pockets and, more chillingly, come for our freedom of expression, the creative freedom to talk about real issues in our art, by trying to get into the personal pockets of the men who financed the label that enabled our music to reach a broader audience. Completely insincere.

As all this played out, we were banned from performing in Texas. But it for sure didn't stop us! The social issues in "Soulja's Story" continued in the saga that we recorded in T.H.U.G. L.I.F.E. The issues were still real and that's precisely why people took to it. That realness resonated, Tupac's sincerity naturally overshadowed the counteroffensive, and no matter how dangerous they thought we were, the people knew what we were saying. Our audience grew, and so did the core group that was contributing to the artistry.

We were still filming music videos while touring and shit, and Pac was cast to star in *Poetic Justice*, with Janet Jackson in the lead. It was filmed in 1992, while we were still working on *Strictly* and starting on T.H.U.G. L.I.F.E. This was just before our full-time move towards Los Angeles, which happened, really, because it was just practical to cut down on the back-and-forth. I was running lines with Pac while running interference with the label. We had a lot going on, always, and I was basically Pac's assistant on *Poetic Justice* because I was the only one who could keep him on track. Even Watani didn't want to deal with him.

Pac was just exhausted, burning both ends of his candle. Music life is night life, and movie sets start with early days. When Pac slept, for example, he was *out*, and *nobody* wanted to wake him up. The PAs were all scared as shit because he'd yell and throw shit at the door when they knocked. He needed somebody around who didn't give a fat baby's ass if he yelled and threw a tantrum. I didn't give a shit, that was my baby brother. And I never saw keeping Pac focused or on track as a distraction from my own career. At that moment it was my job to look out for my little brother. It was beyond seeing our careers as intertwined. I was always creating alongside him; I was part of the crew. But it was really about so much more.

Look, I was well aware of the gravity of the situation, and I had full appreciation of the position I was in. At this point, I had abandoned my solo career to support my brother and what we were building. We were on our third group concept and I was helping him on his second solo album. I knew that the opportunities he was getting were a blessing that most people don't get. Because they were so rare, it was important to me that he be successful. I guess I understood more than most his pressures and where the anger was coming from. Each of these opportunities came with its own set of complications and hard work that would be difficult for any one person to handle by themselves. And Pac was trying to maximize opportunities across music, film, and television, all at the same time. I felt it was worth struggling with him for the benefit of so many who depended on him—Afeni, Sekyiwa, the Lesanes, the family.

Our relationship worked because even though he didn't say it all the time, my brother respected me. He knew that I was smart. He knew I was pretty level-headed. He knew that I was a soldier. He knew that I understood success because I had had a hit record on my own. And he knew that I was Mutulu's son, his brother. Also, our demeanors were complementary—when he was fire, I was ice.

CHAPTER 13

WELCOME TO HOLLYWOOD

Now, my first week of shooting with Pac on *Poetic Justice* was at a beauty shop on Slauson Avenue in South Central LA. John Singleton gave me the location, and I made sure I got Pac there on time. Pac played the character of Lucky, a young, slick-talking mail carrier who got along with everybody in the hood. I was diggin' this character because it was fun. He got to wear his hat backwards and he got to flirt with the girls in the beauty shop, who were played by Janet Jackson, Miki Howard, and Yvette Wilson. Pac's wardrobe was a basic mail carrier's uniform, but he made anything look cool. People were getting to see him be fun and happy and flirty but also sensitive and thoughtful, all things that worked great with this character. I was geeked that we were shooting in the hood, and that I was watching my brother film scenes with Janet mothafuckin' Jackson.

In between scenes, we would kick it in the trailer. Sometimes, Pac would be stressed if he was filming a heavy scene and wasn't fully prepared, or if other things were going on. It would manifest in him lashing out, but I got him. It didn't faze me. Like, one day it was lunchtime, and Pac wanted some fried chicken. Miki was in the trailer with us at the time when he asked me to go get him some fried chicken. This was one of those days where Pac was a little stressed and tense. I was serving as his assistant that day so I hopped on it.

I ran down to Kentucky Fried Chicken, which was close and, obviously, had fried chicken. Now, before you ask, I went to Kentucky

Fried Chicken because, one, Pac didn't specify what kind he wanted, just fried chicken, and two, I didn't know the area well, so that was the only fried chicken joint I knew was there. My only concern was to hurry up and get him something to eat. In fact, I got back so fast, Miki was still in the trailer with Pac. I come in, closed the door behind me and swung around with this big ol' bag of Kentucky Fried Chicken. And Pac let me have it. He roasted me. "Nigga, what the fuck you coming in here with this Kentucky Fried Chicken? You know we eat Roscoe's. We eat the Black chicken. Are you fucking stupid? What the fuck is wrong with you? You know we don't eat that shit." I was embarrassed as a motherfucka, because I—and a whole bunch of other dudes—had a crush on Miki Howard. I gave it right back. "Nigga, you said fried chicken! I got you fried chicken!" But Pac was set on his Roscoe's. I was shelled. So I left and went to Roscoe's, which I get his point, but there was so much shit going on, I didn't think of Roscoe's. Plus, the one I knew was in Hollywood and not at all close. By the time I got back with it, Pac and Miki were gone shooting something else. I sat down and ate my Roscoe's in peace. I'll admit, I was kinda smug about it. If Pac had just eaten the damn KFC, he'd have had a nice lunch instead of spending his entire break waiting around for the Black chicken.

A few days later, after we wrapped the scenes in the beauty shop, we hit the road. John was taking the crew up PCH (Pacific Coast Highway) to the Bay, shooting along the way. That period of shooting was what I would call intimate. Only a few people would be going on the road with us, and the journey would culminate in Oakland for the big scene. John was there, of course, and so was Pac, Regina King and her sister Reina, Joe Torry, Janet and her then-husband René, and me and Mouse. Of course, there was the crew, too, but we were the core group that was together the whole time. Well, except Janet. We actually got to know René more than her. She was just totally off-limits and inaccessible. Even considering how tight we had all become, Janet was simply not to be approached. She had a small team with her, like three or four people plus René. He would hang out, but she wouldn't. In fact, Janet was so inaccessible that anytime she left her trailer to walk on set, the crew got real quiet, John and the producers spoke in a hushed tone, and a seriousness would take over the set. I thought the power dynamic was ridiculous, honestly. But I got a real kick out of the fact that this little Black girl could command all this power on set.

Prior to hitting the road, Pac told me that Janet had invited him to her house to work out. I was excited for him at the time. I mean, *Oh shit, you're going to Janet's house?* I usually went with him almost everywhere, but I didn't expect him to bring me to Janet's, and he didn't. But I pressed him for details once he got back. All he said was, "It was cool. We worked out." The funny thing is that Pac did *not* work out. No basketball, no football, no sports. He liked boxing, but as a spectator. He once bought a whole weight set—a bench bar and a few hundred pounds of weights—but that phase was short-lived. We ended up just using the bench as another seat in the living room. So the idea of Pac working out with Janet was hilarious to me. But Pac was tight-lipped about it, which was weird to me. I never did find out what happened between the two of them, but their relationship was always distant, even when we were all together on the road.

It all came to a head while shooting on the road. Pac and I were in the trailer one day on some downtime, reviewing songs. We were smoking, just listening to music, and Pac was reading the script. There was a knock, and it was John. John comes in and said he needed to talk to Pac. They sit down at the table, and John says it's about the kissing scene he has coming up with Janet. He says that Pac needs to take an AIDS test before filming the scene.

Pac did not like that at all, and I didn't blame him. He said, "Am I fucking Janet? If I'm fucking her, I'll take an AIDS test. But not if I'm not fucking her. Fuck y'all." John said, "Come on, Pac. You know we got to take care of Janet. All of her people are worried. She got a cold after the scene with Q-Tip, so they're taking all precautions from here out." Pac was offended. I felt the same way. So Janet gets a cold after a scene where she kissed Q-Tip . . . if anything, the two of *them* had an illness that they swapped back and forth. So why wasn't the request to test Janet in order to protect Pac? Pac felt, rightfully, that the implication was that he was dirty, or, at least, dirtier than Janet and Q-Tip.

By this time, John and Pac were both on their feet and yelling at each other face-to-face, back and forth. John was trying to point out to him who Janet was, how fortunate Pac was to be in this position, how fortunate they both were to be Black men in that position, and how you have to play the game with these studios. Pac didn't give a fuck about none of that shit. "I don't give a fuck if it's Janet Jackson or Michael Jackson, ain't nobody gonna disrespect me." I was real proud of him standing up for himself. Nobody wanted anything bad to happen to Janet. It wasn't about that. It was about Pac feeling like he wasn't being treated equally. Later, when John addressed the AIDS test "rumor," he said that his request that Pac take the AIDS test was just an "inside joke" between the two of them. I was there when he asked. Pac wasn't joking, and John sure as hell looked serious.

I don't actually remember if Pac took the test or not, but I know he shot the scene. They did it on a cliff overlooking the ocean, and it was set up beautifully. People were anxious because they wanted the scene done right. Things got real still and quiet on set. It even felt like nature got quiet for us, like something big was happening. Pac and Janet sat down on a blanket on the cliff facing the ocean, the scene started, and it was just magic. I was in awe. I knew watching them film it that it was going to be one of Pac's biggest career moments. When he actually kissed her, I thought, *Oh shit, wait till I tell my niggas back in Queens!* Pac had to be intimidated, kissing a woman like Janet that everyone had a crush on. But he sure didn't show it. They wrapped the scene and I remember the crew being elated. I was watching the monitors, and it looked perfect to me, as well. Walking back to the trailer, John and the producers were coming up to Pac, telling him he did great, slapping him on the back, hugging him. We walked in the trailer and closed the door. It was just us. Pac looked at me and said: "Mo, how'd I do?" And I said, "You killed it my niiiggaaaaaaaa!!!"

at the top of my lungs. I just hugged him. That was a true brother moment right there.

That shoot was one of the best experiences of my life. It was not the typical film shoot. It was so *intimate*. John had us moving slowly up PCH doing these scenes, all outside, and I got to see a young John Singleton work his magic. I got to see up close and personal how a real film, with a real budget, is made on location with one of the most beautiful coastlines in the world as a backdrop. I got to see how John still got his scenes while managing the noise from the freeway. I got see a young Regina King do her thing. And Joe Torry was great in it, as well. It was a good combination. Most of all, I got to see my little brother craft this character. The further we got up the coast, the scenes got more and more intense. Though it was getting heavier, Pac had the character on lock. On the downtime, Pac, Joe, me, and Mouse would hang out at these random hotels that they had us in, clownin', smokin', drinkin' and laughing all night. We had enough weed from LA to make it to the Bay, at least a pound. We had so much that when we started the trip we took all these silly pictures with weed in our mouths, in our ears, in our noses . . . literal buds in our noses and ears. We were so high, we didn't think for one second about snot or spit getting in the weed. We just broke it down and rolled massive blunts.

Another bright spot while shooting on the road was Pac's twentieth birthday. He wanted this new Jeep Grand Cherokee SUV that had just come out, and he wanted it in black and gold. Atron was still on the management team with Watani and he had arranged for the car. But it was supposed to be a surprise, so I had to go up to the Bay and drive the truck down to where we were filming. I brought it back to our little raggedy motel in some little town somewhere on PCH. Soon as I pulled up, Pac ran outside with a blunt in his hand, jumping up and down like a happy little boy. "Yo, get out my truck! Get out my truck!" And he hopped in and christened it with some strong weed smoke. Pac was happy because now he could drive back into Oakland in his new truck.

I thought it was a great birthday for Pac, but before long, I began hearing about the day's shoot. While I was driving the car to him, Pac had been shooting a scene with Maya Angelou, and had apparently gotten into a fight with somebody. It was more like an argument, but Pac was threatening to whoop somebody's ass, as per usual. It was so bad that Maya Angelou had to talk to Pac. She pulled him to the side and talked to him about his anger and his temper and that it was interfering in the important work he was doing. The whole crew was abuzz about Pac being scolded by Maya Angelou. I felt like I couldn't leave him alone for five minutes without him spinning off and throwing a tantrum! Normally I would've been on set with him and able to deal with it myself. But if anyone was there to defuse him, I'm glad it was Maya Angelou.

Within a couple of days, we'd made it to Oakland, where it was time to shoot the bigger scenes. There was a lot of excitement when we started shooting in the Bay. It was like the hometown boy coming back as a star. The scenes we shot in Oakland were mostly at night, and had new cast members that Pac was going to be acting with. He had a scene with Tone Loc, which he was geeked about because he was a rapper he respected. And Jenifer Lewis, who was already a star in Black films, was playing his mom. I was thrilled to be working on a film in Oakland with my little brother. I was a little more alert than usual, and I knew Oakland pretty well at this point, though the part of town where we were shooting was rough. I wanted to make sure nobody acted stupid and pulled Pac into some bullshit. As shooting started, things went pretty smooth, and I could see that Pac was happy with his work.

He had a big scene near the end of the shoot where he was alone. He had to show emotion. He had to cry. I thought to myself, *This shit is hard work.* I don't know if I'd be able to cry on point. Shooting a scene like this was way different than performing a song on stage where you can move around and mask your anxiety or fear. An intense drama scene that includes crying took different creative muscles. But Pac was fearless. I looked around and saw how intensely the crew was watching him. John was watching him, the script supervisor was watching the script, making sure he hit all the lines right. The wardrobe people, makeup, lighting, everyone was watching and Pac was the only one in the scene, confined in this tiny frame. I knew that he was tired as shit from traveling and handling music business. I was a little worried that he might be too exhausted. And then the silence on the set. I know I would feel a little exposed. But once again, he brought it. He did so well, there were only one or two takes and they had it. I felt an inner relief when he finally wrapped.

CHAPTER 14

DARK CLOUDS ARISING

After *Poetic Justice* wrapped, everyone was happy. Pac's performance had been great, and now we could focus full time on the music for a beat. We put our energy into finishing up *Strictly* and recording for T.H.U.G. L.I.F.E. We had begun recording before filming started, and while we were filming, we were listening to a lot of rough mixes and selecting tracks from different producers that we wanted to record after filming ended. If we came across tracks we liked, we would start working on them then and there. We didn't record on the road, but we did do a lot of writing and elements of pre-production. But right after *Poetic Justice* wrapped, Pac went to New York for a little bit, while Mouse and I stayed in the Bay. We still had an apartment in Oakland.

There was a lot of pressure on Pac with his sophomore album, but *Strictly* was also a big album for me because it was looking like "Papa'z Song" was going to end up being a single. We had recorded "Papa'z Song" earlier; it was on the demo that got him his solo album deal, but it didn't make it onto *2Pacylypse Now*, and I was kinda bummed. Now, not only was it going to be on the sophomore album, it was going to be a single, which meant I knew I'd be shooting another video with my baby brother, as a featured rapper.

We shot the video in Los Angeles. As plans were being made for the "Papa'z Song" video, Pac had a vision of a few things he wanted to see. What I knew, and I think Pac felt, was that this song was about family, specifically fathers. Our fathers and their absence. In the lyrics, I hear Pac describing what he felt was his relationship with his biological father, to the extent that he knew it to be. In the last verse of the song, Pac used one of his creative techniques, which he came to call the soldier's voice. The soldier's voice was deep and slowed down, and it was distorted. Other rappers would come to use this technique, and they would call it Chopped and Screwed, but we were using it less as an overall musical style than a creative technique for emphasis or delivery of a particular piece of the song. In this case, the soldier's voice was Mutulu. So we end up talking about both fathers in the song.

"Papa'z Song" was one of the last videos to be shot for *Strictly*, and James Michael Marshall had been chosen to direct it, along with his assistant director Tracy Robinson. Some of the scenes were going to be shot in a jail, and all the parts where the soldier's voice was, Pac and I would be outside the bars, talking to the soldier character that was playing Mutulu. James Michael Marshall played that role. I had another scene in which I was in my office, behind an oak desk, and Tracy, the AD, played my secretary. In most of our videos we brought in guest stars, but we were getting the biggest one to date in "Papa'z Song": Vivica Fox. At the time, Vivica was a rising star, and we were excited to have her. She played the young version of our mother; Tracy and Vivica had been friends for a while, and Tracy was the one who convinced her to participate. I was also happy with the video because it was an opportunity to get our new T.H.U.G. L.I.F.E. team some light. Besides me and Mouse, we had Big Syke, Manute, and Serg on the shoot.

To be honest, I was not thrilled that James was gonna be playing the role that was essentially my dad, Mutulu. He looked nothing like him, but he wanted to do it real bad and Pac acquiesced. He used prosthetics and makeup, and he looked crazy. I also thought it was kind of whack for the director to be playing this role. Don't get me wrong, I got a lot of love for James Michael Marshall, but I got to keep it real. Obviously we rolled with it anyway, despite my reservations.

People got what we were doing creatively, and it played a little better on tape than in real life, but still.

The song and the video meant a lot to me, because it was just Pac and I on the record. The two brothers. I was happy with my scenes and the way Pac looked in his. I felt like the song would have touched more people if it had been more upbeat, but it's hard to tell, when you make something so profoundly personal, if the sentiment will land with people in the way you intend it. I know, in a practical, commercial sense, that many hits become hits because of young women, and that teenage girls drive much of the business. But this song was for the guys, about a foundational relationship between men, fathers and sons. I respected that the label picked it as a single, and I was proud to be part of a message that isn't often spoken of in this particular format. Honestly, the record wasn't as commercial as "Changes" or "Keep Ya Head Up," but every once in a while, I'll run into a fan who it really touched. And that's what matters most to me.

By the summer of 1992, we were at KMEL Summer Jam again. I was coming to enjoy it, having a good time because the festival was getting bigger every year. It was a good time to catch up with people and see big artists who weren't just from the Bay. Mary J. Blige was on the bill. We loved her debut album, *What's the 411*, and Pac was obsessed with "Real Love." I mean *obsessed*; he would play the record on repeat for what seemed like hours at a time. As I was walking backstage, Mary and I were just passing each other and I realized, *Wait a minute, that's Mary J. Blige*. I called out, "Hey Mary!" She turned around and said, "Hey, baby!" I said, "Oh, shit! Can I get a hug or something?" And she came and gave me a hug. These kinds of things really made me feel like I was officially in the game.

Later that summer, Pac wanted to attend the Marin City Festival, especially now that he was a movie star. It had been some time since Pac moved from Marin to the East Bay, and while he was doing press for *Juice*, he'd made some disparaging remarks about Marin City on MTV. He was being brutally honest, though perhaps unfairly broad in his characterization, about urban life in that particularly small, poor pocket of the otherwise wealthy Marin County. Pac really wanted to show up at the fair for the kids in a "local boy made good" type of way, and he, Sekyiwa, and Afeni still knew a lot of people in the neighborhood. Nonetheless, we all brought to his attention that some of the neighborhood might be . . . less than happy with him after that interview. He had prior beefs of his own, and even fewer good relationships from before he had moved out of the neighborhood. Pac didn't think it would be too big of a problem. "Yo, it's a fair. There's gonna be families and kids out there. Ain't nobody gonna trip."

This observation did not put us at ease, and we still made sure we were armed. We posse'd up in two carloads and left from Pac's apartment, which was in Point Richmond at the time. We finally got to the fairgrounds and parked. It was a nice summer day, temperature warm, sun shining. The fair was already almost half full, and everyone seemed to be in a good mood. We made a beeline straight to the food. Things were pretty relaxed. Pac was approached by a few fans—kids and adults. The server saw us coming and started getting plates ready. They handed me a plate, and while they were making Man Man and Mouse's plates, I was looking to see what else I wanted. There was the usual chatter coming from behind, typical of a public event, and then I just heard it stop. Subconsciously, the silence set off an alarm inside me, and I turned around to see what was going on just in time to see several dudes approaching. Pac had fans of all types, but this was all guys, and they did not look happy to see us. These were dudes from his old neighborhood. The one in front said, "What's that shit you said about Marin City?" And pow! Just punched Pac in the face.

The first ones to take off on them were Man Man and Mouse. They hadn't gotten their plates yet, so their hands were free. They just stepped in front of Pac and *socked* the guy. I dropped my plate and mushed the last one back, pushing him with my hand over his face. We were so fast, I don't think Pac even had a chance to get a punch off, but he did start cursing them out. "Fuck you niggas! Fuck you bitch ass niggas! Yeah, I said it." While the arguing was going on, other guys were grouping up, preparing to make another run at us. We could see that we were clearly outnumbered.

Some of the Young Thugz had come with us, and had wandered into the crowd to mingle so they weren't with us by the food line. So, Pac starts calling them to come over—not to come over and fight but to come over so we could leave. But as these Marin City dudes were seeing what Pac was doing, they made another run at us, before our guys could get to us. Pac was yelling, "Come on, let's go! Let's go!" And we started running back to the cars. I glanced to the right and I saw that they had heard us and were heading back—K and Big Malc were with us, along with Man Man's little brother and some other youngsters from a kid's group Pac was working on developing. Yaki wasn't with us, and I'm so grateful that happened to be the case. I think about that all the time. He was so tall, he would have easily become a target in what was about to unfold.

Me, Pac, and Mouse were running together, with Mouse in the lead. We had a long way to run, back across this big-ass field to the parking lot. While we were running back to the fence at the edge of the field that bordered the parking lot, we start hearing gunfire. They had assaulted Pac while we had teenage children with us and now they were shooting at us, with children all in the park. Immediately, Pac and I started grabbing for the iron, which was in Mouse's back-pack. I got my right arm in the bag and Pac was reaching in with his left, trying frantically to pull the gun out. Pac popped it out and it hit the ground, and he reached down and put his hand on it.

I saw it all like a snapshot in my head and freaked out. It was like this instantaneous flash of all the bad things that could happen if Pac picked up that gun and shot somebody. Not to mention that the last thing we needed to do at that point was stop running. We had at least a couple of hundred people chasing us at this point, and someone was still shooting at us. I quickly pushed Pac's hand off the weapon, picked it up, and tried to get the safety off and cock it—all while still running, mind you, and that shit is not easy—then shot a couple of warning shots straight up into the air. I was trying to back them off to give us time to escape, because we had yet to climb over that damn fence we were all too quickly approaching. And just to make things more dire, K had a cast on his leg that ran all the way to his hip. Not to mention Big Malc was a sizable young dude. We had to get both of them over that fence.

We kept running. I knew I had to be fast, because I had the keys to the Cherokee in my pocket. I hit the fence, climbed it and hopped over, and made a fucking beeline for the Jeep. Pac was right behind me. I hopped in and started it up while Pac was rushing everybody. "Come on, come on y'all," he yelled, banging his arm against the side of the Jeep. We were trying to wait as long as possible for everybody to get in before we left. In the meantime, the crowd was still coming, throwing rocks as they got closer and closer. I heard a big *booooosh* as they busted out the whole back window of the Cherokee! We heard rocks hitting the truck from all sides, at high velocity. Somebody even threw some shit on the roof.

Next thing I know there's a sheriff with a .357 pointed at the side of my head. He yells at me, "Don't move! Stay right there. Turn off the vehicle and get out." I was frantic, trying to explain to him, "Officer, you have no control of this crowd. They're trying to kill us." Meanwhile Mouse, who had stayed behind to get K and Malc over the fence, was trying to help Malc get the door closed while the crowd was pulling at the door, trying to yank Malcolm out of the car. The sheriff had his gun on me, while the crowd is on the other side of the car trying to pull Malc out, and he's not doing anything about that. Fucking police.

I had to make a decision. I knew if I stayed there and listened to the sheriff, they were going to get Malc. At this point, we were all in the car, so while the sheriff was still talking to me, trying to get me out of the truck, I reached down with my right hand, and with my middle finger I popped the gear in reverse—the gear shift was in the middle of the console on the Cherokee in those days—and I punched it. I caught the sheriff off guard, and he just stood there, stunned. At first the wheels spun and kicked up a lot of dust and some rocks. I think it stunned the crowd for a beat as well, keeping them back as I cut to the left in reverse—just enough to turn around to our right—and then shifted to drive to go around to get to the exit. As I was speeding through the parking lot, the crowd was still approaching, throwing rocks all the way to the exit. We didn't want it to escalate even more, considering we'd already heard gunfire. Thank God I didn't hit anyone, but I was getting us the fuck up out of there.

I grabbed Pac's shoulder and told him and everybody in the car to duck. We could still hear rocks coming as one of them took out the last window. I didn't know Marin very well, besides the few times I had visited when Pac, Afeni, and Set lived there. There was literally only one way to go, so I busted a left. I'm smashing down the street and I hear the cop sirens blasting. I heard them behind me, and I also heard them coming from in front. But there was only one way to go, and that was away from the crowd.

Eventually, the cops did cut us off. They had the street blocked off and were cocking their shotguns, yelling at us not to move, to get out of the car, to lie down on our stomachs.

They got Pac and me out first, and had us some distance from each other. Then they got the young guys out. Everybody's laying on the ground, and the crowd was still coming, still throwing rocks and bottles and cursing us out. It sure didn't look like law enforcement had control of the situation. There was already a riot, and it was still coming in full force. They started targeting us on the ground with rocks and the bottles. And then Pac did one of the most heroic things I've ever witnessed: He crawled over to the young ones and put his body over them to protect them from the rocks and bottles, and the gunfire we knew was coming. The sheriffs went over and pulled him off of them, but still did nothing about the crowd. Finally, the mob took notice of all of the police around, lights flashing and guns drawn, and started to disperse. The sheriffs finally got control and took us all to jail.

While sitting in jail, we got word that a child had been shot. That was the worst news we could have possibly heard. We were all hoping that it wasn't true, but it was, and the child passed away. An already bad day turned into the worst day of my life. We all went to jail, but they held me. We got sued. And it was so fucked up because we didn't start any of it. All we did was respond out of legitimate fear for our lives and those of the kids with us. While I was in jail, services were held for the child. Pac attended with Bone, a well-known and respected street dude introduced to Pac by Watani, who would go on to become an actor and activist. It was the definition of the saying, from sugar to shit. We had been working hard, grinding, having some success, and the next thing you know we're involved with the worst thing that could have happened. It turns out the child was hit with a fragment of a ricochet bullet. After a couple of months in jail, criminal charges were dropped due to the circumstances. The civil suit was settled.

2Pacylypse Now was out in the world and we had been supporting it all through 1992, even while we were recording new material. This period of time would be marked by what felt like a constant clash with the system. We were young Black men telling our truth through our art, and a lot of people didn't like that Pac wanted to talk about things that were real problems for us. In our case, it wasn't just critics or the industry. That was merely a difference of opinion, a difference in the appreciation of a particular aesthetic. *This* was the government—literally. Members of Congress and elected officials: Dan Quayle, Tipper Gore, C. Delores Tucker. It was just the beginning, but they were blaming us for real violence in the streets. As if by talking about the real shit going on, we were somehow responsible for the fucked-up system that had created it all.

I'm going to get into the details of some of these battles down the line, because this continued throughout our careers. But let me just say this here: With all the interest in us for good or for bad, I knew we were making an impact. I knew Pac was making an impact. I knew the content of our music, and I knew where we were coming from. We were young Black men in America, trying to make a stand for our people. Like our parents had done, we centered our experiences as

Black men. I felt that certain people were picking apart our songs—a line they disagreed with here, a line they disagreed with there—as if to make a case for our negative influence on people, Black men in particular. But I think the truth is they didn't like our music because we terrified them for a completely different reason. We didn't create the world we were living in. As we described our generation's experiences, without shame and in the complete vulnerability of our truth, we were actually empowering ourselves and our listeners. It's like the political education my pops did at Lincoln Detox. That scared the shit out of the city, the council members, the elected officials charged with representing us in structures of power, and so they found a reason to shut my pops down. Ultimately, we were talking about power and the powerless.

For example, after the riots, Pac participated in gang truce meetings. He wasn't expecting anyone to leave the gang or to be a former gang member in order to participate from a place of reform. He respected the power of these organizations and, yeah, they participated in violence in the streets, but they also provided material support to their members and affiliates in real ways. He wanted to use their structure and power to achieve a different outcome. And that's a way scarier proposition to the power structure, denying their authority to dictate the terms in which the disempowered participate in a system set against them. In fact, that's probably terrifying to them.

We were consistent in our approach, and Pac was holding people accountable. That year, we attended, and Pac spoke at, the Malcom X Grassroots Movement banquet in Atlanta. MXGM is an organization that my father had co-founded and that has continued to grow in the decades since. Makini, Nzingha, and Chinua were there, and I was so happy to see them. Time and distance really didn't make a difference in our bond, and I loved seeing Mama Makini and my brother and sister. MXGM is one of the organizations that live on as part of my father's legacy, and Pac was not going to let them off the hook on issues where he felt they fell short: their effect on our generation. He took them to task for performing a particular type of Blackness—a revolutionary image that couldn't see or hear what was going on in the streets and how our generation had felt abandoned. He wasn't gonna let nobody forget how he, Afeni, and Set were left without a support system.

We were talking the talk and walking the walk. I can see plainly how, to people elected to positions of power, our type of music—music that makes people think about how they're being neglected and how they want to be represented—would scare them. That's the infectious power of music: People are going to listen to a song they like hundreds of times, and the message is going to soak in. Those in power were coming at us about our music, shitting on the First Amendment, but really it was just confirming their existing bias against us. They were never going to like us, no way.

The first bullshit was over parental advisory labels, which we of course didn't think too much about. We lived and navigated through a lot of adult things as kids, so talking about real shit on a record didn't seem out of bounds for us. It's kinda ironic that this same generation of lawmakers were the same people leaving their kids unattended as part of the same latchkey generation we'd grown up a part of, and now they wanted to stop us from talking about our experiences in that context. This was also, in no small part, a fallout from the crack era. The second—and what would become an ongoing and constant harassment—was over violence and misogyny. As if, again, we'd created it. We literally got blamed for someone killing a cop. Dan Quayle, *a sitting Vice President of the United States of America*, called the label about our music. C. Delores Tucker attacked us for being misogynistic, which is just completely off base if you actually listened to the music. (And Pac would eventually explain this to her directly in "Wonda Why They Call U Bitch.") The truth is the truth and our fans knew what we were saying. They knew who we were. They understood who we were talking to, and mostly they knew a smash hit when they heard it. But this would be just the beginning of the constant push against us as we moved onto the world stage.

And we would always answer, in our way: through the culture.

CHAPTER 15

WONDA WHY THEY CALL US THUGS

Pac's career was gaining more and more momentum, and we were working super hard tryna get the work done. We were getting ready to direct a video for "If My Homie Calls." Because of the name of the song, Pac wanted to have some real homies of his that were well-known on the West Coast, like Above the Law. One of the frontmen and main producers of Above the Law was Laylaw, from Lawhouse Records, and they came up under Eazy-E. Pac had met them while he was out on tour with Digital, and when he came home, off the road, we would shoot down to LA and hang out with them there. Laylaw drove a Jag, and he would ride us around while rolling a fat-ass blunt. I hadn't seen nobody do it like him. I'm lookin' at this nigga, sunroof open, windows down, whip shining, rolling a blunt while steering the car with his knees and the heel of his hands, kush smoke blowing all out the top. I was feeling real West Coast in those moments. They showed us a lot of love, hotel to hotel, party to party, plus some of the dopest music.

In the "If My Homie Calls" video, Pac wanted to have Laylaw driving a lowrider, but we just ended up having an old-school classic Cadillac—convertible, of course. It was a good time in Pac's career. Besides his relationship with John Singleton and Laylaw, he had of course made friends with Janet Jackson's husband, René, while we were working on *Poetic Justice*. So, he got René in the video, too. Why not? René was a dancer, director, and songwriter in his own right, just a well-rounded, talented guy. My scene was me, Mouse, and someone else shooting dice. After all was said and done, the video came out dope, down to John's cameo at the end. I felt good as a big brother to see my little brother shooting his video, rappin' out the top of the drop-top old-school, with Laylaw driving and the Hughes brothers shooting the video. I was happy for him. And that video has one of my favorite shots of me and Pac together. We're walking and Pac slaps and gives me five and we're smiling and laughing. Yeah, that's one of my favorite shots.

Now, a couple of days later, this nigga gets back from the tattoo shop. He was like, "Check out my tattoo! Look, look!" He lifted up his shirt and I saw this huge tattoo across his belly, with thick-ass tattoo ink: THUG LIFE. The letters looked Asian-inspired, and the *I* was a bullet. It was fuckin' massive. I said, rather sarcastically, "You couldn't get a bigger one?" That didn't faze him one bit. "It's dope, right?" I said, "Yeah, it's dope. It's damn sure big. You want all of us to get that?" He said it was up to us.

The very first time the public was introduced to the THUG LIFE concept was in Pac and MC Breed's video, "Gotta Get Mine." The video was actually shot at Left Eye and Andre Risen's house in Atlanta, which would be known for another infamous incident in 1994, when Lisa would be charged with arson after being accused of burning their house down. In the video, there's a scene with Pac, Big Syke, and an early member of the crew, Big Kato, who was murdered shortly after this video. Pac pulls up his shirt so people can see the tattoo and says from his verse in the song: *I live the THUG LIFE, baby, I'm hopeless*. The song was a hood favorite, and it helped give T.H.U.G. L.I.F.E. its own life outside of *Strictly*. We continued rippin' shows coast to coast talking about T.H.U.G. L.I.F.E.

While we were smashing with our creative freedom, Pac started running into a few snags professionally. At this point in his career, he was a movie star with the looks of a model. But this THUG LIFE tattoo made a lot of modeling gigs problematic. On top of the fact, our T.H.U.G. L.I.F.E. gang was getting into a lot of skirmishes, which reflected on Pac and made studios skeptical of insuring him. Salt hand-picked him to be in their video for "Whatta Man," featuring En Vogue. Salt knew Pac from Pepa's boyfriend, Treach. Pac was with it, for obvious reasons, but word was their label was against it. It was most likely due to the reputation my baby brother was developing. He does appear in the video, but they don't show his face. Ironically, the only part of him you can clearly identify is his torso with the big-ass THUG LIFE tattoo as Salt hugs up on him in bed. It pissed Pac off that they cut his face out. Adding insult to the irony was that to avoid accusations of misogyny, music video distributors would decline to air videos when women's bodies were shown without their faces, but there seemed to be no problem in this case. Hypocrites!

My father was still questioning the merits of T.H.U.G. L.I.F.E. at this point, and it was actually getting on my nerves, cuz some of his arguments didn't sound too different from those of the establishment. Pac wasn't too thrilled about it, either. In conversations with Mutulu he would sometimes yell and scream, throw the phone. But truthfully, you had to argue with Pac if you were gonna have a meaningful creative or intellectual relationship. That's just how he worked. He even punched a glass pane in a door and shattered it. He got a rag and wrapped up his hand and said, "Well, yeah, Mutulu, fuck that." He didn't say ouch, he didn't stop talking because he'd just thrown a punch through a glass door. He just kept trying to get his point across. I don't know if Mutulu heard the glass break, but he did realize that it all meant something to Pac. He said again, "Okay. Just make it mean something." And Pac screamed back, "Mutulu, *you* make it mean something! We're out here working!" I'd like to say, looking back, that I can smile about the passion in that conversation. But it was intense. It was a lot. I thought that Pac was being a little extreme, but he did have a point. "You're sitting in there giving us your opinion," he said, "so Mutulu, do this shit, then. Write us a code." We understood Mutulu wasn't going to put his support behind this unless there was some cogent thought and consideration behind it. The truth is, there absolutely was—we just had to fight through the generational rift and the difference between a creative and a political approach. And we had to clean up all of the broken glass.

We were toying with the political concept of the disenfranchised by teasing out what that meant for the so-called "thug." The very nature of how we were working and what we were trying to work with and around ended up building a massive T.H.U.G. L.I.F.E. catalog—a catalog of songs promoting the movement as well as grabbing the attention of our audience. By that time, our crew was so massive, we couldn't all travel at the same time. Schedules and availability would determine who was gonna roll on which show.

With a brand like T.H.U.G. L.I.F.E., we knew we would be tested. For example, Syke and Serg did a show with Pac in Lansing, Michigan, and dudes tried to shoot up Pac's hotel room. So we needed to roll deep, for our own safety. But the movement was resonating nonetheless, and we were getting more exposure. The more shows we did, the more we would feel the love. When we rolled up into spots, people would start yelling: "T.H.U.G. L.I.F.E.! T.H.U.G. L.I.F.E., BABY! T.H.U.G. L.I.F.E.!" I can tell you that felt good. It was really validating hearing that something was resonating with the people we wanted to reach.

While we were recording, Pac shopped the project around. As a group, we didn't fall under his solo deal, so this was a chance to branch out. One of the people he took it to was Eazy-E and Ruthless Records. At the time, Eazy had signed a group of guys from Ohio who each had "Bone" in their names. Signing another group clearly wasn't the right timing for him. Eazy passed on T.H.U.G. L.I.F.E., but the next thing we know, this group has got "Thug" in their name when it wasn't there before. I know Bone Thugs-N-Harmony claims to be the first to use *Thug*. While it is true that their album was first to market, it's in no small part because of the complications I just mentioned. Let me just say we took it as a compliment. Eventually, we ended up making a deal with Interscope—but not before some creative and personnel changes.

Early on, when Pac was an up-and-coming rapper on the scene, he had to do a lot of small shows. When he started to do shows out of state, it would just be Pac, Man Man, and Mike Cooley, just the three of them. In like 1990/91, when he did a show in North Carolina, he was walking around the venue and somebody pulled a gun on him. He was unarmed at the time, and we was broke back in them days, so it's not like they would've got much. But Pac was still shook by the experience, and when he got back home, he told us what happened. He really wanted us to step up our security and self-defense. I didn't think we were at the level to have security yet, but after that incident, I agreed it was needed. Over time, Pac started accumulating his own weapons. He was always going to be responsible with them, but he was going to have them.

By 1992, he had acquired an AK, a MAC-11 with a flash suppressor, and a Mossberg riot control pump shotgun. He also had a .357 and various brands of nine-millimeters. I'm witnessing my little brother acquire all these weapons and I'm saying to myself, *Okay, we need to get to the range.* Brother Watani echoed that sentiment. I knew it was important, being that I was actually trained on an M-16 when I was in the Army. Even I didn't have a lot of familiarity with handguns, but I knew enough to know that it didn't make much sense to have a weapon around if you didn't really know how to use it. Since Brother Watani was from Los Angeles, he was familiar with a range we could go to and not be bothered. Pac was going to the range so he could be proficient and knowledgeable—but he was also excited to play with his toys.

Pac *loved* going to the range. Whenever it was a range day, he would get all excited, telling me which weapons he wanted to fire that day. In the Army, I qualified as a sharpshooter. I had been to the range many times. But Pac hadn't. And he got a kick out of being able to pick his little silhouettes to shoot—he could pick the bad guy or the cop. Pac was actually a good shot. He was anxious to learn how to do it, how to hit a bullseye, and he practiced so much that he did. Pac had a light blue 735 BMW at the time. We both loved that car. I would pack all the weapons and ammunition in the trunk and head all the way across town to the range. We were doing this practically weekly. We ended up at the range so much, Pac once did an interview there while we were shooting. I felt good about having these range moments with Pac, because most of the time it was just me and him. Eventually, Pac became so comfortable and good with the handguns that he felt okay carrying all the time.

In case I haven't already mentioned it, we were known for being copious weed smokers. If our man Big Country wasn't around, we would have to find trees elsewhere. Through the various artists we were getting to know in LA, we met Prince Ital Joe. He was from Dominica and had a juice shop on Cahuenga Boulevard in Hollywood. It was a match made in heaven in a lot of ways, because not only did he have trees any time we needed it, he was an artist in his own right. He had toured with Marky Mark and the Funky Bunch. We would pull up to his shop, get what we needed, and Pac would tell him about the next song and when to be at the studio. This was the missing element from our crew, a Caribbean flavor. Having Joe was like having another tool in the toolbox. Pac would start sprinkling him into different songs for that island flavor. We loved it so much that Joe would end up on some of our most classic songs. Being from New York, we grew up with Caribbean people, and we would hear plenty of patois. But half the time, if Joe wasn't on a record, I didn't understand what the fuck he was talking about.

It's probably clear from some of these stories, but it's worth just saying outright: Around that time, Pac became *a lot, a lot*. He had already been a lot. Shit, we called him King Lear years before, just because of how extra he would get with those of us closest to him. One tipping point came when he wanted to go see a girl in the Bay. The two of us—me and Mouse—drove him five hours up there from LA. We dropped him off at this girl's house and took off for a couple of hours. Somehow, we lost communication, and when we went back to pick him up a few hours later, Pac was *pissed*. "How could you just leave me here and take the car?" After we'd just driven him up there, he expected us to just sit in the car while he was hanging with this girl? Nah, fuck that. We got mad, "Fuck you, Pac, fuck you, fuck you." He wanted to go home, and we didn't say one word the whole way back. The full five-hour drive without a single word!

Pac was demanding, of himself and of everyone on his team. He had high standards, but sometimes his expectations were silly, or even insane. I recall once, for example, we were doing a Pac show, and I had fifteen jobs, as per usual. For all intents and purposes, one of those jobs was DJ, but I was also a backup vocalist, his roadie, his security, his driver, all that shit. At this particular show, the sound equipment was way in the middle of the venue instead of on stage, so I couldn't be Pac's backup *and* play the music. Naturally, this presented a problem. When I knew Pac was ready, I pressed play and made a beeline through the audience to get up to the stage. I got on stage, grabbed my mic, got ready to back him up —and there was no music. It didn't start. I was so anxious to make my run back to the stage, I'd missed the damn button.

Pac looked at me and I looked at him, my eyes popped open. I said, "One second, Pac. Be right back." I hustled back to the sound set up, *actually* pressed play this time, and started coming back to the stage. And Pac got tired of waiting and let me have it. Over the microphone, loud as fuck, no music so you could hear everything he was saying, he announced, "Sorry, y'all. That's my stupid-ass brother on the sound system. I apologize cuz I did come here to bring y'all a good show tonight." He just threw me under the bus, and that shit did not feel good. No recognition of how stupid the setup was. He couldn't fucking ad lib or interact with the crowd? I was pissed. I'll tell you this much: It never happened again. Meaning, I kept my fifteen jobs—but I never had to run through the audience like that again.

Look, I was stressed out with everything we were doing. But Pac would always seem to trump our stress with his stress. The last place he wanted to feel embarrassed was on stage with thousands of people.

So a part of my stress was preventing him from being stressed. It really did piss me off, but I took it in stride. Mostly. I knew how much he depended on me, but I'm still only human and shit happens. Plus, I knew part of the way he fucked with me was only the way a brother could.

It did eventually get to the point where Mouse and I took a break. I want to be clear: The pain-in-the-ass Pac wasn't the only Pac. He was also funny as fuck and full of love—even or especially when he was being a sarcastic little fuck—and he didn't expect anything from me or others around us that he didn't expect 100 percent from himself. Except when it came to waiting around for hours while entertaining different ladies. We just needed some space away, to cool off. Mouse and I left together, first to New York. Our plan was to continue recording. He came with me to Queens first, and then we went to Baltimore together. It was easier to record in Baltimore at the time because Mouse's friend Drake had a home studio.

Meanwhile Pac stayed in LA, recording more T.H.U.G. L.I.F.E. material with Syke. He also shot the video for "I Get Around" with Digital. And my brother had his shirt off again in the video, showing the infamous THUG LIFE tattoo. Mac is in the video with him. Mouse and I were pissed about missing that shoot, but that's the breaks.

I came back to LA after a few weeks. During this time, with Pac being in LA, he was more accessible for production and he started doing more TV appearances. He and I had already appeared on *In Living Color* once, before I left. At his second appearance there was a fight when he was leaving the show. Oddly enough, it was with the limo driver. The story went that they—Pac and the guys, Syke, Serg for sure, and I'm not sure who else—got in the car. They started smoking, as per uge, and the driver got upset that they were smoking in the car. He told them to get out, an argument ensued, and the fellas proceeded to throw him in the trunk.

No surprise, the driver didn't want to drive them anymore, because, um, obviously, and Pac didn't want him to drive them anymore either. So, they were shit talking and throwing threats back and forth, not only with the limo driver but also with his people. The limo company was trying to deescalate the whole thing, but it was a mess. It had gotten so bad that people were calling Pac's house. People used landlines back then and they had his home number. There was a threat involving a gun. I mean, it escalated on some ridiculous shit when you think about it. At the time, though, Afeni was at the house alone. Pac had gotten word they were calling and threatening her over the phone and he called Watani immediately. But Watani was in Atlanta, so he called me to see if I was back in LA. When he reached me, I immediately went to Pac's house in the Valley to protect Afeni.

When I showed up, I could see that Afeni was visibly upset: irritated, anxious, angry. I could see the relief on her face when she saw me, so I think she was probably a little rattled, too. I knew where the weapons were, and I could hold her down if any shit popped off. I was only there alone with her for an hour, maybe an hour and a half, but they never even ended up calling while I was there. Now, Pac had left the situation in Watani's hands to take care of, and he didn't know Watani had called me. I'm not even sure he knew I was back in LA. When Pac and the guys finally got back to the house, they were all irritated talking amongst each other coming into the house. Pac looked up and saw me. He opened his arms and smiled and I went over and hugged him. Regular brother shit.

And *that's* when he tells me that the shit we had recorded was too hard. If we didn't record new material, the album wasn't going to come out. It was back on again.

Turns out, most of the earlier recordings were deemed unfit for commercial release by our A&R himself, Tom Whalley. And in the end, because of the combined sheer volume of recordings and because of the label's hesitation over the themes we were using to illustrate it, there are many early T.H.U.G. L.I.F.E. recordings that didn't make it onto the album. There are also recordings that were intended to be on subsequent volumes of T.H.U.G. L.I.F.E.

After this I became almost entirely responsible for the music. I co-produced the entire album, and we recorded *a lot*. I never had a conversation with Tom directly about that first round of material. He was the person that if we could get him behind us, we could get the rest of the suits to sign on. The thing was, we already had pushback quite literally at the federal level. Those voices—those C. Delores Tuckers, those Tipper Gores, those Dan Quayles, those politicians, the fake-ass sensibilities of the bourgeois and their criticisms—is what brought about the parental advisory ban. But that was also part of what pushed the project to become much harder. They made it appear that our language was the issue, but it was really about what we were saying and who we were saying it to. It was about our ideas threatening to take the seat of their power and let the people sit in it. They did all kinds of things to stop us from distributing our art, which meant taking money out of our pockets. They literally tried to do to us what they did to disco—corny-ass press ops with a steamroller going over our CDs. It was ridiculous.

If I'm honest, however, what was recorded earlier may have been cathartic, but it might have been a bit much. Which shouldn't have mattered. We were exploring the full creative freedom that came with keeping it real, telling the truth about law enforcement. We were talking about crime and the underground economy. We were super pissed about the debate over the crime bill and how Black and brown men were being criminalized. We thought there would be awful long-term consequences for our communities, and that Black and brown men were the most vulnerable. We were so fed up with the respectability politics behind the debate around the crime bill, and we were particularly pissed off at the bougie Black folks who supported it and the so-called progressives who used these Black folks to endorse their bullshit. So, with all that anger, there was a fair amount of imagining violent depictions of a world where the playing field was even and law enforcement was treated the same way that they treated us. We were talking about murdering crooked police officers.

We turned out to be completely right, by the way, but we may have gone beyond bounds just to make the point. There may have been other stuff, too, but it was the rapping about killing cops that really got the label. I chose not to speak to Tom directly about the creative, but I could hear him in my head as Pac retold the story of trying to fight the argument for the first version. *Pac, you're talking about killing cops. I mean, you're making it hard for me.*

Pac was fire, I was ice. My thinking was that Pac had already attempted to turn in an early version and they didn't accept it. He tried to shop it, and even Ruthless and Eazy-E said no. My strategy was to redirect our creativity, and I didn't compromise on the social messages, even when the depictions were violent. I mostly focused on dialing back the cop killing. In all honesty, it was a blessing to have so much material. Turns out, a lot of Pac's posthumous music would end up consisting of unreleased and reworked records from the T.H.U.G. L.I.F.E. project. But that's beside the point. It was back to the studio, and I was responsible for delivering a distributable album. Pac was in New York a lot by the second go-round, filming *Above the Rim*, so I was the creative liaison with the label, delivering the DATs (high-quality digital tapes of the masters) to A&R.

CHAPTER 16

THUGS 4 LIFE

By this time, our team in LA was solid with Big Syke, Serg, Mac, and Rated. And then, to top it off, we had Mutulu and our connections in the pen. We were deep. We had no deal yet, but Pac was able to put up money from what he earned on *Poetic Justice* for a nationwide tour, the THUGS 4 LIFE Tour. Our homie April Walker, who was a pioneer in urban clothing and had her own clothing line, Walker Wear, designed some jackets for us. She was working for Jam Master J, and was always a good friend of ours. They were black denim, three-quarter length jackets with THUG LIFE in white on the back of the bottom hem in big letters. We loved them.

The day we were about to roll out to start the tour, everyone was buzzing, preparing, packing bags and gathering the last few items we wanted to bring on the road. It was a big deal, cuz most of them—Mac, Rated, Syke, and the young homies—hadn't yet been on a real tour. Afeni, in her motherly role, prepared a tour care package for each of us. Honestly, she was so cute: "Come over here y'all. Come get your safety kit." She had these sandwich bags, and in each was a pack of condoms, aspirin, vitamins, ginseng, vitamin E, and maybe a couple of other things I can't remember. Everybody slowly walked over to Fe and got their "safety kit." "Y'all gotta take care of yourself out there now. And drink water, hear? Don't be messin' around and getting all dehydrated with them gals." And everyone was like, "Thank you moms, thank you Fe, thanks Mama Fe."

Then it was time to roll out. In all of the excitement and commotion getting ready to leave, we did not notice one thing until right at that moment. Brother Wa starts asking, "Uh, have you seen the van? Who got the van? Where's the van?" The van transporting us to the tour bus was not out front. I just figured it was parked in a different place or had been moved, and we just had to figure out who moved it. Brother Wa kept searching and found out through some people in the neighborhood, I think, that Kenny Black had taken off with the tour van without telling anyone. I was pissed off. We had everything together at that point and were on time . . . And Kenny Black strikes again! He wasn't even going on tour with us, mind you. And I thought, *This is not how I want to begin this experience*. Eventually Watani tracked him down and got him to return with the van. It turns out, Watani foiled whatever his plans were and we got our van back before anything that couldn't be undone.

The morning after a lot of our shows, we would hold Playaz Court, when all of us, the playaz, would hold a meeting in one of the designated rooms where we would go over the previous evening's pursuits and conquests. "Alright, Playaz Court, Playaz Court," Pac would start it. It was practice in the early days with me, Pac, and Mouse, but with the T.H.U.G. L.I.F.E. clique it was on a whole different level. You see, show night would be when all the pursuits would happen. Either you got some action and the girl is checking for you, or you're furthering the pursuit. In ways it was unfair, because Pac was both a fucking movie star and a rap star. But he always wanted to be one of the guys, so we acted like that part didn't exist. Pac would start out the evaluations with curiosity: "Yo, what happened to Shorty in the red skirt?" Because Pac also had his eye on that same red skirt. So, number one, it was to compare how good the homies' game was and, number two, to see if that hottie was still available. After Pac started, the battery of questions would begin from all sides, to catch those who might have been falsifying information—lying on their dick, to put it more crudely. Granted, we all had our bad nights, but Pac would generally have several rendezvous, often in the same night. Syke would do well.

Yak was a young boy, but he always attracted the ladies. And, not for nothing, I did quite well myself. So well that I was often questioned when the homies doubted that I actually pulled such a bad chick. I was actually a little offended at first. *Why y'all think I can't—excuse me?* I did so well in Playaz Court that Pac was impressed enough to dub me Mopreme, The Ladies' Dream . . . sometimes referred to as the Mopreme, the Ho's Dream (like on the song "Stay True"). We would talk about who had the biggest tits or the biggest ass, who had the prettiest hair. We talked about beautiful faces, too, of course. And while this sounds like objectification, let's be honest: There's a fair amount of objectification on all sides of sexual politics. And for what it's worth, it was a good way for young men to soak up game and learn how to rap to the ladies.

We were rippin' shows across the South, and eventually things got a bit . . . hectic. This particular promoter in Virginia, let's call him Fred, booked three or four shows with us. We were excited about the momentum and success of the movement, so we were all in on it. We had done one of the shows already, and it was time for the second. Now, people in the business know that you get paid before you go on stage. You don't pay, we don't perform. Come to find out, old Fred hadn't paid Pac for the first show and was supposed to make good on the second show. But showtime was coming up fast and we hadn't seen the money for that show, either.

Man Man was our tour manager at the time. When he told Pac that we hadn't been paid yet, Pac was mad as fuck. "Yo, I just gave this nigga a break and he's still trying to fuck me over? Fuck that, let's roll. We're going back to the hotel."

Now, Old Fred heard that Pac was upset and we were leaving, so he came to the hotel to plead his case. We were in and out of rooms, up and down the hallway. We probably had five, six rooms on the floor. When he got there, all he could see was a bunch of black THUG LIFE jackets, Jheri curls, and weed smoke, with loud music filling the hallway. And there's Fred, his briefcase in hand, with the appearance of a businessman. He had one other guy with him, who was like six-foot, light brown skin with a little curly 'fro, wearing high end, trendy hip hop shit. When Fred caught up with Pac, everyone was in the hallway. He began copping his plea. Now, I was a little bit further down the hall, but I saw when they first started talking. By the time I made my way to them, shit had already gone left. I hear Old Fred talking about, "Ah, shit, nigga, come on and do this show. I got another one waiting on you after that. You tripping about this little punk-ass money?" Pac looked at him and said, "What?" Old Fred fucked up talking reckless to Pac in front of his guys. As soon as Pac said that, like five of us grabbed that nigga by his fancy jacket and pushed him into a room.

Pac was a young king, a boss. He shouldn't have been disrespected, and we were going to make sure of that. Once we got Fred in the room, he saw that we were serious, and his tune changed real fast. "Ah, come on, y'all. You know I got it. You know I got it for you. You know I'm gonna take care of you." Pac wasn't interested: "Fuck that bullshit. Where's my money?" Fred insisted that if we just did this one more show, he'd pay us everything, for all four. It was that moment that Pac noticed he was holding the briefcase, which Fred clocked and visibly held tighter. Syke pushed up on him, stopping him from getting a tight grip, and I don't remember who it was, but niggas snatched it up immediately and told him to open that motherfucker. His friend tried to intercede, but Babez hopped onto the desk. Now, Babez is a gangsta-ass nigga from Richmond, California, but he's also like five feet tall. Babez had to hop his ass onto the desk so that he could put a pistol to this tall mothafucka's head "Please, nigga, please. I want you to do something, nigga. Make a move."

Fred gave up the briefcase, because he knew that if he didn't he was gonna get his ass beat and his friend was gonna get murked. When Syke got it open, there was about forty grand in there and a chrome-plated Taurus nine-millimeter. I grabbed the gun because I didn't want Fred or his boy to get any stupid ideas, and Pac reached for the money. Even after all that went down, Pac was insistent that we only take the amount we were owed—we weren't robbing the mothafucka, we just wanted what was due, and we made sure we got it. Now, once we had the money, the new problem was making sure his bitch ass didn't call the police. We sure as hell weren't doing the second show at this point and we needed to get out of town. The first ones out needed to include Pac, of course, and me, Syke, Serg, and Man Man. We had a few of the homies who were leaving later sit on Old Fred in the hotel until we were in the air. Between rushing to get our stuff together and get to the airport and everything else going on, I kinda forgot that I ended up with the 9.

We finally made it to the airport and were relieved to be almost out of there. I remember we were all standing near the restroom, talking and laughing, and all of a sudden, a cold chill started going up my spine. I'm like, "Oh, shit! Oh, shit, y'all. I still got the 9." Pac, Syke, everybody, was like, "*What?*" And I'm like, "Yeah, I still got the 9 in my bag." And Pac went *off*. "What, you fucking stupid? Get rid of that shit. You fucking stupid, why the fuck did you bring that shit to the airport?" I was like, "Nigga, did you not just see all that shit we just went through? You think I meant to bring it?" Pac just kept saying that I needed to get rid of it and he was leaving on that flight with or without me. I knew he would, too. With some quick thinking, I dipped into the bathroom, into a stall, took the magazine out, got some tissue paper, wiped it down good and quick, wrapped the magazine and gun up in tissue paper, and left it at the bottom of the trash can in the bathroom. Thank God there was nobody else in there. When I came out, everybody was asking me did I get rid of it? Where was the gun? Did I still have the gun? I had to hear it from everybody how stupid I was for bringing a gun to the airport, but nobody was thinking about how fuckin' stupid it was to be talking about it while we were still at the fucking airport.

I kind of wish I could say that was the craziest story from our touring days. It was far from it. Now, anybody fucking around with hip hop in the '90s knew about, heard of, or was going to be at the Freaknik convention—this big annual Black event in Atlanta. It was 1993, and Pac was continuing on his meteoric rise to stardom. We were, naturally, fairly popular, and Pac wanted to go. And since we were going—you know how we do—Pac wanted to make a major impact, to make his presence known. He'd just bought a 1960 Chevy Impala, since he'd kinda fallen in love with lowriders and the car culture being on the West Coast. Pac's 6-0 was a baby-blue and white convertible and had a baby-blue and white interior, with a cocaine-white top. She was a damn beauty, I can tell you that much. Pac bought the car after it was used in a video he shot with the Jamaican rap star Patra. I think he paid $17,000 for it. It was a lot of money in those days, but I couldn't deny it was worth it. Problem was, us growing up on the East Coast, we didn't have much experience with hydraulic switches.

So, we wanted to ship the lowrider to Atlanta. But that car, in that environment with thousands and thousands of people, and Pac not knowing how to drive it . . . that was quite a problem. So the remedy, we decided, was to bring our homeboy Country along with us. Country lived in LA but was originally from Pine Bluff, Arkansas. He was basically a super smart country boy—highly entrepreneurial, always had the best weed. And when I say entrepreneurial, I mean entrepreneurial. Country had a used car lot in Arkansas on which he kept a baby lion cub—don't ask me where he got it from—and tied him down right in front of the lot where people could see him, to draw in business for the cars. He did pretty well until animal control started asking questions. Country became part of our crew, and he was also the expert on lowriders. He had his own purple '64 Impala with white interior on sixteen switches that we all admired.

So Country was part of the team to accompany us to Freaknik. By the time we made it to Atlanta, we were probably like twenty or thirty deep. The Freaknik was notorious for causing traffic jams, so just getting the vehicle into the city was a logistical nightmare. The streets were jam-packed, nobody was moving. So much so that people would get out of their cars and party right there in the street, totally unaffected by the unmoving traffic. So one part of the nightmare was just getting the car there on time on a flatbed. The second part was getting Pac to where we needed him to be, unnoticed during the middle of this massive convention.

The offload point was an empty parking lot. Word came that the car was almost there. We started making our way to the parking lot while trying to keep Pac tucked. As the car came through the city, people were *oohing* and *aahing* and wondering whose car it was, 'cause no one in the city had anything like that at the time. By the time the car made it to the parking lot and was stopped, it had done its job and grabbed everyone's attention. Exactly what we wanted. Pac's goal was to hop in his car while it was on top of the flatbed, to make his grand entrance. So while the crowd was admiring the car and wondering whose it was, we enveloped Pac within us and pushed through to get to the front. When we finally made it to the truck, Pac rushed, hopped on top of the truck, and got in the car. People was screaming: "Ah, shit! That's Pac! That's that THUG LIFE shit!"

The problem was that the next part of his plan was . . . totally impossible. Pac wanted the car dropped on the ground, and he wanted to drive away. There was gridlock on every street surrounding us, and we were surrounded by mobs and mobs of people. They would've never let us go. So the decision was made for the car to be taken on the flatbed truck to the hotel and deal with things from there. Which left us, at this point seven or eight of us, on foot, in the middle of hundreds and hundreds of people, most of whom were adoring fans. Many wanted an autograph, a hug, a kiss, a few words, some type of attention from Pac. And Pac loved his fans. So in true form he started signing a few autographs, hugging a few girls. The situation was quickly getting out of control. Man Man, Syke, and I all looked at each other. We knew we had to get him out of there. I tapped Pac: "Yo, we're getting ready to make a move." Syke, the biggest of us, started making a hole through the crowd. We hustled *fast*. Sometimes it's the little things you don't forget. I remember one of Pac's young fans was just so happy, and he screamed out, "Yeah, Pac! That's that real nigga!" And that's what Pac always wanted to be recognized as: a real nigga. Hearing that from this crowd of people who just adored him, I was so damn proud. That was my brother right there!

The seven of us started smashing down on Peachtree Street towards the Underground, which was this big mall, with a whole mob of people in tow. While we're running, I glanced over and saw a random old friend from Queens, my man Big O, who I had no idea was in Atlanta at the time. I was so glad to see him! O is another big, stocky, strong brother, and it was the perfect time for some additional muscle. I yelled at him to help us get through the crowd while we were sprinting down Peachtree. Those fans chased us all the way into the Underground. They chased us until we couldn't run anymore. Mall security finally came out and helped out with the crowd, and Pac signed a few more autographs before we headed back to the hotel. I get why some people would be scared by it, but we were young and filled with adrenaline, and it was the first time any of us saw the impact our music was having on so many people. It was the first time Pac had a reaction from fans like that, and it made us all feel *good.*

By the time we actually made it to the hotel, the car was being offloaded from the truck. People were everywhere, more people were streaming in because they'd found out where we were staying, and we were still being followed by the crowd from before. But even with all of this going on, Pac still could not help but to play with his new car. He hopped up into the car and proceeded to try to use his switches—which he didn't really know how to use—to impress the crowd. It was clear he had no idea what he was doing. The car was making weird noises and moving in ways that were clearly not deliberate. So of course, this smart-ass in the crowd yells out, "Aw, shit, Pac can't even work his switches!" And Pac yells back, "Oh, yeah? But I can work these, though!" and he held up both fists. The dude says, "Nigga what? Yo rappin' ass wants some of this?" At that point, me and the guys put him under pressure. We quickly surrounded him, a few of us reaching into our coats. "Nigga do you want some?"

He finally went back to his guys, but we knew it was time to go, and we hollered at Pac to get inside the hotel and away from the crowd.

By the time we made it into the elevators, that same damn dude was *still* trying to follow us, running up fast. There was no way the elevator doors were going to close before he and his people reached us, and I knew we couldn't have them following us in, knowing what room we were in. So I did the only thing I could think of: I grabbed my weapon and said, "Don't do it. I told you before, don't do it." They froze real fast, I backed into the elevator, and we went upstairs.

When we got in the room Pac was *mad* furious about the guy. That a mothafucka would try him at all, let alone at Freaknik, let alone in front of a crowd of people. We had gotten word this guy was a Gangsta Disciple (GD) out of Chicago, which meant that there were more of them and there was a definite possibility of retaliation. The thing is, we had a show that night in Piedmont Park. Pac's stance was clear: "Fuck them niggas for disrespecting us. Mothafuckas trying to tell me not to perform because they don't want any gang violence. We ain't with letting nobody make an example out of us. Fuck them and whoever they roll with. I want everybody on that stage with me strapped and ready to defend yourself. The show must go on. We go to work."

There was a heavy pause while everybody looked around at each other. None of us thought this was a good idea, but there was no way we was gonna let Pac go out there unprotected. We went back down when the car was ready for us to drive. By this time the crowd had cleared out, and Pac was determined not to let these motherfuckas ruin his good time. It wasn't even an argument that Country would drive; this was not the time to look crazy. Country was also good at evasive maneuvers—just in case anyone ran down on us. So we hopped in and started hitting corners. The system was boomin', too, the car was perfect. We started riding around various neighborhoods, as close as we could get to the action without getting stuck in traffic. There was no drama, just adoring fans everywhere showing Pac love and shouting out, "THUG LIFE."

We rode past a few hotels. Everyone was on their balconies 'cause the city was hot, and they'd yell at Pac to wave. Pac sat on top of the seat like the president, waving to his fans and shouting them out. They were saying how much they loved him, he was saying how much he loved them. Fans on the ground were running up trying to touch the car, trying to touch Pac. It was one of the best feelings. I felt like we'd actually accomplished something. Pac was successful on his own, sure, but we were also successful as a team. It was a special moment.

Everybody that was down with us that came in from California, plus all the fam from Atlanta, showed up to support us, and we were about thirty strong by showtime. We were still on the high of our little parade, but we knew the GDs would come out for the big show. People knew a problem with GDs was no joke. We had our THUG LIFE tour jackets. We looked fierce in them numbers. And the thing about the jackets was, they were so oversized that you could carry big guns under them. So by the time we hit the stage, Big Syke had a TEC-9. Somebody had a riot control pump shotgun. Somebody had a long rifle. There were several 9-millimeters onstage, including mine. And there was one MAC-11. Totally fucking nuts, but the intention was to keep Pac safe. And that's what everybody on that stage intended to do.

Thank God the show went off without a hitch, except for Syke almost dropping the TEC-9 while he was rappin', trying to hold a microphone and a gun under his jacket. Everybody was so relieved there wasn't a problem. After the show, we put away our arsenal and proceeded to enjoy the rest of the evening.

CHAPTER 17

THE LIFE

Given the difference in workflow for music versus film, *Strictly* came out in early 1993 and *Poetic Justice* came out that summer. Almost a year after wrapping, we got to go to the premiere, which felt like a big reunion. I was looking forward to it because I knew everybody was going to be there, red carpet and all. This would be my first premiere. When *Juice* premiered I didn't go; we just caught it when it first came out at Grand Lake Theatre in Oakland. This time it was going to be different, with the director, cast, and red carpet. I remember thinking, *Just be cool, Mo. Act like you're supposed to be here.* I actually did, and the familiar faces I knew from the production made everything more comfortable.

They coordinated our arrival with Janet's, so she and Pac could be on the red carpet together. The premiere was at the Samuel Goldwyn Theater, which is in the Academy headquarters on Wilshire in Beverly Hills. Pac wore a yellow Karl Kani jacket. I wore a brown designer shirt with my brown shades, real chill. Just as planned, we arrived at the red carpet while Janet was there, and a few seconds later, John and Ice Cube rolled up. We had been so focused on *Poetic* that we kinda forgot that Ice Cube was in John's first hit film, *Boyz n the Hood.* Everybody was in a good mood, smiles and hugs all around, while the paparazzi flicked us up. Of course, paparazzi wanted to get Pac and Janet in a picture by themselves, and I'm thinking to myself,

This is it, we're here. This is legit Hollywood. And now Pac is firmly planted in it. Even though I wasn't the focus or the star, I felt like one because I was part of a star-filled project and had been working with these stars for the last few months. I also treasured the fact that Pac and I seemed like we were on this adventure together. The fact that Janet Jackson was happy about working with my brother was icing on the cake.

I was extremely happy and also curious—I wanted to see how all those scenes fit together and how they would flow with the story. And damn, they did.

We did *a lot* of promotion. We were always promoting something—an album, a movie, something. And so we flew to NYC as part of some promotion, probably for *Poetic Justice*. One of the outlets we were doing was MTV. Pac was in a good mood that day, smiling, laughing, and charming everybody on the staff. Stretch and I sat to the side, off-camera, while Pac was being mic'd and seated for his interview. The interview started, things were going smooth, so we just waited for him to get finished so we could hit the city. The next thing I know, I feel somebody plop down right next to me and then I feel an elbow in my side. I turn and look to my right, and it was the one and only Madonna. She was, she is, unmistakable. She's a petite woman, so she appeared quite smaller than me and I had to look down a bit. She was wearing a white tank, a sleeveless tee. And when I looked at her, I just saw her breasts because they were so big on her little frame. She was boobalicious. And she was laser-focused on Pac during his interview. She didn't even turn to look at me, just elbowed me in my side and said, "How long is he gonna be?" I said, "I don't know, it just kinda started." Madonna disappeared and came back a couple minutes later, handed me a note on white paper that had been folded together a few times. "Give this to him when he's finished."

I must admit, deep inside I was fanning out. But I had to be cool. Madonna was asking *me* to do her a favor! You don't blow that shit. After she gave me the note, she got up and left. It was like cinema after that, man. I handed the note to Stretch, because Stretch was closer to

Pac, and then Stretch handed it to a stagehand, who slipped it into Pac's hand and told him that it was from Madonna. Just watching that note get closer and closer, the expression on Stretch's and Pac's and the stagehand's faces as they got that information . . . I could have watched that shit all day! By the time Pac finished the interview and got up, Madonna was heading out. He unfolded the paper to read it and acknowledged her with a motion and a nod in her direction, "A'ight, a'ight."

I would learn later that he had previously been introduced to Madonna by Haitian Jack at some party in New York. When we got back to Los Angeles, Pac mentioned his "new friend" Madonna to Mutulu. Pac was obviously excited, just like the rest of us. Why wouldn't you be? But when we told Mutulu, our father had words of caution: "Pac, I know you want to, but don't sleep with her. Not yet. You want that mind. Sex her *mind*." Pac and I just burst into laughter at the ridiculous shit Mutulu was saying. I thought it was absolutely ridiculous—there might have been a reason for him saying that, some mystic, sixties-era-of-love trick—but I didn't think it was likely Pac wasn't gonna sleep with Madonna. I mean . . . it's fuckin' *Madonna*! As soon as we got off the phone with Mutulu, Pac looked at me and asked, "Mo, how the hell am I gonna do that? Could you do that?" I just looked at him and shook my head and we both started cracking up. Hell no, I couldn't!

And that was how that particular romance started.

I used to drive him to Madonna's house. Understand, Pac never really learned how to drive. I mean, technically he had a license at some point, but he was never really good at it, and would regularly scrape and bump into things. The brand-new Jeep that got destroyed in Marin? Before that, I watched him try to back down the driveway of our own apartment complex in Oakland, with Richie Rich, a legendary Bay Area rapper, scraping the side the whole way and eventually pulling the mirror off. He would get hyped up listening to some music, and gas and break to the music. He would bump other cars, and we were so loud and Pac was acting so crazy that a lot of times, the other driver would just see this guy smoking with his hands in the air, rapping to the music, and just drive off. It was hilariously awful and probably expensive, but I wouldn't say dangerous. He liked fancy cars and bought plenty of them, so I guess he *liked* driving well enough. But that doesn't mean he did it well. So, I was the one who used to drive him to Madonna's house in LA, which at that time was in Los Feliz. I don't think he followed Mutulu's advice; Pac was definitely sexing more than her mind. But they also had a special friendship, and a legitimate connection. They had dealings off and on for some time. He eventually broke it off with her when he was in prison.

Part of the reason it didn't work out is because Pac and Madonna were both so busy. We finished recording *Strictly* after *Poetic Justice* was filmed, but *Strictly* came out first. By the time *Poetic Justice* premiered and during the whole time he was promoting it, we had been building on and were already recording yet another concept and expanding our musical relationships. We weren't ones to take a beat. We were constantly creating, recording, expanding our sphere, and performing—including one very special performance.

By this time in 1993, Mutulu had arranged for us to perform in USP Lompoc in front of him and an auditorium full of federal inmates. We were finally going to be together, all three of us. From the earliest days of my father's organizing in the community, from that corner down the hill where he and my mother met, my father was a man who earned the respect of the people around him. His fellow inmates were no exception. Also no exception were, believe it or not, the warden and the guards, which is for sure part of how this performance happened.

The inmates responsible for the production coordinated through my father and Watani to make sure the equipment was all set up according to our specs. It was me, Pac, Syke, Rated R, and Mac; Serg was there, too. Y?N-Vee, an R&B group from South LA, had been doing vocals for us for a while, and they came, too. Imagine that: a group of beautiful ladies performing in a federal men's prison. Really, it was a Pac show, with me backing him and the girls doing vocals.

It wasn't a big production. They literally just handed us microphones and we walked on stage. But honestly, it was still a lot to coordinate under the circumstances. We only did, like, two or three songs, and our pops had to settle the guys down a couple times when they started acting up.

I remember, after the show, how he was so proud of us. He stood between us and put a hand on my shoulder, his other hand on Pac's. And then we took pictures—a lot of pictures. We were there taking pictures for longer than the actual performance. We had to take pictures with every single crew. The crew from Texas. The niggas from New York. The guys from the Bay. The Latinos. The dudes from LA—Bloods separate from the Crips, of course. The DC Mob. The Chicago boys. So fucking many niggas. But the inmates really appreciated the show. Shoot, the girls had their shirts tied in the front, showing a little skin. For the niggas in the pen that's damn near a strip show! It was a good day, and even to this day remains one of my favorite and most memorable performances.

Seeing our father jumpstarted our consciousness. It was always a part of the very fiber of our beings, but seeing him brought it to the surface in a very particular way. Even before the show at Lompoc, we'd been developing some concepts that brought THUG LIFE into focus for the people. "Uplift" is a common concept for creative materials aiming to bring Black folks forward, but this show profoundly underscored how this work needed to refuse the very premise it's based on. Uplift is rooted in a certain amount of respectability politics that we flatly rejected. We were—I still am—unapologetically Black. For us, respectability politics was a trap designed to have Black folks measuring ourselves against a stick that keeps changing size. Fuck that! Seeing the brothers in the pen confirmed that we were on the right track. We were trying to transcend giving a fuck about how we appeared to others, so we could claim space as our authentic selves.

CHAPTER 18

MOVING PARTS

In the fall of 1993, while we were riding around in New York, we were in intense conversations, not really paying attention to the ride. I wasn't fully aware of our itinerary that day. The driver says, "We should be at the Garden in about twenty." I heard him, but it didn't really register; whatever the hell we were talking about was more important at the time. Next thing I know, the driver's saying, "We should be pulling up in about five." And Pac just casually goes, "Oh, yeah, I gotta do this shit at the Garden." I say, "Hold up. We're going to the *Garden*?" And Pac goes, "Yeah, I'm just gonna do this shit with Biggie real quick." That was huge to my native New York, Southside Jamaica Queens heart. "Oh, shit! We're playing the *Garden*. We're getting ready to do the *Garden*. Ah, shit, T.H.U.G. L.I.F.E. up in the *Garden*." We pulled up to one of the back entrances and security snaked us through the bowels of the Garden until all of a sudden, he opens a curtain and it was thousands of people in the audience. We went right to the stage, no greenroom, no special preparations, no set list. It was the Budweiser Superfest, so we walked onto a full stage. MC Lyte had just finished performing. We were showing up as special guests, to support.

When we got on stage it was just electric. Biggie had just started rapping and he was rockin' it. And because I wasn't aware of any preparation, I didn't know whether we were going to do a song, if Pac was gonna do a song with Biggie, or if Pac was going to do a song by himself. I didn't know what the setup was, but then they handed me and Syke mics. My hip hop acuity told me that they were trying to make it a battle, and I was gonna back my brother. When they introduced Pac and he got on the mic, he made me proud. He lit the Garden on fire. The crowd lost it when he started rapping. And what did he kick? A T.H.U.G. L.I.F.E. rhyme, of course.

> I thank the Lord for my many blessings
> Though I'm stressin', keep a vest for protection
> From the barrel of a Smith & Wesson
> And all my niggas in the pen, here we go again
> ....
> I'm sideways, Thug Life, motherfucker, crime pays

That's us, T.H.U.G. L.I.F.E. And to this day, that rhyme, that moment is legendary!

We were working our asses off pumping out a lot of material, shooting a lot of videos. Pac was on fire, but his meteoric rise was straining his relationship with the Hughes brothers, Allen and Albert. We first met them in 1991, when we were all trying to break out. They had won some type of talent contest that Quincy Jones had for short films. They were young, Black, and they came to our attention by way of an endorsement from a respected voice. Pac always wanted to support young Black creatives. It just made sense to have them direct a video early in his career and they directed his first three, "Trapped," "Brenda's Got a Baby," and "If My Homie Calls."

But since then, Pac had grown at stellar speed, faster than a lot of our contemporaries. *Juice*, which had been shot before his debut album was released, came out shortly after and was a hit. Pac was a movie star. His solo debut had been well received. And *Strictly* solidified his rap stardom. He was a certified rap star. The Hughes brothers had made a short and some music videos, but the young directors wanted to make a feature film. Pac promised he'd be in their film whenever they got their deal, but their shot to direct a feature came *after* Pac rose up as an actor. Pac's success was quite simply outpacing theirs, and I can't help but wonder the role petty jealousy played in the way their relationship got strained.

They finally got the opportunity to make their feature debut, *Menace II Society*, after Pac had already shot *Poetic Justice*, which was his second feature film. Honestly, I also don't think they loved that Pac had developed a creative relationship with John on *Poetic Justice* after they'd already shot three music videos with him. But there is one crucial detail in the Hollywood weeds that's kind of essential to understand the full bullshit scope of what went on between them: The Hughes brothers got their deal, in no small part, by promising Pac to the studio. That's how deals are done. Pac was a proven commodity, and if the studio has confidence that the director can cast the film or package it, that's a big factor in how they decide to do a deal.

At first Pac was happy that the film was full of familiar faces and allies, including Jada. And we were cool with the Hughes brothers, too, but I didn't really pay that much attention to them outside of work. They weren't really part of our crew. Over that period of working with them, we would kick it and share stories and ideas. We would talk about films, classics and stuff we wanted to do that was connected to us, to our story. We even talked about my father's story with them: the rebel part of Mutulu's story, the Brinks robbery, liberating Assata, and putting the expropriations, as we called them, back into the movement. I can't really say if they were the type of critical thinkers to understand the complexity of my dear old dad, but they definitely saw the cinematic value of a story like that. Hell, it doesn't take a creative genius to see what a badass Mutulu was, and how that could make for an epic film.

Cut to the first table read for *Menace II Society*, when everything went left. I personally took Pac on a lot of auditions and table reads, and I used to trade lines with him to help him rehearse. I knew the ropes, and I knew that Pac's role in this film had already been earned by the fact that his commitment to the project helped get the studio backing. He was bankable, and that was a product of his talent and hard work. When we showed up, I stayed in the car. Pac would be playing a Muslim character and had some notes about how the character was written. Pac, being a good sport, with a real work ethic and appreciation for the craft, showed up ready to work. I parked, Pac grabbed the script and ran inside.

I settled in, put the seat back, pulled out a sack, and started rolling a blunt. I got my shit broken down, got the radio on, rolling my shit up, just chilling. Next thing I know, Pac was walking back to the car, fast and hard. I said to myself, *Uh-oh, this don't look good.* Pac hopped in and slammed the door. "Let's go!" It did help that I had a blunt already rolled. I just handed it to him. I hadn't even lit it yet. Pac lit up, took a couple of hits, and then started venting.

"That little punk mothafucka." I knew he was talking about Allen—Allen always wanted to be the leader of the two brothers. "As much as I did for them, I can't believe they tried to play me out. Who the fuck do they think they are? Got they little movie deal and think they hot shit." And I was like, "Word? They tried to play you out?" He said, "Yeah, they lucky that I even showed up for this shit!" I was like, *Damn, this is new.* We never had problems with them before. It didn't even occur to me that there would be conflict at a table read. I assumed they would receive his input without ego, in the sincerity with which it was given and with respect for Pac's relative authority on the matter—probably at least half of our family is Muslim, and it's not like Pac was an inexperienced storyteller. As much as they needed and wanted him in this film, that they would be dismissive simply because they were attached to the words that they wrote . . .

The power of having their own movie must've gotten to their heads. Pac was like, fuck them and their film. I agreed. Hollywood is about the power play and how we, how he, was positioned in relation to them. It was just disrespectful. I mean, Pac had just finished his second film. *Juice* was a huge success, and his second film was with John Singleton, a proven Hollywood director. *Poetic Justice* had all the momentum and talent to be a follow-up success for Pac.

And these mothafuckas were trying to treat him like a rookie. Every music video director wants to make a feature film, and Pac literally gave them that. Are they talented? Sure! But movies get made with the package and the ability to deliver a cast. Pac handed them that, even in a supporting role. The other layer of bullshit is that at that table read, a bunch of our peers from music were there because the Hugheses had cast a number of them in the film: MC Eiht, Too $hort, Yo-Yo, and Pooh-Man. I'm not sure who was at the read, but I do know that none of them rappers had the same acting experience Tupac did at that point in their respective careers. And there were the Hughes brothers belittling him in front of his colleagues, which was both a naked power play and, ironically, a sign of their own inexperience. For them to treat him like that after all he had done for them was unacceptable on a basic level. Up-and-coming directors trying to play out a star? That ain't how this shit works.

In fact, Pac was so much of a star by this point, he was sought after to feature on other artists' songs. Pac, being loyal to the Bay Area and Bay Area artists, was going to make sure he supported our homeboy Spice 1. We had been down with Spice from day one. He would come over to our house on MacArthur back to the early days, and turnabout is fair play. Turns out Spice did a record that ended up on the soundtrack for *Menace II Society*. Pac featured on the song, "Trigga Gots No Heart," and would be in the video. When it came time to shoot the video, the Hughes brothers were directing. I'm sure they never counted on all roads leading back to us, cuz we were running this shit.

Pac showed up to the video accompanied by some of our T.H.U.G. L.I.F.E. crew. For whatever reason, I think I had a court date, I wasn't there. When I saw Pac at the end of that day, he handed me his gold chain, but it was broken. I asked what happened. "Yo, I fucked them niggas up. We fucked them niggas up." I said, "Who? Allen and them? So y'all fucked up Spice's video shoot?" Pac said, "Probably, but I know one thing. We fucked them up." Pac's adrenaline was still rushing. He was still amped. I started getting details from the rest of the fellas. Apparently, when they got there, they basically chased the brothers down, got their hands on Allen, and Albert ran the other way. There was at least six of our guys with Pac when it happened. They didn't hurt Allen too bad, they just lumped him up. Even though Pac had this opportunity for some get-back, he was still mad at them for the insult.

And to make matters worse, Allen decided to press charges against Pac for the assault and sue civilly. It was a sucka move, but we expected it. Pac had been working with a battery of lawyers, because there was always some legal issue, and we were always in court. For this, Pac decided to call on Johnny Cochran, the legendary civil rights and criminal defense attorney. We had a familial relationship with Johnny. He represented Geronimo Ji-Jaga Pratt, and Afeni and Mutulu had worked with Geronimo in the 1970s. Geronimo was both an uncle of ours and Pac's godfather. Johnny represented Geronimo in a case in which he was accused of killing a couple on a tennis court in Santa Monica. He was convicted and served time, but it was a setup for which he was eventually exonerated.

All the preliminaries had been done in regard to Allen's lawsuit, and now it was time for Pac to actually appear in court. On court day, I drove Pac as usual, and when we got out of the elevator in the elevator bay, I got to meet the legendary Johnny Cochran for the first time. When I shook his hand, he had a great big smile on his face, and he was very cordial, very warm. Pac was all stressed out—we both were; you'd think we'd eventually get used to showing up to court, but you never really do. Johnny was cool as a fan. Smiling, joking with the court clerks, not a care in the world. I was hoping his energy was going to help calm Pac. We went in the courtroom, and Johnny and Allen's lawyer addressed the judge. Albert wasn't even there. I don't recall the specifics of what happened case-wise, but when we walked out of the courtroom back to the elevator bay, Pac was heated. No surprise. He was explaining his position to Johnny again, and then all of a sudden, Allen and his lawyer appear in the elevator bay. And Pac lost it. "You punk motherfucka, how the fuck you gonna sue me? I should have my niggas fuck you up again." As Pac lunged to get in his face, I grabbed him: "Pac, hold up. Don't make it worse, don't make it worse." At the same time, cool Johnny was like, "Hey, hey! Pac, man, Tupac, be cool." I think Pac's reaction kinda shocked Johnny. He knew of Pac, but he definitely didn't know him like this. The elevator came, and Johnny and I both pushed Pac into the elevator as he continued to verbally bang on Allen's ass.

Pac had to do some time in county shortly after this. I believe it was over this case. But it also could've been a gun charge. I think you're getting the idea that there was always some legal shit going on. It got hard to keep track! He was in county for like two weeks. He was in protective custody with—get this—Rick James, T.K. Kirkland, and the Menendez brothers. He said the Menendez brothers were actually cool, and that one of them gave him stationery. It had Erik's name on it, I think. Such a strange world we were in here in Hollyhood.

Pac was, at this point, thinking more about his film career and the different creative disciplines attached to production. I could tell from the way he would choreograph some of our stage shows that he would be attracted to directing. I don't know how it actually happened—whether Mac Mall, this young up-and-coming artist from Vallejo, asked Pac to direct the video for his song "Ghetto Theme" or just appear in it—but Pac ended up doing both, and he took the task seriously. He created a nice treatment for the video and he recruited Tracy Robinson to AD and produce. He cast me and Stretch as characters in this story. Everybody in the crew loved the song. It was about two good friends who go to war with each other after things go left. I played Pac's character's brother, who was trying to keep him from doing something stupid. A little on the nose. Stretch played the friend with whom he'd had a falling-out. Pac had everybody involved that he had wanted and we started to shoot.

Things got a little tricky right away because the filming location was a block in the Jungles, a notorious Blood 'hood in LA that's kind of cut off from the city, in the sense that there's only one way in and one way out. The problem was, no one spoke to anyone from the neighborhood before we started filming. That was a real learning moment. Tracy had innocently chosen the location, and didn't really understand 'hood politics. Naturally, a few brothers from the neighborhood decided to come have a chat with us when we started unloading our cameras and shit, and they weren't too happy. When you go into a neighborhood, people want to know who the fuck you are, what the fuck you're doing and, mostly importantly, what the fuck they get. They were threatening to shut down the set. This totally freaked Tracy out, to the point that she started crying. Pac went and talked to the Bloods who ran the block, and I tried to console Tracy.

Once we put out that fire, Mac and Rated visited the set. It was all good at first; we thought they came to hang out and support Mac Mall. Turns out they had something else in mind and wanted to talk to Pac about it. I was already in the trailer as Pac, Mac, and Rated came in. They had originally come to us as a duo called Double Jeopardy, and now they'd been offered the opportunity to leave our group and go on tour with Coolio. They wanted that freedom, and they brought some paperwork for Pac to sign. Pac had agreed when they first asked him, but he didn't really expect them to leave. Now that it was real, he was angry because he had so much love for them as part of his crew. All I remember him saying was, "Y'all gonna come with this shit now?" They pled their case and Pac was so pissed, he just said, "Just give it here. Give me the paper." He signed it, got up, and walked out the trailer. Mac and Rated were trying to tell him that it was all good, it's all love still. They weren't leaving us behind so much as they were pursuing a great opportunity of their own. But they were part of this T.H.U.G. L.I.F.E. family Pac was building, so how could he not feel betrayed? In retrospect, there probably was a way for them to do shows as a duo separate from the group without them leaving the group entirely, but nobody thought about that.

In the midst of all this, we ended up getting the video shot. And to this day it's still one of my favorite songs and videos. Pac got to do a separate director's cut of the video, Stretch did a good job, and it turned out to be a classic.

Later, Stretch performed with us on our March 1994 Arsenio Hall date. That combination—T.H.U.G. L.I.F.E. and Live Squad—was hard to beat. Live Squad were *very* talented rappers. The song that we performed was one of Stretch's—his remix to Pac and Stretch's soundtrack single "Pain," from *Above the Rim*. During that period, it was on and cracking, coast to coast. It was our second time on *Arsenio Hall*, and we were stage vets at this point. It's still always a thrill to perform on TV when there's a live audience. It's a true blast. There are cameras on all sides, and a live audience happy to see us. The energy of that is different, even from a concert. There's just something about that combination that's uniquely fun, where you can find and play to both the cameras *and* the live audience. My comfort level was super high; by that time, I knew all our material back and forth, which made it easier to engage the crowd and let loose a little. I called my mom and a few other close friends on the East Coast to check me out. My mom was always excited and happy for me, but to be honest I don't remember if she watched it. She was happy that I had become successful at what I loved to do, but I don't know how engaged she was in it all. I would find out later that she talked about me regularly with the ladies at work, one of whom, coincidentally, was ODB's (Old Dirty Bastard of the Wu-Tang Clan) mom. I know she heard "Feels Good" on the radio, but I didn't know how much rap she heard. Any way you look at it, the fact that she was happy for me made me know she was proud of me.

I did get to see her when we'd go back to the East Coast to work in New York. Once, we even did a show at Trafalgar Square in Queens. It was a personal high point for me, coming back to my hometown with me and my brother on top. Even if my mom wasn't coming to a show, I'm pretty sure she would tell her friends about it. Stretch was from Queens, as well, so it meant a lot to him, too. That show was a madhouse, man. It was New York'ed out. Queens was in full effect. Goons and gorillas everywhere, a gangsta party. I felt bad cuz somebody ended up stealing Pac's leather jacket that night, but we still murdered the stage.

T.H.U.G. L.I.F.E. was expansive, and we wanted to take it into another medium, even before we had released our first album. We were full of confidence, sure that we were on to something. Pac's creative juices were ever flowing, and one day he tapped me on the chest: "Mo, we're going to Catalina to write this movie. The T.H.U.G. L.I.F.E. movie." Well, that was the first I'd heard of it! But Pac had already talked to Tracy, and he wanted to bring along James Michael Marshall and Lisa, another creative who was friends with Tracy, to help with the writing. Pac wanted us to go somewhere where we could have a certain amount of focus, like on a writing trip. He chose Catalina Island, which is off the coast of Los Angeles. I was happy about that because it was close and I hadn't been there before. The five of us took the ferry over, just like everyone else does. Pac had rented a condo in Hamilton Cove. It was cool because we weren't really that distant from our daily lives, but it did kind of feel like a faraway, sleepy beach town. Golf carts came with the rental, which was cool because you can't really get around the island any other way, and we'd take it back and forth to the store to get food and booze. It kinda felt like a vacation, which I had not had since about 1989. But really, we were working. When we finally got started, we all sat down at a table and Pac started relaying his vision. He started listing characters—most of them were actually us—and Tracy and Lisa started writing down notes, trying to structure the narrative. I was listening to Pac's ideas, and gave him insight on different people, types of characters, that we should include in the movie. The second day, we worked some more. We didn't go out to dinner. No parties. After a week, although we didn't end up fully building it out, we did have an outline, character descriptions, and a few pages of organized thoughts. We never did get past that point in development, but a T.H.U.G. L.I.F.E. movie was part of the plan and would've broadened our audience.

In April of 1994, Pac was recognized by *The Source* magazine and was nominated for an award and asked to perform at the awards show. This was a big deal in the rap community because a Source Award was the only award that was truly ours, for the hip hop community. By this time, we were still promoting Pac's second album, *Strictly 4 My N.I.G.G.A.Z.* Pac had recently done a bunch of songs, and the one he wanted to perform for the awards was called "Out on Bail." It was kind of perfect for the time, since Pac was—and it always felt like he was—out on bail. This time, I think it was a gun charge, but there were so many situations, it's hard to say. Honestly, we spent almost as much time in the courtroom as we did the studio in those days.

The Source Awards were happening in New York, so about twenty of our guys flew out from California, in addition to the ten we already had in New York. Pac felt good having all his homies with him, he kind of wanted the New York crowd to feel his power. I felt the same. Old friends and foes were getting to see us in our full glory. Before the show started, Pac wanted to walk through the audience and feel out the crowd. So, all of us proceeded to follow Pac and walk through the audience. There were a lot of *oohs* and *aahs* and cheers. But you could also sense that there was a bit of fear because we were so deep. Me, Big Syke, Stretch, Maj, Country, Manute, Paint, Bill Bang, Biggie (not Smalls), and others that slip my mind. We were on the slow stroll through the audience—slow enough for niggas to roll a blunt while walking, which some actually did, talking to girls and just seeing how big the audience was.

When Pac and the whole crew hit the set to perform, our presence was felt. And when it got close to showtime, the stage director came and told us to go backstage and wait to hear our music. Our cue was literally the first notes of our music. Pretty clear. When we were backstage, we had no view of the stage, and there were no monitors. We were paying zero attention to who was on stage at the time, A Tribe Called Quest. They were receiving a Source Award and making their acceptance remarks. Before they were finished, though, someone (the sound engineer, most likely) mistakenly started our song. That was our cue! Pac's favorite song at the time, the one he had been champing at the bit to perform. The song dropped and we rushed the stage. There were so many of us, we totally overwhelmed A Tribe

Called Quest, the podium, and whatever they were talking about, right in the middle of their speech.

Pac started rockin', and me and Big Syke were on backup vocals. We was feelin' it! But while doing my backup vocals, I started to feel a mood change in the crowd. I started hearing a few boos here and there, and then they actually grew a little bit. *What the hell was going on?* The boos didn't overwhelm the people who were loving it, but it was definitely noticeable. Pac heard it, too, which I know because he started rapping with some anger behind it. By the time the song was over and we were leaving the stage, I wound up my right arm with my mic in my hand and slammed it to the ground. I know I broke it. We didn't give a fuck. It felt like the audience was on some East Coast–West Coast shit. We got offstage and went backstage and were ready to fight.

While I was standing there talking to Pac about what was going on in the audience, Doug E. Fresh rolls up. And Doug E. was telling Pac to calm down, everything would be alright, everyone's just there for the show and to have a good time. Doug E., being the consummate peacemaker that he is, was tryin' to cool temperatures, because they had already spread through the audience. T.H.U.G. L.I.F.E. was about to set it off in that motherfucker. They had already seen how deep we were, so if we set it, it was gonna be ugly. Doug E. is a real one, so Pac listened. Apparently, what people were mad at was that they felt we disrespected A Tribe Called Quest by mobbing the stage while they were still accepting their award. Hand to God, we heard our cue. In fact, there's no way we would have begun our performance if they hadn't cued the music. It was totally unintentional. Once we realized what the problem was, we got the whole visual of the situation and we realized it wasn't some East Coast hater bullshit, so we rolled out peacefully. But the audience never knew that. To them, it looked like we'd dissed them.

The whole thing was a big mistake, and our reputations took the hit for shitty production skills and a lack of organization. These were still early days for rap awards shows, which were already fraught with high energy, tension, and a whole lot of testosterone backstage. We had no ill will towards A Tribe Called Quest, but to this day people still have feelings about it, which is kinda fucked up, because it really wasn't our fault.

As you can tell, this was a busy era for everyone involved. But it was even busier for me, for one reason in particular. While working on the album, I met China. I met her at Blue Palm Studios in North Hollywood. Back then, it was owned by Norman Whitfield, the legendary Motown producer. He was one of the few Black men of his day who owned his own label, and he was just cool as fuck. At the time, China was working for Paisley Park. It seems Prince had heard we were working on something and sent her by to check us out. She came over to the studio in jeans, boots, and a bolero jacket. She was beautiful and had a fun and bubbly personality. Around that time, Mac, Rated, Syke, and Johnny were there recording a lot. All the guys were interested in her, both because she came from Paisley Park and because she was beautiful. In a studio full of young guys, she was the center of attention.

We struck up a conversation. Because her job was to check out Pac, and I was co-producing the album, a lot of her questions came to me. Questions about the group, what the T.H.U.G. L.I.F.E. movement was about, what Pac was about. Eventually, our interactions became more social. She had visited three or four times before we started spending time together outside of work. We realized that we had a lot in common: Our parents and grandparents were from the South. She was also into oils and herbs and a lot of natural shit, and that was familiar to me because of my dad's side of the family.

It developed into a relationship from there. She was a real rock for me. I was spending a lot of time flying back and forth, working and recording. She was living in a guesthouse in the Hollywood Hills, and with whatever free time I had, I'd go over and spend it with her. It started out casual, but when you're making a point to spend all of your free time with someone, you get pretty close, fast. China got pregnant in those early days, and thank God I was in Los Angeles this day. I had gone to get her ice cream, and luckily that's a quick errand, because when I got back to her house I found her passed out on the toilet, blood everywhere. I picked her up and saw this bunch of unformed flesh just sitting in the bloody toilet bowl. That image will always stick with me—seeing the future that we'd planned to have together, just there in the toilet. I called an ambulance but had to carry her up the steep hill from the back house up to the main house. Thank God she was okay. I still don't really like talking about it. I have rarely felt that scared, that helpless, in my life. We had both been so excited because this would've been the first child for both of us. We were hopeful for the future and, for the first time in my life, I started thinking about how to be a father. After the loss we were both shelled, stunned, and we consoled each other through it.

CHAPTER 19

T.H.U.G. L.I.F.E. BAAABY

We were busy as hell and each day felt busier than the last. Our success was established in music and Pac was hitting his stride and was completely comfortable as a professional actor, too. The third movie Pac filmed was *Bullet*, even though it came out fourth. We were recording two albums—*Me Against the World* and *Thug Life vol. 1*—doing shows, and partying a little in between. And because of that, I was back and forth to NYC, where *Bullet* was being filmed. I was looking forward to going to the set because this film was grittier than anything he had done thus far. It was a crime thriller, with a respectable, grown-up cast that included Mickey Rourke, Ted Levine, Donnie Wahlberg, Adrien Brody, and, at that time, up-and-comers Peter Dinklage and Michael K. Williams. Pac and I hadn't talked much because he had been spending a lot of time in New York, so I was a little out of the loop on what the film was actually about and his role in it.

When I got there, they were filming a shoot-out scene. As I looked at the set, I swear Pac was wearing an eye patch and kinda looked like Slick Rick. Stretch was in a scene with him. I felt some type of way that he didn't have me in the scene, but then I thought maybe he had something else planned for me, so I waited patiently for my opportunity. When the clapperboard sounded, everybody went into action and Pac stood up and delivered his lines. I think he pulled out a gun and there was a shoot-out at the table with him, Stretch, and the other actors, and they flipped the table over. I was like *Oh, shit, this is fucking action!* I was impressed. I thought that shit was real dope.

Only thing I really hated was Pac's costume. Pac was skinny, about 165, 170 on a good day. And wardrobe put him in a tight-fitting brown two-piece suit with a blue button-down, collared shirt. That shirt might have even been fluorescent—yuck! He was supposed to be a boss, some type of gangsta. Instead, he looked like a caricature. Everybody was doing their part, but it was hard for me to take Pac seriously in that suit, with the eye patch and hat looking like a busted Slick Rick—no gold on! I was hoping it didn't look so ridiculous on film, because the movie had some real good actors in it.

After they wrapped the scene, we linked up in his trailer. When I got there, there was this girl named Spawn hanging out. I would later find out she was beginning her porn star career. Stretch and I rolled up blunts, and we kicked it a little until Pac had to leave and prep for the next day's scene. Before he left, he said he wanted to talk to me later about Spawn. She and I stayed in the trailer and talked for a little while longer. She told me she had met my cousin Billy Bang and we were all going to reconnect back in Los Angeles. I headed back to LA a few days later, and I never ended up being able to get into the film.

One of the friends that Pac made on *Bullet* was Mickey Rourke. They apparently bonded on this film. I believe it was a kindred spirit type of thing. Even after filming, Pac and Mickey stayed in contact. Sometimes I would hear Pac laughing real loud and I'd be like, *Who're you talking to?* It was almost always Mickey. One of the last days I was in New York, they planned to meet at an Italian restaurant somewhere in Manhattan. So Pac got me, Country, and Stretch and we went off to meet Mickey. On our way there, Pac let us in on the fact that Mickey had been having problems with his then-wife Carré Otis, so it seemed like we were going to try and give Mickey some relationship advice. When we got there, a small restaurant with couples snuggled up at small tables, we kinda felt like fish out of water. It was all these big guys, in baggy gear in this little restaurant with little-ass tables. As soon as Mickey saw Pac, a big smile came on his face. He got up and they hugged. Pac introduced us and then we tried to fit our oversized selves into the chairs in the tiny aisles. Mickey introduced Pac to his wife; Pac proceeded to be his usual, charming self. Mickey and Pac got up and stepped to the side of the table to talk privately. After a few minutes they came and sat back down. They laughed and joked for a few minutes more. And then we got up to leave. We didn't eat or order anything! Shit, I was hungry. On our way out, Pac got some flowers from somewhere and gave them to Mickey to give to his girl. I said to myself, *Good thinking, Pac, good thinking.* A small example of the type of friend Pac was. If he considered you a friend, he'd always try to help you. And as far as I know, Pac and Mickey remained friends until his last days.

After getting back to Los Angeles from New York, I got a call from Pac. He said, "Yo, Mo, I meant to tell you while you were out here, that chick Spawn wants me to manage her. But I want you and Bill Bang to manage her instead." I'm like, "Manage her? Ain't she tryin' to be a porn star?"

"Yeah, look out for her."

I'm like, "I ain't tryin' to be in the porn business, so I'm gonna let Bill Bang handle that, and I'll oversee it, I guess." I don't recall if Bill Bang did any actual management work. I think Spawn ended up managing herself, but we remained cool. We actually wound up living close to each other in Hollywood. Eventually, Spawn introduced me to Ron Hightower, who also lived close by. He was one of the few Black adult film directors at the time. We would hang out at his house, shooting pool, kickin' it, and I got to meet a lot of people in that industry. This coincided with one of the times when Pac was in jail. I was laying low and this friendship would come in useful down the line. I would meet Ron on set from time to time, and I'd watch some of the scenes. There was always the smell of strong soaps, lotion, and lube. Other celebrities and rappers would come through and we'd go offset to smoke weed most of the time.

In September 1994, weeks before the long-awaited release of *Thug Life vol. 1*, we had a big show in Milwaukee. It was at MECCA arena: Xscape, Spice-1, H.W.A., MC Eiht & Compton's Most Wanted, B.O.S.S. Big Mike, and Scarface, among others, were performing. Pac was set to headline. Early on the day of the show, Pac had read an article about a young fourteen-year-old girl who had been murdered by an eleven-year-old boy in the crossfire of a gang fallout in Chicago. It fucked with him all day. The lineup was long, the crowd of 12,500 had been waiting on Pac, and he had been spending all that time backstage just stewing about this young girl. Finally we took the stage, but Pac almost immediately started having issues with his mic. The crowd saw a performer frantically looking for a mic, but the tension on stage was the highest it had ever been. We knew he was in a fucked-up mood. At the same time, the crowd was rowdy, and not in a good way. The whole vibe was just wrong. Pac got a new mic and kept performing, but at one point, he just stopped the music and started to give the audience hell: "You better stop killing those babies or else I'll murder you myself! I taught you about harming those babies. Keep it up and I'll murder all you muthafuckas!"

Pac was seriously pissed the fuck off, and maybe people didn't realize it until that moment. It was one of the things his fans loved most about him: that he really cared and that he always held a mirror up to people if he felt they could change and improve things. But, man, this audience did *not* want to see themselves in that mirror. I didn't even have time to think about how wrong this could go, it happened so quick. As soon as Pac finished his rant, they just started throwing coins at us. I remember a quarter hit my head; it landed on its side, so the edge came down on my bald skin hard. Before I could react—before any of the rest of us could react—Pac jumped right back in and went off. "I don't know who the fuck you all think I am. You can flash them gang signs if you want, but I'll kill all of you muthafuckas! This is THUG LIFE!"

There was this incredibly potent silence, and then all of a sudden the air just broke with these wordless screams. *AAAHHHHHH!!!* The crowd started to rush the stage. There was not a second to think: It was fight or flight. We chose the former. Billy Bang was smashing people over the head with full Heineken bottles, spraying glass and beer everywhere. *Boooosh! Booosh!* Pac was holding his mic stand and swinging it like a club. We had to get the fuck out of there. Security ran us back to the greenroom and we ended up stuck in there for a little while with Spice 1 and, randomly, Jubu, one of the musicians from the Tonys. The cops busted in and searched the place looking for weapons but eventually let us go. Man Man and the venue staff piled us into the van. "Come on! Let's go back to the hotel," someone said. Then came, "You can't go back to the hotel! They're tearing up the hotel!" The whole van erupted, laughing and screaming, "OH SHIT!" We went directly to the airport and had to send Man Man back to the hotel to pack up and get all of our luggage. The mayor sent word that we would get paid for the show, but we were banned from Milwaukee. Come to think of it, I still might be banned in Milwaukee. So, yeah—Pac being Pac, being pissed at the wrong people for the right reason, took it too far, at the wrong time.

All the hard work we did, recording for almost three years, politicking with the label, promoting, touring, bringing the fans along with us, came together when we finally released *Thug Life vol. 1* in late September. It charted on Billboard 200, hit number 6 on Billboard's R&B/Hip Hop chart, and remained charting through 1995. I was happy we were able to get it done, release it, and that we didn't miss the opportunity after working so long on it. I was proud to be behind the helm of a project that meant so much to me and Pac; after all, he had the very words THUG LIFE tatted across his belly. After

I saw how well it did when it came out, I felt vindicated. It resonated with the people. It began with the people, from what we had experienced from the ground up. And we had so many obstacles along the whole way—my own father had questioned us, the system had opposed us, even banned us in some instances, and the label fought us—but the people saw us through, believed in us, saw themselves in what we were making, and embraced the truth of the work.

CHAPTER 20

THE TRAP

That whole "Pac being Pac" thing—and us being who we were, growing up as targets as Mutulu's kids, as Afeni's kid—I don't know that I was surprised when I heard that Pac had been shot. Actually, at first I thought they had the story wrong. I thought *Pac* shot someone. I had just gotten to Los Angeles from Atlanta when I got the word. I was worried and I was also furious. I knew he would be okay, weirdly. As his brother, I just felt like he would. But I was still so worried about him, and I needed to get to him fast. I got on the first plane out with my man Big Country. Pac had been going into Quad Studios in Midtown Manhattan when it happened, but that didn't make any sense to me, because we had plenty of people in New York. In fact, he was with Stretch, Zaed, and Nickels. There's no fucking way he should have been exposed and unprotected in that way. He was also spending a lot of time around these real gangsters, Haitian Jack and Jimmy Henchman, who were supposed to be looking out for him.

The thing is, we had built a reputation in our brief, meteoric rise for kicking up dust and not taking no shit from nobody. Off that alone, you make a lot of enemies. And besides that, let us not forget, Tupac and I were the children of Black revolutionaries, which made us feel like enemies of law enforcement. We fully understood that cops don't protect the children of people like my parents. Mind you, all my father's New York cases were investigated under the NYJTTF (New York Joint Terrorism Task Force). We felt like targets even as we were making legal money.

There were other factors also that might have led someone to want Pac dead, for sure. There were jealous artists who wanted to take Pac down because he was on top. Or it could have been that someone simply wanted to rob him. In New York City, in 1994, Pac would walk around draped in jewels. In fact, right before the shooting, we were both in Atlanta and I didn't realize that Pac was headed to New York at the same time that I was headed to Los Angeles. I asked him where he was going. He had chain after chain after chain, just draped in gold and diamonds. He told me he was headed to New York and I asked him, "You're going like that? To New York? Home of the stick-up kid? Draped in jewels? Looking like Mr. T?" He said, "That's why I got these." He lifted up his shirt, showing me two ten-millimeter Glocks he called "the twins." I just shook my head. So, as I reflected on that, I thought it could've been a robbery. Pac was also outspoken and brash. Sometimes he would step on the wrong person's toes. But the thing is, all of this considered, it pissed me off that he was unprotected. We were from New York and we had people there. Stretch was there. He and Notorious B.I.G. were building a relationship. He felt safe. And he should have been protected.

It turns out that when he was entering the studio, two guys approached Pac, Stretch, Zaed, and Nickels at gunpoint in the lobby as they were waiting for the elevator. When Pac went to draw on them, his own weapon fired and he was shot in his leg. They fired on him, and two bullets grazed the top of his head. Nickels got shot, too. The guys took off after taking some of Pac's jewelry. I'm unclear where the other three of them went after the shooting, but when Pac made it upstairs, bleeding, he sat down to roll a blunt while the guys he was supposed to be recording with looked on in shock. From his perspective, they looked shocked that he was alive, not shocked that he made it upstairs. They looked like they saw a ghost. He demanded his money. Someone called an ambulance. It was those Junior M.A.F.I.A.

niggas in the studio and there were Bad Boy people, amongst others, all in the area. Pac felt like it was a setup.

So even though Afeni met him at the hospital with Yas, our aunt, and Watani, and even though Watani showed up with FOI (the Fruit of Islam) security on point, Pac didn't feel safe. On top of that, he learned news of his childhood that he hadn't known before. Right there in the hospital at arguably one of the most vulnerable moments in his life, up to that point, in walks his biological father. He just walked in. I wasn't in New York yet, so I cannot speak for what conversations were had leading up to this; my understanding is, many years later, that he just saw on TV that Tupac had been shot and went to the hospital. I don't even know exactly who happened to be in the room at the precise moment he showed up, or if someone had a conversation with Pac to tell him he was coming, but somehow, some way, he walks into Pac's room.

Pac had always believed that his biological father had died when he was little, too young to really remember him well. It turns out that he was alive, living on the East Coast—and not at all who Pac thought he was. Pac believed his father was a man named Legs, an all-around hustla, man of the streets. His mother raised him and Sekyiwa to hold Legs in high regard, and up to that point, he believed himself to be the son of a respected man of the streets *and* the son of revolutionaries. And now in walks his biological.

Let's not forget that Afeni became pregnant with Tupac when she was on bail, defending herself and her codefendants in the Panther 21 trial. Her bail was revoked when some of her codefendants absconded, but she successfully defended herself and the other members of the Panther 21 and was released from custody shortly before Pac was born. It turns out, his biological father was another Panther from a different chapter who had been assigned to guard her when she was on bail. For reasons that I am certain were complicated for her, Afeni told Tupac that his father was Legs. I don't question her judgment in choosing to tell Tupac what she felt was best to keep him safe as a child. But make no mistake, it had a significant impact on his state of mind as he was in that hospital, coming out of surgery and suspicious about who had shot him in the first place. Then, at the same time and out of nowhere, the identity that he'd built through his life was uprooted, and he was questioning if he could fully trust the people he'd trusted most. For most people, this alone would lead to soul-searching of the existential type. Pac was burdened with so many crises. It had to have been disorienting at a time that really required clarity.

He wanted to get the fuck out of there. He also had a court appearance the next day and even though the court would have surely delayed the case, this one was too important. (I'll explain more about this later.) It was too much, so he checked himself out and they all went to Jasmine Guy's house uptown. Pac and Jasmine met when he filmed a guest arc on *A Different World*, and they had been tight ever since. He felt safe there because only his most trusted knew he was there, and that made us all feel a little safer. Thank God for Jasmine Guy and her courage at that moment. I will always have love and respect for Ms. Jasmine Guy. Cuz as far as she knew, niggas was trying to kill him.

When Country and I got to New York, it was late at night, and Pac had already left the hospital. I called Watani and he told us to come to the courthouse in the morning. We headed there and saw a big group of people, amongst them FOI, and we headed in that direction. When we got to the crowd, we pushed people out of the way, even FOI, to get to Pac. Have I mentioned that Country's enormous? He just parted that crowd. We finally got to Tupac and he's sitting there in a wheelchair. In that moment, I was so happy and relieved, because he looked up at us and just started smiling, even as he was wincing in pain. I know he felt safer with us there. He had a cast on his arm and a bandage on his head. I was thinking, *Look at this little warrior*. We rolled him into the courthouse with FOI behind and on our flank. He had a hearing, so we didn't have a chance to talk in the courthouse.

While we were there waiting for him, someone told us to meet him at Jasmine Guy's house after. That's when we finally got a chance to talk, and that's when he told me what happened. We spent a lot of time going over his suspicions about who was behind the shooting. It felt like a setup to him, and to me. We went through a lot of details, gathered and rehashed information to get to who was behind it. Pac was on the couch, in pain and complaining, "Yo, where the fuck is Stretch? Will somebody call Stretch? I need some fucking weed. What the fuck?" No one had anything to say, because nobody had heard from him since the assault. That seemed weird as fuck, cuz the nigga was there when Pac got shot. In the meantime, we all tried to keep Pac comfortable, running errands, sending the little homies to find some weed, and watching Pac's back.

I soon left to get back to Los Angeles and keep the machine running; I knew that Watani, FOI, and everybody else had Pac secure. When I reached LA I kept checking in with the little homies to see if Stretch had surfaced. What I ended up discovering was that Mutah was there when Stretch finally showed up and delivered a message from Jimmy Henchman saying, "If you wanna go to war, you better get your money right." That's when things started crystallizing for Pac.

While we were in Jasmine's apartment, we had spent most of the time reflecting and dissecting anything and everything, big or small, that was out of the ordinary or the slightest bit strange. There were a series of odd events: To start with, Jimmy Henchman was blowing up Pac's phone all that day, pressing him to be sure to make it into the studio. Now, Pac took his recording time seriously. Sometimes he ran late, but if he was gonna be there to record, he was gonna be there to record, no question. Jimmy knew that. We were never sure why all those Junior Mafia niggas were all gonna be in the studio, either. Bad Boy had a video shoot around the corner, and it was possible they just hung out after they were done shooting. But there wasn't a *reason* for all of them to be there.

Pac said that when they pulled up to the studio, before they got out of the car, Stretch asked to hold the twins, the Glocks. He said, "Yo, God, you don't need to be going up in there like that." Pac said, "I looked at him like he had three heads." Stretch never, ever, ever wanted to hold the iron. He was a big-ass Black dude and felt like that would make him a target for police. At the same time, Pac was usually armed, especially if he was with someone who wasn't. That was the standard rule amongst the clique. Everybody knew. And after they robbed Pac, it took forever for Stretch to come see about his best friend. Two of the guys that were with Pac at the time, Stretch and Zaed, disappeared right after the shooting, and we had no idea where they went. And when Stretch finally pops up, when Pac's best friend finally surfaces after he got shot, it's to deliver a message from the people who apparently set him up. Things were already bad, but putting these pieces together made it worse. I knew how Pac felt about Stretch, and I thought I knew how Stretch felt about Pac.

Something wasn't right. Pac was livid. By the time he got back to Atlanta, he was almost completely healed and was full of anger, rage, suspicion and, rightfully, paranoia. He had become more certain and more passionate about his feelings on the situation. I would watch him pace and stomp around the house, yelling about it. Once he turned to me, no shirt on, sweating and yelling, both fists balled up in front of him. "Mo, he asked me for the twins!" He knew that I knew what that meant: It looked like his best friend was trying to disarm him before sending him in to be ambushed. Even then, even then, I was still having doubts about Pac's theory, and the main reason was that I knew how close we all were. It was very hard for me to live with this theory. Everybody loved Stretch, most of all Pac. In our whole crew, there wasn't any one of our guys that didn't get along with him. Even Afeni. Pac and Stretch would shake the crew and have their own separate capers. They would shake the rest of us and be at a yacht party or somewhere off in another state. I would be pissed, but we all trusted Stretch that much. At the same time, I was a realist. I knew about the guys that Pac and Stretch were around. I had to consider it seriously.

If I'm being honest, it burns me to this day that the cops did not lift one finger to investigate this attempted murder. Let's be clear: If anyone else had injured themselves, potentially fatally injured themselves while defending themselves in the commission of a robbery, or worse, an attempted or foiled homicide where the perpetrators fired on him and bullets grazed his head, there would be an investigation. I don't even recall hearing about the cops interviewing the witnesses. They didn't give a fuck. And if there's any part of Pac's or my theories about the crime that seem confusing, understand that the lack of clarity is completely the fault of the NYPD who never really investigated this crime. It was like self-fulfilling, circular destiny—we don't trust the cops because they often misuse their power in policing us, and then when they should do their job to protect us, they don't do shit. Just another affirmation of why we don't fuck with the police.

And because of this, this incident would have a lot of fallout down the road—on so many levels.

CHAPTER 21

THUNDERSTORMS

Now, I have to back up a little bit here. One of the reasons Pac wanted to leave the hospital so soon after he got shot was because of that court date the following day. Obviously, being shot would have been a legitimate reason to delay a court date. But this was a unique situation, and a precarious time. It wasn't that being arrested or having to go to court was a new or unusual thing for us; we had been defending ourselves against crazy charges from day one. As you'll recall, Pac got beat up by the cops and arrested in Oakland as he was crossing the street to cash his first check from *Juice*. Pac shot at cops in Atlanta who were beating up a guy on the street. Pac got into it with the bitch-ass Hughes brothers, and they pressed charges. There was a long list of legal bullshit.

This situation was different: Pac had been arrested in New York on rape charges, and his drive to show up in court that morning to defend himself was because he really couldn't understand these particularly awful charges. I wasn't in New York when the incident allegedly happened, but I didn't believe it could be true. My understanding was that Pac knew the girl from before. She'd met him in a club when he was out with Haitian Jack and he introduced them. She gave Pac head while they were on the dance floor. After that, she was trying to link up with him and they met up at his hotel, the Parker Meridien in Manhattan. They hooked up and then Pac left the room. Haitian Jack and Man Man were the other two brought up on rape charges and Pac said what happened with her and the other guys happened after he had left the room. I believe it's possible, even likely, that she was assaulted, but I do not believe that my brother had a part in it.

There were a lot of niggas around that never, never, ever should have been in our sphere. Period. Grimy-ass mothafuckas. And now here was Pac having to defend himself while recovering from being shot. It was the worst possible accumulation of circumstances. As the trial progressed, Pac's codefendants separated their cases and that made all of us suspicious. The woman's prior relationship with Haitian Jack already piqued distrust, and then the separation of the cases escalated those suspicions. Then Afeni recognized someone in the trial proceedings from her time defending herself as a member of Panther 21.

I need to be clear so that I'm not speaking out of turn about this, because Mama Fe is no longer with us to clarify. And I only know what I was told at the time and how to interpret that through the lens of my life experiences up to that point. It is documented that the FBI started watching my father since he was sixteen. Mutulu, Afeni, and others did the legal research to access files using FOIA (the Freedom of Information Act) to prove COINTELPRO's existence when they established the National Task Force for COINTELPRO Litigation & Research. But they only proved this after they had already been subjected to its destructive effects. Afeni famously defended herself as a member of Panther 21—while pregnant with Pac—largely by rightfully questioning how and why they gathered their evidence and who they had embedded as an informant, who was a bad actor. The cases that Assata won before she had to be liberated and live in exile were won on similar grounds. They knew it was systemic, and they proved it. I remind you of this history to be crystal clear about how completely confident I was in Afeni's ability to identify a plant when she saw one. I believed her when I was told that she'd seen someone in court, at the rape case proceedings, that she recognized from her Panther days. Someone who, even back then, she suspected was a plant. And of course I understood this to mean that the government was up to its bullshit . . . again.

It was all too much. On December 1, 1994, Pac was acquitted on the more serious charges of sodomy and the associated gun charge, but was convicted of two counts of first-degree sexual abuse for "forcibly touching the woman's buttocks" in his hotel room. The judge gave him the maximum possible sentence—one-and-a-half to four-and-a-half years—which was highly unusual; in almost every other similar case, the sentence was commuted to time served. Later, it was basically established that the jury only found him guilty of those particular charges because they assumed Pac wouldn't get any jail time. But the judge in the case was one of Rudy Giuliani's guys, and we all know how they felt about young Black men. I heard the same ringing in my head that I did when my father was captured: *All great Black men go to jail.* It was scary and infuriating, thinking that the feds could be involved in this in some way. We mostly just had our suspicions, but on some level we all knew: If we discovered that the feds were definitively involved in this, it meant the fight was *on*. I felt the stress and anger of insecurity about what would happen next and where our future was headed.

Pac was sent to Clinton Correctional Facility in Dannemora, in upstate New York, which began a very difficult, stressful time for all of us. Clinton was nicknamed "Little Siberia" since it's so far upstate. There seemed to be only two seasons there: winter and July. The building itself was this depressing, imposing thing, like something out of 1800s Europe. It was made of big stone blocks, crude stone, ancient and cold. It was built by prisoners in 1845. The interior was somehow even more depressing, just this dank gray, almost devoid of color. Pac had to wear this ugly puke-green two-piece with his number printed on his chest in white. When we would visit Pac, we'd stay for a week and see him every day. Coming from Los Angeles, we'd have to fly into Burlington, Vermont, and then drive into New York to get a hotel in Dannemora. I remember everyone there just looked so *angry*, and the prison reeked with that institutional smell:

nasty cleaning products and cold stone. We were led into the visiting room, a big space with metal benches and tables and a floor of old stone tile. There was no glass between visitors and prisoners, but we couldn't touch each other. They didn't allow pictures. I had never been in a New York state prison before; I'd been to county jails and federal prisons and holding facilities. This was different: older, danker, grayer, drabber.

But when they would finally bring Pac out, he usually had a big-ass smile on his face. He was so glad to see us, and that gave me comfort. This was early on, so we talked about his case, where he was on the appeal and getting all that legal shit out the way. Over the course of our visits, we also discussed the status of business, music, and what our next step should be. He kept telling us, "They love me in here! Where they have me at, they call that the 'thug tier.'" Pac was never unsafe in the pen, not as far as his other inmates were concerned. Let a nigga who did time with him say otherwise. Pac's music was always for the poor and disenfranchised—who more so than the brothers locked up? They had love for him and it was genuinely mutual.

While my brother was in Clinton, China and I got married. We figured, after the miscarriage, that if we were going to have a child, we should make our relationship official. I proposed, but after everything we'd been through, it was nothing elaborate. She didn't even want a traditional ring. We were at her house; she was sitting on the couch when I got on one knee and I proposed. We were married by a friend of hers at her house, which doubled as a small venue for weddings in Los Angeles. Only one other person was there—and I don't even remember who that was! China wore a nice dress, I wore a suit. We wanted to get married as soon as we could and then maybe have a big wedding or reception later, when things were less stressful, maybe once Pac was out of prison. We just didn't want the stress of planning a huge wedding on top of everything else.

After we were married, we got our first place together on Detroit Street and Sunset. I don't remember when I first found out she was pregnant again. I just felt like I was immediately on alert, because of the prior miscarriage. But when she started showing, I began getting really excited. She got pregnant in August of 1995, so she started to show around the late fall of that year. We were really cautious about telling people, but I did tell my brother when I saw him in October, even though she wasn't out of her first trimester. I told Set, who was also pregnant at the time with my nephew Malik, and who had already welcomed my niece little Nzingha a couple of years earlier. They were both so happy for us. Pac was real excited to be an uncle to my kid.

With a new wife and baby on the way, in some ways I knew where my life was headed. Pac and I talked a lot during those visits about his plans when he got out, too. He talked about getting back at mothafuckas. It didn't help that he was hearing rappers from New York talking about him on the radio. People don't realize that Pac got the radio up there. The same radio they had in Manhattan, Queens, Bronx, and Brooklyn, he could hear up there. People love to fuck with someone when they're down, and petty rappers are no different. I'm thinking, *They think they can do that with impunity, that he can't do shit cuz he's locked up even if he does hear it*. He was kind of fucked up over that. He felt betrayed but, you know, people ain't shit. I was telling him that people out there still loved him. The people, not the fakers in the business. I told him, "The streets are still rooting for you regardless of what you heard on the radio." He had a lot of anger, and rightfully so, about the shooting at Quad Studios. These feelings of betrayal didn't just go away when they sent him upstate. I kept telling him what we all knew: The radio may have been talking shit, but the streets were still his. But that was a turning point for Pac: He became angrier, more withdrawn, more focused on getting back at people.

And while all that was going on, Pac wrote. Not music, but screenplays and monographs, long letters and correspondence. Reflections. Meanwhile, his legal team went straight into putting together an appeal. This is a point I cannot emphasize enough: *Pac got an appeal*. There was enough suspicion of prosecutorial misconduct that he was granted an appeal. That's a big deal by itself. After nine months, he was also granted bail. Being granted bail, in any amount, on an appeal is a very big deal, and genuinely points to there being something amiss in the way the case was prosecuted. Still, the bail was 1.4 million dollars. For the average person, that's a lot of dough. But *Me Against the World* was released in March of 1995 with the first single, "Dear Mama," a smash hit from its release the previous February. And that train had not stopped rolling.

We were producing music videos while he was locked up, for Christ's sake. His shit was *charting. Thug Life vol. 1* had come out earlier in the fall right before he was convicted in late November of 1994, and we were still pushing it into 1995. The singles were selected, but two of the four videos were shot after he was sentenced. So the team told the label what Pac wanted and we were executing. Two videos I remember we shot almost back-to-back: "Shit Don't Stop," from *Thug Life vol. 1* and then we went directly into "Temptations" from his solo album, *Me Against the World.* Instead of us, the talent, the label used a bunch of cameos: Adina Howard, B-Real, Bill Bellamy, Cheryl "Salt" James, Coolio, Crystal Waters, DJ Spinderella, Ice-T, Isaac Hayes, Jada Pinkett Smith, Jasmine Guy, Kenya Moore, Shock G, Joe Torry, Taye Diggs, Treach, Warren G, and Yo-Yo. Despite what he was feeling in the isolation of prison, Pac had a lot of love, and people wanted to show support.

The decision to keep things moving was Pac's, and I know the label was happy to have product to promote and revenue to bring in while he was locked up. Which is why there should have been—there's no way there wasn't—money in that bank. The bank being the label, Interscope. There were *two* new lines of revenue, from *Thug Life* and *Me Against the World.* Shit, if I had the money, I would've posted it myself and it definitely crossed my mind why I *didn't* have it or have something to put on it with the rest of the crew. But, most crucially the label wouldn't come up with his bail, even with a number-one record, two albums charting and multiple singles charting, and even if it were to be applied against the earnings the label was collecting to be paid in the subsequent months. It was bullshit, and Pac knew it.

It was all hands on deck, trying to find him another deal so that he could pay the bail with his advance. Interscope's position, as they tell it, was precarious: Around this time, Warner Music Group had recently been bought out by Time Inc. Atlantic Records, the distributor of Interscope, was a wholly owned subsidiary of Warner. They claimed they were under pressure to distance themselves from rap, as it was too controversial and didn't fit nicely with the "clean" image of what would become Time Warner. For their part, Interscope separated from Atlantic and Time Warner because they wanted to keep the cash cow that was their rap roster, and they eventually went to Universal. But while the timing was close, the deal with Universal was done by this point. And years prior to Interscope leaving Warner, but after Interscope had signed Pac, they made a label deal with Suge Knight for Death Row Records, and Suge was now making a play for Pac. I guess having Pac one layer separated from the distributor and Interscope would make a difference? To my mind, the money was all coming from the same place at that point. But what do I know?

Watani wanted Pac to wait until he saw what the other majors had to offer, but Suge had made the effort to visit Pac in prison to make his case, and that made a difference to Pac. It made Suge a real nigga in his eyes. On the one hand, I felt that it would be good to have someone with that much power on our team. I was aware of Suge's reputation as a hardcore dude, but we knew a bunch of hardcore dudes, so that didn't influence me either way. I felt, business-wise, that he had already done good business with Pac on the *Above the Rim* soundtrack. That sat well with me. And we all liked the idea of going with a Black-owned label. On the other hand, I wanted Pac to be on an even bigger label, like a major and not an imprint. We were already at Interscope, and I didn't love the idea of going one layer under. I felt like a direct deal with a major could give Pac opportunities with his music and his film career. But we had also always been pro-Black business and maybe, on top of everything else, we saw more in Suge than may have been there simply because we wanted to see a Black businessman succeed. I didn't know too much about Suge other than Death Row and the rumors. But I was about to find out how influential he would become to Pac personally.

They signed a deal from Dannemora, handwritten. Suge posted his bail as an advance on his solo recording deal for three albums, and it also included a deal specifically for me and for Big Syke to carry on the T.H.U.G. L.I.F.E. brand. Actually, Pac is the one who had told me and Syke how the deal would break down. Basically, what we discussed on that visit is what ended up in that handwritten contract. I didn't talk to Suge directly about it. As far as I was concerned, I still only had one boss, and that was Pac. I was pleased with what was supposed to happen, and as long as Pac was getting what he wanted, I assumed that we would get what we wanted. I didn't really have any feelings about Suge either way, cuz I didn't know the man.

Now, when word came that Pac made a deal for the bail, everybody was waiting to see where he was gonna go. He was from New York, he'd lived in Baltimore, he'd lived in Atlanta, came up in the Bay, was working in LA. I wanted him in LA, away from all the shit in New York, where he hadn't been protected. LA was where Death Row was based, and I knew we'd both loved LA even back when we first came to shoot *Poetic Justice*. Sunshine, palm trees, in the ragtop. We were on the same sheet of music. I knew where he'd end up. But everyone else in the country was on pins and needles wondering where Pac was gonna go. DJs on the radio were announcing every move like they were calling a game. When they heard Pac was free, when they heard Pac was on the plane, it was *We don't know where he's gonna go, but he's free.*

When Pac got out of jail everybody was so damn happy! Tupac had really been caught up in New York. He caught a case. He'd been set up. He'd been shot. He did time at Rikers and Clinton Correctional Facility. Yo! The kid had gone through it in New York. Back on the West Coast where he came up at, where people were pulling for him, his people were waiting anxiously for their boy to return. When Pac hit LA, it felt like the whole city was celebrating. It was like a holiday or something.

Pac went straight to the studio. He got fresh—new clothes and jewelry—and then he came to swoop me up. I had a balcony, and all of a sudden I heard that rumbling *boom boom* of a bass that you can feel in your stomach. I walked out onto my balcony and saw Pac standing there, looking up with his hands raised, in a shrug, a smile on his face. He had on a Rolex, jewelry, bracelet, fresh. And behind him was his new ragtop 500 Benz coupe. I got in the car and he was bumpin' "Ambitionz az a Ridah." He threw me a sack and said, "Roll something." I'm like, "Nigga, you know we're in a drop top?!" But it was like we were invincible, like the whole damn city was on our side.

As we rolled through town, it felt like every car was bumpin' Pac!

CHAPTER 22

THE NEW LABEL

Soon as Pac got out, it was all about releasing his first album to make a statement—to represent for everyone who was rooting for him and to let niggas know he was back and in effect. It was also about showing that part of the industry that didn't believe in him—both the corporate side of the industry that wouldn't post his bail and the rappers who were trying to come for him—that they'd fucked up and underestimated him. He wanted to show them all how this shit is done, take it up a level, cement himself as the greatest rapper of the time, period. This album was a big deal and he knew everyone was watching him for one reason or another, so *All Eyez on Me* was a perfect title for the moment.

People forget, because he was charting while he was in prison, there was a lot of talk on the radio that Pac heard while he was locked up. This whole East Coast–West Coast shit wasn't *our* shit, we didn't start it. And people love to forget that we were New Yorkers. So hearing all the shit that people were talking on the radio felt like they were talking way out of turn, greasy, like talking behind his back and not realizing he was hearing almost all of it. And he definitely felt set up by those New York niggas. So fuck them. If they were gonna start shit, he was gonna bring it from the West and dead that shit. Show them all how this is done. That was what this album had to be. It was a big deal.

I was feeling the same feelings he was, because I understood his perspective. I understood why he was angry with the New York rappers. I knew we had been trying so hard to make sure that they knew he didn't forget about them and that we knew our roots, even though we came up in Cali and formed a group with LA niggas. For example, Pac wrote "Old School," which was on *Me Against the World*, to make precisely that point. We felt that with our sincere alliances with Live Squad and Treach and Naughty By Nature, it was just stupid for this to be made into a geographical beef. We tried to make an alliance with Biggie, in addition to all of our other, older hip hop relationships from New York. So, yeah, I understood why he felt set up and attacked. He and I would have none of it. My mindset at the time was very much *Hell yeah, Pac, let's ride.*

He was still recovering from the gunshot wounds, though, and I worried about his health. Real talk, had he not been sent to prison shortly after being shot, most likely he never would've sat down long enough to heal. And then there's this disgusting truth: It felt like that shit, the people coming for him, was petty jealousy. We were making real money in rap and having real success and, though both of us were from New York, we were bringing that success back to the West Coast. The more popular we got, the more successful we got, the more scrutinized we felt. And we were in Hollywood, able to cross these worlds in a way that hadn't been done before. I felt like a lot of the shit was just hateful-ass jealousy.

At the time, Pac was accusing Biggie and Bad Boy of being behind Quad Studios. I felt a little confused and troubled by what Pac was saying, by the rumors that were circulating. Even though it felt like something bigger was going on, it was hard to believe that Biggie had the balls to participate in something like that. Pac had first met Biggie back when we were trying to figure out who would be included in the T.H.U.G. L.I.F.E. movement, and Biggie was definitely on the list. Pac had even pulled Biggie in on a song with Stretch and the little homies, "Runnin." It was produced by Easy Mo Bee and also featured Dramacydal: Katari, Yaki, Big Malc. Big had come out to the West

Coast and stayed with Pac. This was before Biggie had a deal, but we were familiar with his music, what he was doing, that he was coming up on the New York rap scene. Pac would check in on Biggie and Big Stretch whenever he was in NYC; at one point, remember, he showed Biggie love, doing a T.H.U.G. L.I.F.E. freestyle with him at Madison Square Garden. It was important to Pac to keep those connections strong, to show that the whole East Coast versus West Coast thing was something drummed up and he didn't buy into it.

The thing is, remember that when Pac had that recording session at Quad, Bad Boy had been shooting a video around the corner. When Pac made it upstairs, there were a bunch of industry people there—I heard it was Puffy, Andre Harrell, Jimmy Henchman, and a host of others—and all of them were connected in some way to Bad Boy. Pac's whole reason for being there was to do a feature for an artist named Lil Shawn, who was managed by Jimmy Henchman, an associate of Haitian Jack. From our perspective, everybody in the area at that time worked with or was associated with Bad Boy Records. I think Pac assumed that Big and he were close enough friends that if Big suspected some shit was going to go down, he would've warned Pac . . . unless he was involved. I mean, he was claiming to be King of New York at the time.

It seemed inconceivable that Big was behind this escalating beef, unless he was just a petty, jealous mothafucka on a level I hadn't seen coming. But shots had literally been fired, and Pac had a lot of time to think about all the players behind it, including the possibility that even Stretch was involved. I couldn't entirely dismiss the things Pac told me. Even if I didn't think Big had the balls to orchestrate the whole thing, I did feel like it was entirely possible that he was being used. At that point, it didn't matter. I rode with my brother no matter what. *Fuck 'em* all! This was THUG LIFE, bitch!

All Eyez On Me was a double album written and recorded quickly, with about twenty more records that didn't even make the release. The work was nonstop, with a lot of the OGs. Getting the features was like the longest who's who hall of fame musical genius session ever, everyone from Dru Down to Wu Tang to DJ Quik to George Clinton to Roger Troutman. Some were friends, some were musicians we'd always wanted to fuck with, and they were all coming to Can-Am Studios in Tarzana. Because the studio was so deep with talent, it was like battling to be on a track. And Pac was a beast. His work ethic was like no other. Ideas were flowing back and forth and the first best verse was the shit we laid down.

During the early days of Death Row, it was on and crackin'. *All Eyez On Me* was out, and people loved it. Now it was time for the monster single, "California Love." We heard the record first and knew it was going to be a smash hit. I especially loved the song because the original version was produced by my man Laylaw from Above the Law. Dr. Dre ended up producing another version, but the original was my favorite. The people were eating it up like candy, so the video had to be *good*.

I remember one night with Pac and Dre at a club on Sunset. I think it was called Le Dome. We were there hanging out and Dre pulls out a few sheets of paper to show Pac. It was sketch outlines of storyboards for the video, in black ink, hand drawn. Dre was explaining to Pac how it was going to be a Mad Max Thunderdome theme. Pac was looking at it and got real excited. Dre was explaining how they were gonna be in dune buggies, smashing through the desert. Pac got real excited, damn near jumping up and down. I was standing back between the both of them and thinking to myself, this was going to be a major, major video.

We didn't talk about the video long before we were distracted by the commotion we were hearing because Mike Tyson had walked in. I had heard that the champ was going to be in the house. The three of us walked over to Mike and greeted him. I was excited to meet the champ and figured his attention was gonna be on Pac and Dre, so I gotta make a move. I ended up between Mike and Pac, but to the back a few steps. I nervously whacked the champ on the elbow and I knew immediately—oops, that mighta been too hard. I threw a big-ass smile on my face, like, *hey, what's up, champ?* He did not return the smile. Pac introduced me as his brother and Mike kinda nodded and moved along with the conversation. But I'll never forget seeing Mike Tyson looking at me like that, his brow all lowered. It was like staring at a bull about to charge.

A few days later, I started hearing more buzz about the video. It was gonna be shot at El Mirage Dry Lake in the Mojave Desert, and it was going to be a million-dollar video. I'd heard about Hype Williams directing, but I didn't know that Jada was originally supposed to direct it. Eventually, she backed out because she had other obligations and felt that when she directed one of Pac's videos one day, it deserved her full attention. Shoot day, I hopped in the van with a group of people headed to the desert. It was a pretty long drive, but I was anxious to see what a million-dollar video looked like, especially one that my little brother was the center of. We got there late afternoon, early evening. The area the production covered was expansive—big tents, bigger than the average film tents. Honestly, it resembled more of a movie shoot than a music video. I looked around and saw all the props. There was a group of four dune buggies. There was a big structure, shaped like a dome and netted with camouflage. There were different smaller setups around the compound. This shit was *major*. It didn't quite hit a million in the end; I believe the budget was more like $600,000.

There was nothing being shot at the time, so I headed over to where all the trailers were. I saw Dr. Dre dressed in his Mad Max costume with an eye patch on, walking around. I saw my homegirl Sonshine from Y?N-Vee who used to rock with us in the T.H.U.G. L.I.F.E. days. Someone pointed me towards Pac's trailer. He was sitting there at the table. He looked tired as hell, but he looked happy. He got up and he too had his Mad Max costume on, with fake dust and dirt all over him. He gave me a tight hug and a poof of dust came out of his vest. He's like, "Mo, you see this shit?" I just said, "Damn, nigga!" We had a quick drink and smoke and then he had an interview to do with Suge. He hopped out of the trailer and walked over to Suge and they started shooting this interview, talking about the making of the video and promoting the new album and Death Row. In the middle of it, he pulled out all of this money and started counting it. I was glad that Pac was finally having bread, but I knew the haters were gonna hate him for throwing it in their face like that.

Then it was time to shoot the dune buggy scene. Pac really wanted to drive. The techs started gathering around him, telling him how to drive the buggy and what not to do. And Pac was just nodding his head. *Mm-hm, can I go? Mm-hm, can I go?* He was ready to tear shit up. I found it kind of appropriate, being that Pac was such a notoriously bad driver. So him driving around in a Mad Max world kinda fit. Hype called action, and Pac took *off*. The problem was getting him to come back to do another take. The kid had fun, clowning around in the car.

I started looking around for the other guest stars that were supposed to be in the video. I was looking for Roger Troutman, because I was a big Zapp fan. I was wondering what his role in the video was going to be. It was really hard to tell who was who, though, cuz everybody was in their Mad Max shit. I saw Clifton Powell and then I ran into Chris Tucker. I barely noticed him, but there was no mistaking that voice. I had known him from the days hanging out in Hollywood at the Comedy Store. Eventually, it started getting late, and there was a van leaving soon to go back to the city. I really wanted to see Pac shoot his scene, but didn't know if I was gonna make it. I ended up having just enough time to catch him doing one take of his verse. I was so damn proud: *Look at my nigga!* Between the location, the budget, Pac, Dre, the story, I knew it had to be good. After it was cut, I finally saw it for the first time, and the first scene is Roger Troutman, leaning out of the helicopter singing "California Love." It was just as good as I thought it should be. I started trippin' off how fucking big Pac was gonna be from this. The world hadn't even really heard it yet and I knew everyone was going to love it.

We were reaching new heights in our careers, and it was just getting better. It appeared that Death Row label-mates and staff were regulars on the Las Vegas scene. One day we got the word that we were going to Las Vegas for a fight. It was the third Bowe–Holyfield match, "The Final Chapter," and I had a ticket. The trip to Vegas was on another level. It was a convoy of high-end vehicles—like seven or eight—speeding across the 10 from LA. Pac had his rag 500 Mercedes-Benz, which was his new favorite car at the time. Once we got there, he wanted to ride around because the sun was still up. Pac said, "Mo, come on." And I hopped into the passenger's seat as we headed towards the strip, rolling in with the top down. But I don't think he was ready for the fans. When we got stopped in traffic, people recognized him immediately. The car was already hot and loud and drew attention . . . and then they saw Pac. He was in a good mood, smiling and rapping, and the fans started surrounding us. It was all love. Girls were telling him they loved him. Dudes wanted to shake his hand and touch him. Rappers wanted him to take their CD to hear their music. Girls were handing me numbers to give to Pac cuz they couldn't get to that side of the car. People, of course, were taking pictures. It was a real good moment, just us brothers loving it all.

When we walked into the arena for the fight, there were thousands of people. At least a third of them were smoking cigars inside the arena and the smoke mixed with the smells of a variety of expensive colognes in the air. It smelled like money. We had great seats, and the fight was everything I expected, even if I don't remember any of the details. Afterwards we ran into the new champ at the roulette table. We shook hands, took pictures, and it ended being a great night.

Pac came to me one day with an idea for the video for "How Do U Want It." He wanted to do two music videos for it: one clean, and one X-rated: "Ay yo, Mo, what's up with that porn director that you was kickin' it with when I was in jail?" I said, "Yeah, he's still around, what's up?" He said, "I'm about to shoot this video on some freaky shit. I wanna invite all the porn stars. Can you hook that up for me?" I called Ron and told him what was up. And of course he was with it, so I plugged him with Pac, and Tracy produced it. Ron came through with the top actresses in the industry at the time, including Nina

Hartley, Heather Hunter, Nadia Cassini, and Angel Kelly for "How Do U Want It." The girls were happy to do it; I didn't realize until later that they got paid more for this music video than they did for performing in porn! That's some shit. When the X-rated video hit the streets, it felt like it was all people were talking about. *Pac and porn stars?* Viral wasn't a thing back then, but if it could've been, it would've been. The word of mouth was mind-blowing. For the life of me, I can't even remember how it was distributed.

The work I did on that album was less than previous albums. We had to make room for all of these features from the label to get on the album in some way or space, and at the time, China was pregnant, so I was naturally spending more time with her. The one song I did record that made it onto *All Eyez On Me* was "When We Ride," produced by DJ Pooh. But beyond the recording, there was also that Hollywood shit. We were happy to be back in the studio and Hollywood was happy for us to be back. Just as people love to kick you when you're down, they'll hold onto a ride when it's on its way up. That's not to say that there wasn't genuine love. But damn, we partied, too.

In the early days of recording the album, Pac called me saying he was at Miyagi's, a type of club that doesn't really exist in scene-y parts of Hollywood anymore. It was massive, styled like a Japanese pagoda. Downstairs was a restaurant where you could have mediocre sushi and California–pan-Asian food, greasy fried shit to soak up the strong drinks. It was fine. But nobody was there for the food—you were there for the scene. Upstairs there were dance floors, bars, karaoke. It was sprawling and open, with balconies looking down onto Sunset Boulevard. It was all wood, and the inside was dark, almost dank. You could really hide out, only be seen if you wanted to be seen. It was definitely a scene for the well-heeled, but it wasn't posh or luxe by any stretch of today's imagination. I was living down the street, not too far down, and was at home with a very pregnant China when Pac called: "Yo, what's up? Whatcha doin'? Meet me at Miyagi's, I want you to meet somebody."

When I got there, we ordered some drinks and Pac introduced me to the girls he was with. It was Faith Evans and her sister. I'm thinking, *You're something else*. It was hard to believe they were hanging out, because Faith and Biggie had been married for a little bit by that point. But at the same time, there were rumors about Biggie and Lil Kim, so I guess it made some sense why Faith was with Pac. She seemed like a fish out of water, though, just hanging out and not really into the scene. Her sister was acting cool and just fell to the back. After Pac introduced me, I was watching Pac and Faith to see how they interacted. They were talking, really just talking and hanging out, no dancing or affectionate behavior. Honestly, it was all pretty awkward. In hindsight, I wonder if Faith was having second thoughts about being out in public with Pac. I know Pac had his own agenda. In his mind, and up to the day he died, he believed that Biggie betrayed him with the Quad Studios shooting. So doing a record, and whatever else, with his wife seemed like fair game—even if it was deliciously petty and messy. That was the whole point. And, honestly, it was brilliant from the position of pure revenge, taking up space in another nigga's head. I'm sure there was some double meaning in having Faith featured on the "Wonda Why They Call U Bitch" track, too—although eventually they pulled her off the track and re-recorded it, calling the version with Faith the demo. It all just underscored the point: Having her in the studio, in Pac's sphere, on his arm anywhere in public, was a message to Biggie. That wasn't about the music.

It wasn't all work and partying. By that time, our little cousins had been with us for a few years, out in California—Katari, Malcolm, and Yaki, plus Yaki had brought out Mutah. Pac and I were young men, still in our early twenties, holding down and providing whatever guidance we could to these teenage boys. It didn't matter if we were up for it or not. Our situation was better than what they had back home, and we had an obligation to help. It was a lot, but I loved those little son-of-a-bitch kids. They brought drama, but also fun, inspiration, and a youthful optimism we needed. Over time, Pac had been bringing them into the game, first in a younger crew of their own and eventually merging them together with Pac, Syke, and me in the Outlaw Immortalz. He made sure they had a shot to get on the album, even if they had to work for it like everyone else.

Sure, we made mistakes with them. It's not like there's any manual for how to do these things. The music game is dirty to begin with, and when you consider where rap came from, the street side didn't make shit any easier. They grew up fast around us. They drank and smoked as teens. We cut them off if they got sloppy and stupid with it, but they probably had too much latitude for their age. They came by it honestly, though, growing up around and meeting celebrities, gangstas, people big in popular culture. We also had all kinds of traumatic life experiences, some just a part of life, some particular to life as Black men, some unique to who we were as the children of revolutionaries. And in spite of all that, or maybe because of it, we had a remarkably cohesive core group at the heart of the machine that was the business of Tupac Shakur. It was absolutely organized chaos—but it fucking worked.

The little homies had been with us as Pac developed and grew different concepts. Just like T.H.U.G. L.I.F.E. grew from 50 N.I.G.G.A.Z. and the Underground Railroad before that, Pac was working on creating the Outlawz at that time. When Malcolm and Katari—Edi and K—first came out, they were gonna grow into that. Then, when we learned that we were gonna have Yak come out, too, Pac realized that we needed to make them their own group, their own entity. Young Thugz came out of that, although that soon became Dramacydal, because other rappers started using *thug* in their names and Pac wanted to do something different. I honestly have no idea where Dramacydal came from. They started fine-tuning their skills, really hunkering down and making a solid demo for a record deal. I even produced a song for their Dramacydal demo and started to executive produce what would have been their album. They also did a feature on *Me Against the World* and *All Eyez on Me* as Dramacydal. But there came a time when Pac wanted to merge everyone together, so instead of changing T.H.U.G. L.I.F.E. and keeping Dramacydal, he incorporated it all into Outlaw Immortalz.

At that time in hip hop music, a lot of artists were using mafia names and monikers. Pac, being ahead of the game and globally conscious, decided to give us all names of controversial world leaders. Katari “K-Dog” became Kastro after Fidel Castro, probably because the alliteration of the two names appealed to him. Yaki “Young Hollywood” became Kadafi after Libyan leader-turned-dictator Muammar Gaddafi, because they shared physical attributes, both being tall, light-skinned, and having curly hair. Malcolm “Big Malc,” who was on the larger side and dark-skinned, became E.D.I. Mean after Ugandan dictator Idi Amin. Mutah “Lil’ Mu” became exiled French emperor Napoleon, and yeah, it had a little to do with his stature. Fatal became Hussein Fatal after Saddam Hussein. Storm, the only woman in the group, had met Pac in 1995 and he immediately made her a member, but never gave her an alias beyond what she already called herself as an artist. Syke became Mussolini after Italian fascist dictator Benito Mussolini. Noble joined the group last, so Pac never gave him a name. I was Komani after the Iranian revolutionary leader Ayatollah Khomeini. My brother literally said, “Khomeini, he blind, so you be him with your blind ass.” Ayatollah Khomeini famously went blind long before becoming the spiritual leader of Iran during the Iranian Revolution. I mean, I could admit my vision wasn’t the best, but to be clear, although I would eventually become legally blind, I was not even low vision back then. I was just a little nearsighted! And Pac, of course, became Makaveli after the fifteenth-to-early-sixteenth-century Italian diplomat and political philosopher Niccolo Machiavelli.

It was late 1995, and the New Year was fast approaching. Pac came to me and said, “Mo, we’re going to Cabo for New Year’s. I’m going down with Suge on the boat. Y’all niggas are flying in.” I’m like, “Cabo? Word? Not for a show or an event or some type of work? Bet. *Now* we’re ballin.’” I met with the Outlawz at the airport. I think Mutah, Fatal, Malcolm, Katari—everyone but Yaki and Syke—were there. We landed in the evening and Death Row had the whole airport shut down for our arrival. At least it felt that way. It was a small airport at the time, but still. I found out we weren't going to be staying in a hotel. We were going to be staying on a couple of yachts.

Suge had his yacht named *P-Funk*, and David Kenner, the attorney for Death Row, was there with his yacht. I don't remember the name, because it sure as shit wasn't as memorable as *P-Funk*. We first got settled into Suge's yacht, which had a master suite in the back and a couple of other bedrooms decorated in white and red. I don't remember how many feet it was, but it was respectable. There was a captain and a small crew, but not like a luxury yacht crew there to take care of us. They were just there to keep the boat floating. Suge's captain was a sunburnt, sun-bleached blond white dude who just talked about going marlin fishing and hustling marlin down the coast. When we got in, Pac and Suge weren't around, so we chilled until we figured out what was next. While we were getting settled, I was just thinking about how far we came. All the shows, all the events, all the music, all the taping and filming. It was starting to feel like we were at the top. I mean, how do you *not* feel like you're at the top when you're hanging out on multiple yachts in Mexico?

When we got up the next morning, everybody was hungry, so we tried to find some breakfast. Before we left the yacht, the captain started handing out these sweatshirts. I was glad to get some swag, but they were ugly as fuck: thick black sweatshirts with the name of the yacht on them in red gothic letters. The captain started explaining that's how it's done down there. You on a yacht, you represent the yacht. I was all for that, except for the fact that we're in hot-ass Cabo San Lucas, Mexico, and they got us in heavy black sweatshirts. I'm like, "Yo, y'all ain't got no white ones, or a different color?" Nope, that's it.

We got off the yacht and started walking down the dock and I began to see what the captain was talking about. There would be two or three guys from a yacht, all in the same color shirt, and there was a few dudes from another yacht all in the same color shirt, with the names of the yachts on them. Everyone was wearing light clothes, light and bright colors, airy fabrics, and here we go wearing these sweatshirts. I know they're looking at these big-ass Black niggas in these big-ass black sweatshirts like, "Who are they? Where'd these niggas get money? Who is that in the slip? Who is P-Funk?" I often find a bit of humor in being conspicuously Black in very white situations.

The plan later on was to ride some Jet Skis. I was excited, cuz I'd never ridden a Jet Ski. And in that environment, I knew it was going to be fun. Suge's yacht had four and Kenner's had four. We got our life vests on and took the skis out. It was me and the rest of the Outlawz, and it seemed like where we were riding was a small area, too small for all the Jet Skis that were in the water. It was enough for me, cuz I wasn't sure I could ride that well anyway, but the rest of the guys were going buck wild. I stopped my Jet Ski for a minute and just took a look at everybody wild'n out. And when I faced forward again to take off, Fatal was coming straight at me at high speed. I was caught completely off guard and my Jet Ski was at a dead stop, so I couldn't really move, and Fatal's Jet Ski came up the nose of my Jet Ski. I moved my body just enough where it didn't hit me dead in the face. I could actually feel the Jet Ski slide across the side of my head, and I could hear a bunch of people yelling, "Oh, shit!" Fatal made sure that I was alright, and I said, "Yeah, I'm good. So good that I'm getting the fuck off this thing right now. I ain't about to get killed in paradise!"

On New Year's Eve, all of us were going to get some drinks and toast to the New Year. That night we all started walking to the neighborhood, me, Pac, Suge, Napoleon, Fatal, and Edi. We came across a street with several bars on it. We all filed into the first bar and started drinking, and I don't know if it was on purpose or not, like to keep us drinking, but we kept being given the wrong time. We kept trying to find out what time it was so we could cheer at midnight. We were getting double shots of tequila, all in our own world, really only paying attention to each other, and someone yelled out, "It's almost midnight! It's almost midnight!" So we'd do a round of shots, and then we'd realize it wasn't actually midnight. We went to the next bar. Same thing. Suge got another round of double shots. Someone said it was almost midnight, again, and we did another round of double shots of tequila. And *again*, it was *not* midnight. But we were getting fucked up! So we went to *another* bar, and we barely caught *real* midnight. But by then, we were too drunk to enjoy it. I mean *drunk*. There were, of course, other drinks in between the double shots. A couple of the guys started throwing up. We're stumbling down the street, trying to make it back to the dinghy so we could make it back to the yacht. We were so drunk that getting into the dinghy was a whole ordeal. The slippery, bouncy, moving dinghy was hard to maneuver, drunk as we were. Not to mention, we weren't exactly a group of small dudes. Guys were puking in the water getting into the dinghy before we even left the dock. They were all off the side of the dinghy, throwing up into the water while the guy's driving. The driver's like, "Let me get you to the yacht, let me get you to the yacht." When we finally made it to the yacht, we struggled getting out the dinghy, trying to make sure we weren't going to fall into the ocean, but we were all still happy and laughing at each other. We stumbled onto Suge's yacht laughing, throwing up. I mean like three to four of us were throwing up. One of them being myself. I headed straight for the rail and let it blow. One of the guys was in the bathroom. One of the guys was in one of the bedrooms. There was puke everywhere.

Suge's yacht wasn't big enough to house everybody, so me and two of the fellas went and crawled into another dinghy to get to David Kenner's yacht to sleep there. Kenner was known for working real closely with Suge. I didn't know him much. He was hardly ever at the studio, at Can-Am, but I was well aware of who he was and his power at Death Row. I was also well aware of his alleged connections to the mob in Los Angeles. When we got to the yacht, a crew member told us which rooms to take and we passed out. When I woke up in the morning, I oddly didn't have a hangover. It was so early in the morning that the sun had just come up, so I decided to go to the front deck and catch the sunrise. And when I got to the deck, there's nobody there but David Kenner, wearing a pair of swim trunks and no shirt. He had a cup of black coffee in one hand and with the other hand he was smoking a Churchill. And I was like *Damn, look at this dude. He on some master of the universe type shit.* He nodded to me and I nodded back, but we didn't speak. I also saw this crazy scar he had on his back, going laterally across his lower back from one side all the way to the other. It was gnarly. It was straight and looked surgical, but the size of it was disturbing. I was like, *Did someone try to saw this dude in half?* To this day, I wonder what the fuck did that.

We both stood out there on the deck for a few minutes. I caught the sunrise and checked out the view and then headed back to my room. When I was walking back, I was thinking to myself, *Okay, these niggas are having it their way.* This ain't no rented boat video-shoot shit. This is the type of money Pac is supposed to be having.

CHAPTER 23

SHIT DON'T STOP

After recording *All Eyez on Me*, Death Row organized a small tour. Really it was a couple of spot dates, but it was with other Death Row artists so it was branded under the umbrella of a Death Row tour. We went to Ohio first, and then to New Orleans. I have no idea why these two places were picked. It's strange routing for a tour, you know. As T.H.U.G. L.I.F.E., we had done a show in Dayton before, but this show was in Columbus. I had also been to New Orleans before. But even having been there before, I was excited. Any new show, new production, new lineup, should be exciting, or what's the use of being in the game? It was our first time going on the road with The Row and there was a lot more people than ever before. We knew a lot of the artists on the roster, but we hadn't spent that much time with them before. It was Dogg Pound—without Snoop—DJ Quik, Jewell, Pac, me, Syke and the Outlawz—K, Edi, Yak, Fatal, and I think Mu was there by that time, too. The Ohio show went good, it was dope, we killed it, murdered it. It was at a medium-sized venue of around 6,000–8,000 people. And then we went on to New Orleans.

We had just gotten to New Orleans and everybody was getting settled in. After everybody dropped their bags, people started to go their separate ways. Before sound check, there was some milling around in front of the hotel, as usual. Some of us went to smoke or to find something to eat before the show. On my way back, I found out that one of the crews had been shot at. Apparently some words were exchanged between them and a passerby, a local, and there was gunfire.

I ran into Pac near the entrance to the hotel. He told me what had happened and asked where I had been, "Cuz Suge called a meeting and he wanted y'all to be there to see how things go down over here," meaning The Row. I was like, "Alright, well, I wasn't around or else I'd've been there." It wasn't any of the main artists that had gotten into this altercation. It was people with the tour or the crews of one of the artists. And it was clearly a situation with a local, not even on some shit with some history or background. Of course, security was always an ongoing issue, but this didn't seem like that. Much less did it seem like something that was that crucial for an artist, particularly an artist of Pac's caliber, to be spending his time or energy on leading into a show. But it was clearly important to Pac that I see this new way of doing things. It seemed uncharacteristically important to Pac to have some other guy's meeting set the tone. It stuck with me, even if it didn't concern me at the time. I found out later that supposedly someone got slapped. I don't know who. I thought that was an alarming way to handle things, even on some street shit.

The show in New Orleans was a huge venue—like a 70,000-seat type deal. It was at the Superdome, which would eventually become the Mercedes-Benz Superdome after Katrina, and then Caesar's Superdome. It was a testament that Death Row had Pac looking good, that they took it up a notch. It was the first time we had our own pyro on stage. Look, tech is different now and people have pyro at much smaller shows, but we had our own damn fire shooting up in the sky, sixty feet in the air, and that was a big deal in the '90s. The show had bigger production value and that was a change for the better. The pyro feels weird when you're on stage with it, but it was dope. I felt great, because the size was what I expected from a label like Death Row. To be able to book and fill a venue that size was meeting with my expectations. Plus, "California Love" was out, so it felt amazing performing that onstage. People were everywhere I looked and they was loving it. There were no crowd incidents to speak of, everyone was just having a good time. In this moment, I was happy with what my career was doing, cuz part of my career was helping Pac get to the top. And it was starting to feel like he really was at the top. Which meant I was at the top, too.

The interesting thing about that New Orleans show was that we ran into Rated R. Remember, back in 1994, Mac and Rated R had left the group and had gone back to their careers as Double Jeopardy. That was part of the reason why we folded T.H.U.G. L.I.F.E. and Dramacydal into the Outlawz. Since then, we hadn't seen them much. Rated had gone on tour with Coolio and they went to Africa and had brought back a video of them on the Nile. So when Rated popped up backstage at the show we were shocked to see him. It was only me and Syke at first. Even knowing that some of his family is from New Orleans, we were surprised to see him, especially with Pac having made a point of talking about The Row's different security protocols, but it was also good. He was impressed with the show and how we killed it. It was all love. Pac walked up a little later and we all kicked it for a few moments. I don't know for sure, but I felt like Rated might have felt a little regret, because we had clearly moved up from where we were when he'd left.

It was on our way back home from those shows that shit started getting *weird*. The shows were over, the general consensus was that we killed it, and everybody was pretty upbeat. We were boarding the plane—me, the Outlawz, Pac, Death Row label-mates and staff. It felt like our people were filling up the whole flight. When I got on board, I went directly to my seat and started positioning myself to, hopefully, go to sleep. Mind you, by this point I was a veteran of the road, doing shows, catching flights. It was all part of my job. I got to my seat and people were still boarding on both sides of the plane. People were laughing, cracking jokes, excited and anticipating getting home. Apparently, while we were boarding, some people who were with us started taking alcohol from the carts in the galley as they boarded. I didn't actually see anyone going into the carts, but I did see people passing bottles back behind the seats, a drink for the next person. I wasn't quite sure, because Death Row as a label had money to buy drinks for everybody, so it didn't really enter my mind that they had actually been stealing it. When somebody passed a bottle of Bailey's over the top of the seat to me, I accepted it happily. I didn't even know who was sitting in front of me, I just knew most everybody on the flight was our people. I was going to wait to drink my little cocktail later, once we got in the air, so I put it in the seat pocket, snuggled up next to the window, and closed my eyes.

Next thing I know, somebody's yelling, "Come on, y'all, everybody off the plane!" *What the fuck?* Apparently, the flight crew started complaining and we were being kicked off the plane. While everybody is exiting and gathering at the gate, Pac starts separating all the Outlawz, all our people. He wanted us to have a group meeting in the bathroom, of all places, but it was where we could have the most privacy. When we got in there, I could see Pac was mad. He, Syke, and I were veterans of the road, doing shows, catching flights. It was the job. This was some rookie shit.

Pac starts asking me and the Outlawz who was taking alcohol off the cart. And nobody said nothing. I definitely didn't say nothing, cuz I didn't see nothing. But Pac kept going: "Come on, y'all, we got kicked off the motherfuckin' plane cuz people were stealing alcohol off the cart. Everybody got alcohol. Somebody was stealing alcohol off the cart. Who was stealing alcohol off the cart?" I'm not gonna be specific because I don't remember who said what, but slowly people started coming clean and admitting that they were drinking. And then Fatal says, "Well, I think everybody that was drinking at all should be responsible, because everybody had some." And then Pac looks at me and asks, "Mo, was you stealing shit off the cart?" And I said, "Come on, man, hell no! I'm too old for that shit. I had a drink because someone passed it to me, but I didn't steal shit from the cart." And because I didn't say I had no alcohol *period*, Pac got mad and was acting like I was trying to get away with something. Which pissed me off. "Are you fucking kidding me? I'm too old for that shit. You gonna sweat me for some shit I didn't do?" Pac was like, "Fuck that, you should have said that from the very beginning. Matter of fact, give me that vest." Some of us were wearing bulletproof vests, and I took it off and threw it at him.

I guess Pac felt he should be exercising some type of discipline, being that the Outlawz were the youngest on the tour. But I was mad as fuck. You're gonna make me give back my vest? Your brother? Your frontline soldier? Over this bullshit? He normally would have thought about everything, the totality of the situation, but it seemed like he was just focused on showing he could exercise discipline. When we did get on another flight, there wasn't a lot of talking. At that point, everyone was just trying to get home and be on their way.

A short time after, while recording at Can-Am, Pac was not around, and Yak came to me. He pulled me aside, and said, "Yo, Mo. Pac said we gotta discipline you for that shit that happened on the plane." He was looking down. He didn't want to have to say or do the mission that was put upon him. I actually started laughing and trying to console Yak. "Oh, yeah? Really? Disciplined?" Come *on*. Because now I was mad.

Again, this was not the norm, this language. This is how gang-bangas act and the language they use. This was not us. I couldn't believe Pac was calling this shot, because I raised these fucking kids. Yak was telling me this at the entrance to Studio B. I started wildin' out. I think Kastro and Edi were waiting in the studio, so I said, "Come on! All y'all! Come on! Let's go right now." Apparently the other Outlawz knew what was up. All of them threw some lackluster blows that had no effect, because their heart wasn't in it. This wasn't the way we had been operating for years. It wasn't the way we were raised or how we had raised them. It was almost like slap boxing. I didn't hit the ground; there was no broken skin, no bruises, nor scar on me. Every time someone touched me, I touched them back. But we weren't really trying to hurt each other. We scrapped for a few minutes and then we all just decided to stop. It was pitiful, really. Pac wasn't around, so they could say they successfully carried out his orders. I didn't call Pac. I was waiting to see him. I stayed at the studio a few more hours and walked past Suge a couple of times in the hallway. When he looked at me, it looked like he was trying to see if I was fucked up, which put me on alert in a whole 'nother way.

That was only the beginning. Shit got weirder after that. And I got it: Things were being run differently at Death Row and Pac was trying to fit in. We had never claimed a gang. We had always claimed T.H.U.G. L.I.F.E. so that we'd have a line of communication with *all* the gangs, nationwide and worldwide. Because of our background, how we were raised, and that we were raised in multiple cities, we weren't from a particular hood; we repped *the* hood. I'm not stupid—I could see how things were going down—but everyone knew we weren't gangbangas.

We kept working, back and forth to the studio. One day in the studio, the little homies told me that we were all supposed to go to Snoop's house that night. Pac wasn't around, so I got the message from them. I was ambivalent at first, but they said that Pac told them to make sure I was there. I was a little suspicious, but I hooked up with Pac and the fellas that night and smashed out to Snoop's house in Clairemont. When we arrived, Snoop, Kurupt, and the other members of Tha Dogg Pound were there. It was a big house, but you could see there was a fair amount of people there. We were cool with Snoop and Dogg Pound. We'd been around them on a day-to-day basis for a few months at this point, so everybody was just chillin', drinking, smoking, and playing video games. Snoop loved him some video games.

I started wondering how long we were going to stay here. I could see there was no attempt being made to leave. Next thing I know, they're talking about just spending the night and leaving in the morning. I was a little pissed, because I didn't plan on spending the night, but I'm like *Fuck it, I'm with the fellas*. Everybody found a spot to fall out in until the morning. And at that point, I started realizing that I hadn't seen Pac all night, since we had first arrived. But the house is big, and Pac didn't really play video games, so I figured he was moving around the house somewhere else.

Everybody went to sleep. The next morning comes and the guys start waking up, moving around. I'm making sure that I've got all my shit as we're getting ready to leave. And then Pac comes to me and says, "Yo, Mo! That shit you did on the plane was fucked up, so you got to be disciplined. That's how we do shit now." I'm like, "Nigga what? Are you fucking serious?" "Yeah, cuz when the little homies got at you in the studio, they didn't do a good job." I'm like, "Pac, are you serious with this bullshit?" Dudes started seeing us argue so I just said, "Come on, let's go." He was saying they were waiting for me out on the basketball court, and I wasn't about to look like no punk. I was angry and I was hurt by my brother and these little bastards that I helped raise. And this was not us. This didn't feel like us and this didn't feel like Pac. But in this moment, I had to handle it for what it was.

I got out to the basketball court and there was niggas lined up. Everybody knew but me. Seeing all of them enraged me even more. I said, "Come on, you little punk mothafuckas! Come on!" Pac was to the side smoking a blunt, telling the little homies, "Y'all go ahead." We start fighting, they all start swinging on me. They was popping me and I was popping them back. Honestly, they weren't even fighting hard, again because they weren't into it. A few minutes go by and it was obvious they hadn't done any damage to me. I didn't even hit the ground. And then at the very end, little Napoleon swung from my rear right side, around to my face, and caught me under my right eye. I started to bleed. Up to that point, I had been restraining myself because it was my little homies who I had love for. But now blood was drawn, and I was getting ready to go in. But that's exactly when Pac said, "Alright, that's it," and broke it up before I had a chance to return the blow.

Everybody was huffing and puffing, licking their wounds. I wiped the blood from under my eye and realized it was a small cut, nothing major. I looked at Pac and I looked at the little homies, just shaking my head. Pac and the rest of them came over and started hugging me and shit. I pushed them off, went and grabbed the basketball, and started shooting baskets just to let them know I wasn't fazed by them little fuckers. I was fucking pissed, man. I didn't want to hug anyone.

After the fight, everybody left, and Pac wanted me to ride back with him. He knew I was pissed, so he let me drive his ragtop Jaguar to get us back home. He knew I loved that car, so I wasn't going to turn it down. We rode back and honestly didn't talk much. I'm thinking, *He should have something to say to me right now. He ain't talking, and I can't believe he ain't talking*. That was when I started to get really worried about the influence of Death Row and the culture there. It fucked me up how he could do that to me, his brother, after all the shit we'd been through. And if Pac was changing like that, how else was he changing?

CHAPTER 24

SUGAR TO SHIT

Things at Death Row were, to put it mildly, not what I expected. I wasn't feeling how they did things, and I didn't like the fact that Pac was spending a lot of time with Suge and not us. I knew he was handling his business, but usually some of his team would be around, too. Not anymore. This was not coming from a jealous place; we were all uneasy about who Pac surrounded himself with, especially after everything that had happened in New York. It produced a lot of uncertainty, not knowing who out there was trying to hurt him. It felt like Pac was alone with a bunch of new people and the big brother in me didn't love that. I also didn't like the fact that Suge used physical discipline to keep people working. I thought that was counterproductive to a creative work environment. We were making art, after all, and art can't flourish in an environment that's not a safe creative space.

And I *really* didn't like that there were so many law enforcement people who were part of Death Row's security. I'm not just talking retired law enforcement either; it also included off-duty law enforcement. They were mostly Black, but still—COINTELPRO often uses Black law enforcement officers to infiltrate Black organizations. I'm talking about plants, infiltration, operatives and, ultimately, setups. With cops like that, you never really know whether they're on the level or not. There was also just an ideological inconsistency to the presence of law enforcement. It would have seemed less out of place to me if it was former military. Maybe it was simply the extent to which they seemed to be within the organization, I don't know. Look, I caught some slack because my mama was a 911 dispatcher. She worked *with* the police (and firefighters and paramedics) not *for* the police, yet there were still more than a couple words about that on the political side. Death Row was on some street shit for sure, so it seemed inconsistent for law enforcement to be so integrated into the organization, and placed in positions of prominence, too. I'm a logic person. The contradiction made me uneasy. And I knew Pac had to see that, too, at least in some way.

I also didn't like the fact that Death Row's security left us unarmed at a time when Pac was a walking target. Sure, having full-time security detail wrapped into the label's structure meant our family didn't have to do security and Pac didn't have to pay for it out of his pocket. But in the end, wasn't he paying for it anyway? And sure, not having to carry our own heat and still being protected definitely felt like we'd leveled up our success. But it also left us unarmed and vulnerable.

Up until then, Pac listened to me a lot. For what would end up being, sadly, the majority of his career, I was his sounding board. He would often come up to me, smack me in the chest, and say, "Yo, Mo, check this out. Tell me what you think." And then he'd test out a rhyme on me and I'd give him my thoughts. Either it was fire from the jump—and it often was—or he'd rework it. I was part of his process and we each cared what the other one thought. We pushed each other to better our craft. But now he was asking me for less advice at precisely the moment when I thought he needed it most. Watani was no longer managing Pac; Suge took up that role. Which is totally frowned upon in the industry, by the way, since it's not considered ethical to manage an artist and advocate for their interests which, from time to time, are likely to come into conflict with the interests of the label. But Suge clearly wanted to have my brother all to himself. It wasn't just me; his influence over Pac isolated my brother from a lot of people. Pac was "the precious," and Suge wanted to be closest to him. Either way, it was a whole new team. I didn't like it, but I understood it. I realized he was growing into his manhood; he wanted to make his own decisions and be responsible for those decisions all on his own.

In February of 1996, Pac was booked to appear on *Saturday Night Live*. I was super excited. I grew up on that show and had been a fan since the beginning. Being from New York, getting to perform on *SNL* was a legitimate benchmark by which to measure our growing success. I wasn't surprised that I was going to be part of this performance, since I had performed with him more than anybody there. The crew that had been chosen left for New York. It was cold there, snow on the ground. We stayed at some hotel off the beaten path. I was actually surprised at that, because we were in one of the outer boroughs and *SNL* tapes at Rockefeller Center. You'd think that a show like that could have sprung for something a little nicer. After we made it in, a group of us went out to get something to eat. We came back and were hopping in the elevator to go upstairs; Pac got off on his floor and Suge wanted the rest of us to go with him to his room, where Pac was supposed to meet us later.

As soon as we stepped inside, I was turned off by the energy. I felt uneasy. So uneasy that when I walked in, I stayed near the door and scanned the room. It was a big-ass suite, and in each corner on the farthest side you could see that there was someone being intimidated. Other people were just sitting in the room, hanging out, chillin' while this is going on. Syke and Suge were behind me, talking low about something, and then Suge got on the phone. I started moving around to make some space, because we were still bunched up by the door. Suge got off the phone and started walking up on me. In that moment right there, everything illuminated in front of me. They'd been trying to get me. From the shit at the airport, the shit in the studio, the shit at Snoop's house, this shit had been coming from the top. I had done nothing wrong, it was about who I was: Pac's brother. My choices were to fight this big mothafucka—with not a great chance of winning, since I'd get rat-packed by his goons for sure—or see if Syke would back me up, which would put him in a bad position, too. He was an Inglewood Village Crip and I wasn't. It was gonna be a whole big thing if the Crip card got my back. I was looking at three possible outcomes: get humiliated, get beat down, or get killed.

When Suge rolled up on me, he snarled, "Get out there," motioning to the balcony. Like if I didn't, he was gonna beat my ass. My street IQ told me, *You know what it is, Mo. Survive.* I gave him a little grin, but I went out onto the balcony, in the snow, with no coat on, like he wanted me to. I was being bullied, but I was outnumbered, and that shit isn't safe. I was going to have to take the L—for now. He kept looking at me to see if I was gonna cry or beg for mercy. I just kept my little grin on my face. I had a lot of dark thoughts running through my mind in that moment. He made me take off my shoes, my shirt, and my pants, and told me to make a snowball. Out there in my underwear, I didn't actually make a snowball, like, *What the fuck, this shit's weird.* That was kind of my form of rebellion, like, my way of saying that he had enough power to get me to a certain point, but I wasn't just going to roll over and follow every last command. I just picked up some snow and threw it in the air. I took the humiliation route, all the time planning to get him back. After Suge had his fun, he backed away from the door so I could reenter the room. I looked around the room seeing all these niggas laughing. And I'm thinking to myself, *These niggas have no idea what they've done.* When I got inside, I stopped, still had the grin on my face, and started slowly shaking off the snow. Suge said, "Don't get that shit on my rug!" I just got my shit back on and walked out of the suite.

I went down to my room, processing what had just happened. The things I was thinking about were all going to end with me either in jail for a long time or dead. *Why is Pac's boy doing me dirty?* I thought we were allies. I had had no beef with Suge. We rarely even talked. I knew it was a power play, plain and simple. I was sitting, thinking things through in my room when there was a knock on my door. It was Big Syke. "Cuz, I told that nigga not to fuck with you," he said. "But he said, 'Let me see what Pac think.' When he called Pac, I guess he asked him if he could fuck with you out in the snow or some shit.

And I guess Pac said, 'Yeah, if you can get him out there.'" *Are you mothafuckas serious with this shit?* That's all I could think. Pac called Syke at that very moment, and Syke let him know that he was with me. Right away, Syke handed me the phone, and Pac started going off on me: "What the fuck is wrong with you, Mo? How you gonna let a nigga do you like that?" I'm like, "How am *I* gonna let him do me like that? The mothafucka been trying to set me up the whole time. You already know. I'm too small to be fucking with niggas that size. And you know they're making sure we're all unarmed. I would've handled my shit, but I was outnumbered. The fuck you talking about? You know what, don't trip. I'm good. Last straw." I hung up. Syke left. I sat there with a whole bunch of shit to think about.

But then it came to me. I had made the right decision in how I handled it and I knew I was about to walk the fuck away. From the moment I knew China was pregnant, I had tried to be extra cautious. Simply being in the rap game, in the streets, let alone at Death Row on the daily, there were a lot of dangerous environments. Knowing I had made the right decision, thanking God that I had made the right decision, made it a little easier to live with. Honestly, who wants to go through that? I survived.

By this point, I couldn't tell Pac shit. It fucked my head up that he could be so deceived by Suge. Pac thought he knew what he was doing, that it was under control. In that moment, I couldn't say anything because it wouldn't be effective. If Pac didn't see it for himself, it would backfire and just make me look petty—like I was the one trying to control my brother. I had to give it time. So I fell back, even though it stung to do it.

I'd spent the last five years watching over Pac and guiding him through, but I also felt that he had come to a point where he needed to be on his own. He was at the top of his game. Here he was at this big label, and everybody there wanted to work with him and spend time with him. I missed Pac, missed recording with him, missed our constant camaraderie. But I was his brother—I didn't feel no permanent detachment. And the fun and funny Pac was showing up less and less anyway. Stepping back felt strange but necessary, especially since China was pregnant again. Even if I had wanted to be involved in Pac's day-to-day, my wife needed me more at home. I was happy for it to be that way.

China didn't have any difficulties during this pregnancy, but we were on high alert because of the earlier miscarriage. We were really on top of all of the pre-natal stuff, all of the nesting, all of the gadgets. We started preparing to buy a house, which we did in Palmdale shortly after Cheyenne was born. When the day of miracles came, she went into labor and we went to St. Joseph's in Burbank. I couldn't believe this was happening, that China had finally made it. There were a few nerve-racking moments, especially when they told me that she needed to have a cesarean. But I remembered what my mama and Aunt Jo always told me: *Don't forget to pray*. I stood right outside the operating room looking at her through a window. The doctors had put up a curtain, but I could see her head, and I was laser-focused on China as I did exactly that.

After the procedure, they gowned me up with the cap and smock and everything and brought me into the room to see China and meet my new baby daughter. The room smelled like burnt flesh; I think they used a laser to make the cesarean incision. China looked flushed and exhausted, but she had a smile on her face. That eased some of my tension. I got to cut the umbilical cord, and once they cleaned Cheyenne and wrapped her up like a little seven-pound burrito, they put her on China's chest. That's when I got my first good look at her. She looked calm, this little light brown bundle of peace. She looked just like a little chickpea with a little black, curly, fluffy 'fro. That's her nickname still, to this day: The Pea. I held her for the first time in that operating room. I remember feeling so happy, blissed out, and privileged: *Now I'm a parent*. It was all of the big things, the joy and the happiness, the excitement and the fear. The pride. Cheyenne felt warm, like she belonged in my arms. I felt like the luckiest man in the world. *How the hell did my crazy ass help make this beautiful little person?*

My daughter's timing was utterly perfect. I loved having a baby. I loved being a new dad. I loved taking care of her, playing and just having the time to spend with her as a baby. I loved giving her all my love and attention. She was *such* a good baby. She wasn't fussy, but even if she had been, I wouldn't have cared. In the industry, it's easy to lose perspective. It's not just that unimportant things can distract you, it's that setting out to accomplish a particular mission or goal can come with baggage that's particular to the business and you can really get caught in the weeds. But once my daughter was born, my perspective was locked in: She was my everything and my reason. Mind you, we were coming from a place where Pac didn't think he would see twenty-one. He talked about his death all the time and, frankly, that shit got on my damn nerves. Even so, I didn't think I would see twenty-five, but I didn't talk about it all the time. Young Black males were—are—an endangered species. To make it to the point where I was married and had a child was very fulfilling. Cheyenne was my reminder of the reason we were doing this shit in the first place.

Honestly, I probably only fell back from Pac for a month or two. But for brothers as close as we were, it felt like a long time. As soon as Cheyenne was born in early May, he wanted to see the baby. He called me, but we didn't talk about work at all, or anything like that. He told me he had been dating Kidada Jones, Quincy's daughter, and he wanted to tell me about her. The two of them had gone to Italy, where Pac had done a performance at the Versace show. Since he knew I wasn't coming to the studio, he would invite me to come over to the house. I liked visiting at the house anyway because Afeni, Jamala, and the cousins would be there.

While recovering from the bullshit in New York, I started focusing on the important things. I sank myself into acting, which was the only other thing I had skills for at that time. I had a few roles as a glorified extra. My friend Donovan and his cousin Chris were doing the extra work hustle. It wasn't high paying, but I genuinely enjoyed it. I worked on *Primal Fear*, *Star Trek* (the movie), and *The Nutty*

Professor. While working on *Nutty Professor*, I ran into Jada, who I hadn't seen in a couple years. We hugged and chitchatted for a few minutes on set and I got to see her do her thing with Eddie Murphy. In one of the funniest scenes I had ever seen, I got to experience a young Dave Chappelle just starting out.

I was still keeping in contact with the Outlawz from time to time, and I was hearing that Pac was starting his new label, Euphanasia. I started hearing about Makaveli Records. These were very good signs to me. It was telling me the Pac was about to make his move away from Death Row, that he was seeing a future that didn't include Death Row, and I didn't have to guide him that way and risk him resenting me on some stubborn baby brother shit. He had started making these moves shortly after *SNL*, which told me he didn't need long to see it, either.

Very good signs, indeed. He had even opened up a small office on Beverly Boulevard and had our aunt, Yaki Kadafi's mom Yaasmyn, running it. I liked the idea. I was all for it. I barely knew what Euphanasia meant, but I was with it. He even had shirts made up with Makaveli Records and the Outlawz on them and business cards for Euphanasia. The office was actually in an apartment that Pac rented for Yas, in a cool area by CBS Studios. I felt comfortable going to the office because I knew I was working with family. A friend of ours, who ended up becoming a writer, Dream Hampton, was also in the building. I would go up there with the Outlawz and we would hang in the office or at Dream's apartment down the hall. Things were starting to feel like the old days again, everyone around working on the same goals, lifting each other up. I thought things were going to be alright.

Eventually, inevitably, Pac called me because he wanted me to hear what he'd been working on. He was going to call the album *The Don Killuminati: The 7 Day Theory* and release it under his alias Makaveli. Little did I know it would be his last album—at least, the last album that he would work on before he passed. I often wonder if Pac knew. I swear, it felt like he was trying to tell us all the time that he knew he was going to go young, that he wasn't going to be here for long. Early in his career, we used to literally think Pac was prophetic. He would rap about some shit, then it would happen. For example, there's a song where he says, *[pop pop] Pac drops two cops*. And soon after he did just that in Atlanta, while protecting a stranger, and he was exonerated. That's just one of several examples of why his lyrics were so powerful.

I met up with Pac to listen to the new album. He knew I hadn't been at the studio in a while, but he really wanted me to hear it and we listened to it right. We got a sack, like a half ounce of weed. Got some blunts and some Hennessy. Went up to his room. He threw me the sack and said, as usual: "Roll somethin'." The sound system in his bedroom was, of course, as close to a professional studio system as possible: clean and loud. He played me every single song except for "White Man'z World," cuz that was still being mixed. Looking back, he probably made a point of mentioning regretting that I couldn't hear that record because he shouted out Mutulu and Sekou. Through all the shit, he never forgot our roots.

When we were finished, he asked me, "What you think?" Honestly, it scared the shit out of me. I mean, it was a masterpiece. So good, but so dark. There was a sadness to it, too. And I said, "It's dope as fuck. But yo, are you ready for what's gonna happen after you drop this album?" He looked at me and said, "Yup." And I'm like, "Naming names, you know what's up with that, right? You know how it's gonna get." He was like, "It is what it is." I had been working with Pac long enough to know how serious he was about his music and his messages and how all eyes *were* on him. I knew that album was gonna cause a lot of beef, a lot of drama.

It wasn't so much that Pac was mentioning these names, it was who they were and the context in which he named them. *That* made it explosive. He mentioned Jimmy Henchman and Haitian Jack, which were two well-known, serious cats. Some call them gangstas. Even though they were legitimately in the music business, they were some real niggas. And he accuses Haitian Jack of being a snitch. He accuses

Jimmy Henchman of setting him up. On top of the things that he says about Puffy and Biggie. These were some very serious accusations, especially in our world at that time. Accusations like those could lead to real violence in the streets. But there already had been violence.

Everybody was gonna hear and have a feeling, one way or another. I didn't want to see that for him, but I understood what he was going through. We kicked it for a little while longer and then I left. On my way home, all the way back to Palmdale, I couldn't stop thinking about that album and all the titles of the songs. And where his head and his heart were. I mean, oh man, just the mood of the album, the tone was all dark, the vibe of it. The song "Hail Mary" really shook me. I felt like he was throwing his life up, and talking about his death in a way that made me uncomfortable. I felt like he was saying, *Here I go. It's a Hail Mary on my life. I'm throwing it up*. I mean, he often talked about death and put his death on songs and different records, but this was different to me. It was scary—real scary.

At the time, I didn't know why divine intervention was working this way, cuz I wanted to be there for him. And he knew it. I never thought about what it would've meant to me personally had I been more involved in the creation of this album, cuz I was gonna ride with him regardless. That's what I loved about that little nigga: When he said *I don't give a fuck*, he really didn't give a fuck. In a real way.

CHAPTER 25

MAKAVELI'S LAST RIDE

I got the call from Syke in the middle of the night on September 7, 1996. I thought they had to have it wrong again. I thought that with Death Row as his label and the way they operated there, that they mobbed on someone else. For real, I thought, *Pac must've shot somebody*. Same thing I thought the first time he was shot, like the reality of that first time still hadn't sunk in.

I knew he went out to Las Vegas for the Tyson-Seldon fight. The one sport Pac really dug, like actually followed, was boxing. I knew he had recorded something for Tyson, for the match. Honestly, before Suge opened his Club 662, we weren't in Vegas much because there weren't really any venues for hip hop in Las Vegas and certainly not of the size and caliber that would be appropriate for us. Plus, it was well-known that, at the time, the city of Las Vegas wasn't really open for business when it came to urban music. We had been to Vegas for shows at Club 662 since it opened in 1995 more than we had been in Vegas in our whole careers up to that point. I mean, once in a while we would go to gamble and enjoy Vegas, but Club 662 was the first time there was business for us there. Which meant, to my thinking, more of our people. More protection. I knew Big Syke had homies out there for the fight, too. Pac was with the Outlawz. He had people, security, with him. Somehow, even though this had happened before, I was even more convinced this time that the story was wrong. Hadn't everyone learned from that, figured shit out to keep Pac safe?

But I got up and immediately started getting ready for the drive out to Vegas. Syke said they told him Pac had been shot off the Strip. Me, China, Cheyenne, and our friends Donovan and Ladawn packed up for the drive and got there the next morning. The whole drive there, I was just shook. I really felt Pac was a lot stronger when he got out of jail. On the one hand, he had more power. He had more money, more security, more love from the people in general. He had sold over ten million records! Tupac Shakur was now the king of rap! On the other hand, The Row didn't seem to be a safe environment, not underneath all the outward bluster. There was too much fuckery, weird petty bullshit sidetracking people from the mission, and what appeared to be a concerted effort to bring the drama of the streets into the boardroom. Pac should have been more protected. What could have gone so wrong?

The reports were, of course, true. When we got to town, the five of us went directly to the hospital. The core people were there: Afeni, Watani, the Outlawz. When I walked up, our cousin Jamala and Pac's fiancée Kidada were outside on the phone. Yaki was, understandably, a wreck. Pac was alive, but in very bad condition. Still, I thought he'd live. They had Pac on the first floor, which didn't make us feel comfortable. Watani had our people posted at the entrances and access points. We set up a security detail throughout the hospital and even tried to get security onto the roof. This was not, to be clear, The Row's security that had come with him to Vegas. This was Pac's people. The level of emotion was at a completely different level than when he had been shot in New York. There were news vans and reporters, and paparazzi, too, all outside. The fans started showing up out of love and support. It was difficult, honestly, to maintain some level of calm in all the chaos.

We were at the hospital every day, all day, for close to a week. It was traumatic for us all, for a variety of reasons. The emotional weight of those days at that hospital, hanging on any and every word from the medical staff, is impossible to put effectively into words. We prayed, we cried, some people sang. We were all there in love . . .

painful, anxious, and bearing the weight of the knowledge that life is fragile.

One day, while there were fans and supporters waiting outside, Yaki and I went out front. The crowd had grown, and it was probably too big for the hospital to manage, so the cops started harassing us. You know, "Get out of the street, get on the sidewalk, don't stand here, don't stand there." My man Donovan came outside, too. But young Yaki banged back on the police. He was like, "Man, fuck y'all. Y'all see we're grieving." He was right in their faces. Yak was young, but he was, like, six-three. I went to pull him back, and the cops started trying to jack me, too. I tried to talk to the officers. I let them know that emotions were high. I told them that we were family, that my brother was up in there. We were grieving and didn't mean no harm, in the hopes that they would leave us alone. Even with so many of Pac's fans there, it didn't feel intrusive. Their presence was comforting because of their extreme loyalty. They knew him. They knew his music. They had been supporting us the whole way and at this point were almost like family. There was a closeness. His words touched them deeply, and we were all consoling each other. I even saw my man Puug from Oakland. That touched me especially, because I hadn't seen him since we first started out.

My brother had been in and out of a lot of surgeries, and at the beginning, when I first got there, he was still conscious. I was anxious to go in and see him, but I was also still bracing myself for whatever condition he was going to be in. My sister Sekyiwa and I went in to see him together. While we were walking towards the room, she grabbed me and said, "Don't let him see you cry. Don't let him see you cry!" We both knew that he was in bad shape. When we entered the room, I did not like what I saw. The light was very bright, so everything was vivid and raw. Pac was laying there with a tube down his throat, bandages on his arms and head. I was soaking in the situation and I did see two Death Row security guards posted against the wall. Pac had all the machines going and tubes all in him, but he was conscious. Set talked to him while I was looking at him, assessing his situation. I was thinking to myself, *If God pulls him through it's going to be a hell of a recovery.* He had been hit several times in the lungs. When Set finished talking to him, he looked over at me and his eyes were trying to tell me something. His eyes were wide and wild—and everybody knows how expressive his eyes were—glaring at me. He was trying to verbalize something to me, so much that you could hear him gurgling muffled and unintelligible words through the tubes. His arm that was closest to me was bandaged up in a sling, but he was moving and trying to communicate so much that he started actually shaking the bed while he was trying to talk to me. I could already tell, of course, even with no words, he was pissed about something and was trying to tell me something about what happened. I know that. We wanted him to calm down and I told him, "Don't worry, Pac. Heal up. And when you get out, we're gonna handle business." He calmed down some, but he still wanted to tell me something. At that point, despite my promise to Set, I started crying. She and I left the room and embraced each other in the hallway. We didn't really know what to do but pray.

On the morning of the sixth day, China and I made the decision to go back to Palmdale to refresh, pick up fresh clothes, and pick up some stuff for Cheyenne. We hadn't intended on being in Vegas for that long, having no idea what Pac's condition was before we drove out. And when we made the decision to drive back, we thought Pac was stable enough. We thought we'd quickly get shit in order at home and come right back.

We had just driven into Los Angeles when we heard the news on the radio. As soon as we pulled up at 4:07 PM to drop Donovan off, literally unpacking the car, we heard the news that Pac had passed. I was in shock. He had taken a turn for the worse, coded twice, and the decision was made to take him off life support.

I was, I am, devastated. There is no reflective clarity from looking back on that situation that makes the pain any more bearable. There is no comfort in the idea that things happened the way they were supposed to. Fuck that. No mother should bury her son, no brother should bury his baby brother. Loss is human and a part of life, but burying a twenty-five-year-old man is not and should not be. I pick myself up, I move on, I cope, and I process that loss because I have to. I have no choice. But that doesn't make it normal. It should never be normalized. The loss of young life is tragic and reverberates through the lives of all the people they touched. In my brother's case, that is just massive. He still lives in so many people's hearts. That is a beautiful thing. That is also a real painful thing to process. I take my moments to grieve my brother by myself and with my family. But I also share that loss with the world in a way that, maybe selfishly, I sometimes resent.

Following his murder, the Las Vegas Police Department, who were entirely responsible for investigating, made no attempt to do so. To be clear: I didn't have any faith that they would. But it's important to state the obvious, simply because it's a truth that isn't said often enough. *They did nothing.* For decades, they blamed the Outlawz for not being good witnesses, which is bullshit considering investigations are completed and charges are brought against suspects every day in murders without any witnesses at all. The Outlawz, by the way, had seen the incident, but from a separate car. They were teenagers, barely adults. But the police treated them like fucking suspects, claiming that they needed to "secure the scene." They were traumatized, forced into an unthinkable position of having to be witnesses without trusting the cops, and for very good reason. The police blamed the community for not cooperating with the investigation, which is ridiculous. Because what investigation was there? I wish they would give a fuck about a Black man. I know they don't.

The family, at Afeni's direction, decided to cremate Tupac. That happened very quickly after his death. There were multiple plans for different services over a period of time, but it was a very difficult thing that nobody was prepared for and that nobody, I think, could wrap their brain around. It was a delicate thing, doing something that balanced our need for privacy with the scale and size of the service that he deserved. Over the subsequent years, we would have to learn how to balance our devastating personal grief with that of a public that adored and grieved him, too, even if they didn't know him. I don't think there's a person on earth that has the emotional maturity for something like that.

One of the first family and friends services very shortly after Pac's passing was at Jasmine Guy's home, off Melrose. She had a California-style bungalow—there was a nice living room, and you went through the kitchen, to the back of the house. It was fall and at dusk, so I couldn't see all the flowers, but she had a beautiful garden, with a well-kept lawn and shrubbery. It was very peaceful. It fit a good twenty people, and she had set up the backyard for everybody. There were chairs on the grass, facing a small altar with pictures. There were a couple floral arrangements throughout the yard and the house, elegant and not overdone. Jasmine took the spiritual lead. Somebody read something. People spoke. There really weren't many people there. Afeni, Sekyiwa, and I were there. And, of course, Jasmine. Jada, Yaki, and Syke, and maybe Yaasmyn were there, too. Syke, me, and Jada were hugging, telling each other it's gonna be alright. Fe was talking to everybody, trying to be strong. Honestly, it's all a blur. I was emotionally spent, just going through the motions.

I do remember that at some point me and Yak went out front and talked, just me and him. It was strange, cuz we were about to leave and he said, "Mo, look out for Set." And I'm thinking in my mind, *Yeah, nigga, we gonna look out for Set, of course. Me AND you.* Two months later, Yak would be gone, too. As if we needed any more pain, the young prince, my nigga, one of the little homies, our cousin, our brother, was gone. Apparently, while home in New Jersey he got into an altercation over a girl. Yak had his vest on, but the dude shot him in the head, point-blank. Devastating. When he passed, he had two little girls on the way. I helped carry his casket. My last bit of respect I could show while he was on this earth. It was like he was telling me that he wasn't gonna be around. I didn't think about that until later.

In the weeks that followed, there was a lot of grief as the family was trying to settle on how to say goodbye to Tupac. I don't think any of us actually wanted to, to be honest, and maybe it's fitting that there was never a definitive service, because Pac really is still living on, you know? There's no closure in that sense. We, the family, had these very private services for him. The biggest service, the closest thing to a public service, was in Atlanta at the Atlanta Civic Center. It too was a blur. Part of me would have loved to have had a big-ass service, with thousands of people. He definitely deserved that. But we, his family, still carry his loss publicly, regardless. One of them nights at the mini-mansion in Calabasas, one of the houses he lived in, we smoked some of Pac's ashes. I guess we were trying to feel close to him, just being in his space. It was me, Jamala, and Mu. We sprinkled his ashes on the weed and rolled on up. Pac always talked about it, that's what he told us to do. He said it often enough that we knew this was his wish: "Y'all smoke my ashes. Y'all get higher than a mothafucka smoking my ashes. When I go, when I die, y'all need to smoke my ashes. Roll a blunt and smoke me up. All this good weed I be smoking, y'all be higher than a motherfucker."

Mostly, it warms my heart how much he's loved, although there's a piece of me, a small piece of me, that hates the conspiracy theories that he's still alive. Like, yo, you don't think we, his loved ones, would fucking know if he was alive? Of course, I'd love for him to be alive somewhere, but it stings a little when I think about the fact that that means people, his fans, really don't understand how loved and how lovable he was to those who knew him. How fully he loved his family and friends.

There have been moments of depression along the way, for sure. I got divorced. I picked myself up and started a new life. I reflect on this part of my life daily. There's no way not to. I know we created something big, vast, and beautiful. I also know the world hasn't even seen it all. So I plug away, trying to do what I can to keep alive the things that are important to me, the things that I think we shouldn't forget. I intend to thrive in surviving to tell the tale.

I know this: As long as there is inequality, Pac's music will touch people. And as long as his music keeps touching people, he's still alive in people's hearts. I have faith in people to keep my brother's spirit alive. I have clear eyes about the systems of inequality that keep the need for his voice as pressing today as it was in 1996. And I see the reverberations of what we did in every person who is brave enough to live this life in their authentic truth.

I always wanted to make my mother and loved ones proud of me. I hope I did not fail them. I am proud and honored that me and my brother took what our parents gave us, good and bad, and transformed it into something that touched so many people. We are the cornerstone in what would be the foundation for telling the Shakur family's story to a broader audience through entertainment. The Hate U Gave Little Infants Fucks Everyone. T.H.U.G. L.I.F.E. Everyone was getting all bent out of shape about the name, missing the fact that it stood for making sure we look out for our kids, for our most vulnerable. My brother's work always included socially conscious records, but by consistently standing by the most vulnerable and recognizing the spaces where so-called polite people are willing to let the disempowered be left behind, T.H.U.G. L.I.F.E. is arguably our most political work. Say what you wanna say, it comes from love, love of the people. The presence of or the lack of love will alter reality.

From time to time, I think about the "27 Club," the group of musicians who died at twenty-seven. Jimi Hendrix, Janis Joplin, Kurt Cobain, Amy Winehouse, Robert Johnson. The list is long, and there are a bunch of factors involved that I promise I'm not trying to simplify. It's not like they all lost their lives the same way. And there are many more who weren't quite twenty-seven, but whose deaths were too early. What I'm saying is, the mid-twenties are a vulnerable age. I don't know how honest we are as a society about that. Sure, we're adults in our twenties, but we're just figuring out who we are. Or at least trying to. I was twenty-two when I recorded "Feels Good" and linked back up with my brother and sister. I was a baby, really, but

I thought I was grown. I was figuring out who I was, entering into manhood. And Pac was twenty-five when we lost him. He always knew he was going to leave us early, which is why I think he pushed us to work so fast and hard to get out this thing we were creating. It was a breakneck speed. We had a hell of a ride, and I consider myself fortunate to have been a part of the music industry and to be part of something so influential that it's for real historical. I am appreciative and grateful that I can contribute to something in this world of entertainment that endures and that is powerful enough that it still matters. We still matter. It was so much material, so much creativity, so much . . . truth.

We pay a price for that. We make ourselves vulnerable when we tell the truth, especially in a system, in a society, that doesn't want to confront those uncomfortable, those painful, those exploitative truths. I have never been willing to step back from my Blackness in the face of a situation or circumstance where dabbling in the politics of "respectability" may have afforded a different or more advantageous outcome. And I have always told the truth and been my authentic self, representing the broad and conflicting range of my Blackness through my life's work. And I continue to be proud of and celebrate my baby brother's brave unwillingness to step away from his authentic Blackness. His determination to show this world just how shitty we are to poor people, to women, to Black people, to brown people, to anyone disempowered, made him a target. We thought we'd never make it past our twenties, simply as Black men in a society where the chips are stacked against us. But add in my baby brother's relentless need to tell the mothafuckin' truth . . . it was liberating, it was empowering, but it also made him a target.

My brother was determined to reframe our childhood traumas, our life's traumas, and to never allow himself to feel disempowered. Being a young, Black man trying to figure things out, coming into that much power when you don't fully understand how to channel it is a dangerous thing. Our King Lear missed a pitfall, one that the few people who experience his level of success often do. He was seduced by those who would have him sacrifice himself for their gain. But even so, he was never so blinded that he didn't return to what's real. At one point, he was driven by revenge, which he came to honestly: through sincere and profound betrayal. He chose a path that would see him respond to the betrayal, maybe not in the healthiest way. But he was twenty-five! He was figuring shit out! Honestly, it's not easy to see all the pitfalls in a busy life when you're moving so fast and with a lot of adrenaline. It's like if you're driving too fast in a car, you're going to miss some signs.

Once we made it, we learned the lesson that all the great Black leaders learn—whether it's Martin Luther King Jr., Malcolm X, or Fred Hampton. Those leaders who truly want the people to be empowered become targets. I chose survival as the ultimate power play. I know my brother had my back, even when he was so blinded by revenge that he made some questionable choices. I also know that towards the end he was making every move to take back his power. I was told, and it's no secret, that towards the end of his life, he wanted to own his masters and to leave Death Row. In the grand scheme of things, it took him a couple months to figure that out . . . but there just wasn't enough time. Life is fragile, and we don't appreciate that when we're young. Tupac had yet to learn that we have to adjust around pitfalls to protect ourselves or we waste our dreams. In my father's day, they screamed, "Power to the People!" and "Free the Land!" We honestly felt that the war cry of our generation was "THUG LIFE!" And in this thug's life, I learned a lot about survival, and how powerful it is to simply still be here.

THUG IN PEACE Tupac Amaru Shakur, Afeni Shakur, Mutulu Shakur, Assata Shakur, Joseph "Uncle Joey" Harding, Fulani Sunni Ali, Yafeu "Yaki Kadafi" Fula, Sekou Odinga, Quincy Jones, Lisa "Left Eye" Lopes, Clarence Harris, Tommy "TC" Cox, Tony Taylor, Michelle "Mimi" Wheeler, Derek Mouldin, Andrea Jones, Shock G,

Big Syke, Stretch, Johnny J, Deon "Big D" Evans, Nate Dogg, John Singleton, Saafir, Fatal, G Money, Young Noble, K-Blunt, KMG, Laylaw (California Luv forever), Jewell, G-Nut, Brother Marquis, MC Breed, Yakisezwe Tyehimba, Big Kato, Johnny Cochran, Michael Tarif Warren, Jonathan Lubell, Peter Schey, Njeri Farlice, Chokwe Lumumba, Yuri Kochiyama, Geronimo Ji-Jaga Pratt, Bilal Sunni Ali, Delores "DP" Parker, Cleo Silvers, Musa Mil, Sherri Mitchell, M. Elena Duarte-Ruiz, Ian Alexander, Jr., Jenni Rivera, Coolio, DMX, D'Angelo, Angie B, Polo, Catfish, Bushwick Bill, Niko McKnight, Albert Golston, and Mary Francis and George Holmes.

EPILOGUE

My family and my life's work have always been intertwined. Like many artists, I come from a family with a lot of musical talent—my grandmother DP and my Aunt Jo played gospel music and my uncle Bilal played with Gil Scott-Heron. In the first part of my career, I made music with my brother and later my cousins, which actually isn't that unique in music. Though because my brother's and my father's contributions to culture, to society, are so massive and special, I have spent the better part of the second half of my career honoring their legacy. My greatest strength has been the way that I use my voice in my work, and that's forever through my culture and my art. As I grow creatively, I also continue to process my experiences: my pain and my joy. I expanded into other mediums, but that's never an easy road. I don't think it ever is, for any creative balancing the art and the business. I wanted and always endeavored to center my people in the stories I want to tell, and to do my best to advocate for productions to make space for those people to participate in telling their own stories. I've had lots of ups and lots of downs in an industry that's mostly full of people trying to tell you what you can't do—that just because you can do *one* thing doesn't mean you can do *another* thing. I'll keep putting my faith in the work. I'll keep it pushing.

I produced an episode of a popular series about my father, convincing the executive producers of *American Gangster* to rethink what they mean—what we as a society mean—when we call someone a gangster. This is not dissimilar from the way we wanted folks to think critically about who a thug is. In 2014, Afeni worked with a group of creatives to produce a play that used Tupac's works to tell an urban story. My music was on Broadway at the Palace Theatre. Dig that! This little Black boy from Queens had his music on the Great White Way. I have always viewed Broadway as the purest expression, the pinnacle of entertainment. I know my brother did, too. And I had *music* there!

I've toured Asia, Europe, and South America and the one thing that continues to amaze me is the way our music resonates with audiences across the world. Of course, Tupac has sold millions of records, and I am humbled and proud to have contributed to this body of work that continues to have a massive global impact. Even as I struggle in a business often at odds with the very artists who fuel it, my greatest pleasure is knowing I'm part of a legacy that has touched millions and will continue to do so long after I'm gone.

While I was writing this book, my father was released from prison after almost thirty-seven years of incarceration. From the time I saw that poster in the subway calling for his freedom until the day he was released on December 16, 2022, my father had a network of supporters fighting for his freedom, seeking appeals, pardons, parole, and any legal action that would secure his freedom. I pitched in, in any way I could, and I also dedicated myself to ensuring that people understood my father's full story. I wanted them to understand him as a kind, generous, loyal, principled, and brilliant soul so that the world might understand the sacrifices he made for Black Liberation and for freedom and fairness around the world. I was one of the producers of a film about his work at Lincoln Detox called *Dope Is Death*.

Diagnosed with multiple myeloma, he came to live with me and spent his final months surrounded by love. I got to see him free in this world—eating ice cream, taking meetings, doing speaking engagements, going to film screenings and premiers, recording an album, meeting the mayor, seeing me and Sekyiwa unveil my brother's star on the Hollywood Walk of Fame, and living the last of his life free and to the fullest. My Dear Old Dad passed on July 7, 2023.

On what would have been Dad's seventy-third birthday, August 8, 2023, I got a call from the detectives in Las Vegas, the city that had neglected my brother's case for over twenty-seven years. They were going to seek an indictment in my brother's murder. For decades, I pushed back against the way the media framed my brother's murder: *He was an artist who got killed pretending to be a gangster. He got himself caught up in the streets and was over his head.* And for decades, as far as I could tell, Las Vegas wanted no part of an investigation, portraying my brother's murder as something that gangbangers brought to their city. That's not the whole story, and I refuse to let my brother be remembered that way. Afeni worked tirelessly to preserve his legacy through his work, and I always had the support of his fans in my endeavors. His fans pushed to solve his murder and to expose those at its heart, making a commercial space to produce multiple TV series investigating his murder when the police would not.

There's a part of me that believes that the very people whose hearts we touch with this music are the ones that won't let it go, that pushed the police to investigate and ultimately make an arrest. And to be fair, nearly thirty years later, the office of the district attorney is a whole different generation. We'll see what they do. I'm determined to hold everyone accountable—all the actors in this tragedy. What that means for law enforcement is still unfolding.

Either way . . . I have more story to tell!

ACKNOWLEDGMENTS

I've been on a lot of missions, but this one would not have been possible without you. Thank you, I love you: Talia del Carmen Rodríguez-Shakur. Specifically, I would like to thank you for your writing expertise, skill and all-around awesomeness, for your bomb ass cooking, dope cocktails and your relentlessness, pushing me when I didn't even know or remember what I had in me. I couldn't have done it without you. I love you.

Super big thanks to Kevin Powell for setting me on this path to get this story out in the first place. A special thanks to all my loved ones who helped me dig up old memories and check facts: Dana "Mouseman" Smith, Serg Bryant, Erroll Jackson, Dedan Gills, Money B, Atron Gregory, Charles "Man Man" Fuller, Leila Steinberg, Karen Lee, Babez, Mike Cooley, Roland Brooks, Mama Gunz, and Peron Williams of the High Power Two. Much gratitude to Tracy Danielle Robinson and Stefany Baclaan for helping me with photos and for being so organized when I am . . . not so much.

I would like to acknowledge my family, friends who are my family, and loved ones for all the love and support over the years and on my journey in this world: My mommy Sharan Golston, my dear old dad Dr. Mutulu Shakur, Joanna "Aunt Jo" and Eugene "Uncle Gene" Evans, Cleo "Big Mama" Haley and the McDaniel 13, Afeni Shakur, Tupac Shakur, Makini Shakur, Sekyiwa Shakur, Nzingha Shakur-Ali, Chinua Shakur, Talib Shakur, Ayize Jama-Everett, Malik and Nzingha Shakur, Assata Shakur, Mary and George Holmes, Jean and Johnny Schaal, Jermaine White, Gretchen Schaal, Jessica Roberts, Ian and Natasha Davis, Fall and Run Missionary Baptist Church, Aunt Sharon and Nicole, Albert and Ligia Rodríguez, Bertita De Landa, Uncle Pete Cetani, Brandon and Mama Gibson, Albert Golston, Chui Ferguson, Dingus and Sekyiwa Shakur, Susan Rosenberg and Dawn, Walter Bosque, Dr. Tatsuo Hirono, Juan Cortez, Steven Wheeler, Randy "Ran Chan" Chandler, Big O, Cash, David Lewis, Jeff, Benji, Butter, Todd, May Turner, 146 Jamaica Fam—The Reverse Oreo —Breeze and Julio, Nicole and Yvette Taylor, MC Razzamatazz, Mona Conway, Watani, Ahadi and Asinia and Ife Simon Tyhemba, Akinyele Umoja, Veronza Bowers, Nobuko Miyamoto, Oshun Farlice, Debra with the Black Subaru, Super Friend Naomi Ramsey, Laura Troy, Echo Hatttix, Keisha Morris, cousins Bill, Scott, Kenny, Greg, Jamala "Moo," and Mai Ling, Dina and Imani Cox, China Myers, Aiyisha Obafemi, Efua Ata Ayanna Ayo Sunni-Ali, Chaka Zulu, KofiAta Shakur Sunni-Ali, Zayd Akinyele, Yaasmyn Fula, Derek, Bobby and Helen Mouldin, Donovan Fordham, Bo Brown, Wayne Vaughn, Sean Mead, Steve Shockley, Jamaica, Big Paul, the whole Brooks Family, especially Chris, Uncle Vic, Sherril, Lil Vic, Benjamin, Julie and BJ McKnight, Decio, The Malibu Crew: Merlin, Marcia, Carey, Lori, Mikke the Mayor, Maggie, Karen, Steve, Jordan and the Graces, Adrienne Pieroth, Belinda Ma, Angelica Hale, H Ryda, Michael "Hawk" Hawkins, Ron James, Gregory Mitchell, Michael "Cali" Callihan, Andrea Jones, Tiwan Parker, Vera and Michael Parker, Mama and Papa Syke and Sabrina, Gregory "Big Country" and Kennisha Martin and family, John Weathers, Steve "Precise" Morris, Pete Stone, Shomari Pass, Big Mike Mike, Judah and Makaya, Greg and Camron Jackson, Buford "Big Duke" Carter, Lena Miller, and most especially Cheyenne "the Pea" Harding.

I must take a moment to thank God and recognize my heroes—the people whose work, art and perseverance paved my path in this world: Paul Robeson, Marcus Garvey, Malcolm X, Emmett Till, Martin Luther King, Jr., Nelson Mandela, Robert F. Williams, Yuri Kochiyama, the Republic of New Afrika, the Black Panther Party, the Black Liberation Army and the heroes in my own family: Mutulu, Sharan, Tupac, Afeni, Assata, Geronimo, Zaed, and Lumumba. Free them all!

Free the land!

Huge thanks to my agent, Jon Michael Darga, for staying in the fight from the beginning, through the proposal and every edit and rewrite, pushing me and Talia to put my story into this world. I would like to thank Mark Bryant and the Scribd team for the work they did in the early stages of crafting this book. Many thanks to my editor, Denise Silvestro, especially for staying on top of every detail and for approaching the whole process with practicality and sensitivity—Queens kids stick together! And thanks to the marketing team at Kensington, Michelle Addo and Vida Engstrand.

And finally, as an artist I have collaborated, created and worked with so many wonderfully talented people, without whom I wouldn't have this story to tell in the first place. In no particular order, I would like to acknowledge and express my sincere gratitude to each of you for all that you do: Kenya Baker, Macadoshis, Rated R, Big Syke, Yak, Edi, Kastro, Fatal, Mutah, Noble, Storm (T.H.U.G. L.I.F.E. Outlaw Immortal 4 Life!), DJ Pizo, Tony! Toni! Tone!, Treach and Naughty by Nature, Ray Luv, DJ Dizz, Spice 1, DJ Xtra-Large, Shock G, DJ Fuse, Cleetis Mack, Raniece, Jimi "Chopmaster J" Dright, Master Z, the whole Digital Underground Crew, Danielle Field, Regina and Reina King, Boots Riley, Davey D, Big D the Impossible, Shorty B, Go Mack, E-40 and the Click, Too $hort, MC Hammer, B-Legit, Sway & King Tech, Suga-T, Rappin' 4-Tay, RBX, Paris, Dru Down, The Gov, Richie Rich, Jada Pinkett Smith, Yolanda "YoYo" Whitaker, Jasmine Guy, Medusa, Sylk-E. Fyne, Ms. Toi, Mr. Tam, Easy Mo Bee, Prince Ital Joe, Keyshia Cole, Nuttso, Rakim, Wu Tang Clan, WC, Cypress Hill, Mellow Man Ace, Magic, Cle "Bone" Sloan, Matt Nye, Marlon Wayans, Peter DiStefano, Treacherous Three, Thyrifa, LL Cool J, Pharcyde, De La Soul, Kent Butts (King Records), Taj, Sauve, Buckshot, Boot Camp Click, Onyx, Papoose, Sean Stone, Oliver Stone, Darris Love, Lyndsey Labrum, Michael Tarrif Warren, Iris Crews, Peter Schey, Brad Thomson, Mark Kleiman and Stephanie Fletcher, Stuart Hanlon, Truman, Shakim Compere, Flavor Unit, Busta Rhymes, Spliff Star, DJ Bobcat, Above the Law, Laylaw,

Battlecat, Kurupt, Daz, Big Hutch (Cold 187um), KMG, Kaos, Terrell and Pat "Pop Masters," Lil Monster Coty, Nate Dogg, Norman Whitfield, Y? N-Vee, L.V., Alicia, Joe Torry, Eddie Griffin, Martin Lawrence, Luenell, Faison Love, Chris Tucker, Dru Down, Don Omar, Tea Time, Demarco, Trick Daddy, Pitbull, Purple, Bone Thugs-N-Harmony, Ron Hightower, Yukmouth, Brian "Beavis," Patrick PhD Hawkins, The East Bay Dragons, Geto Boys, Curtis Blow, Kool G Rap, Guru, Biz Markie, KRS One and BDP, D-Nice, Kool Moe Dee, Big Daddy Kane, Tim Dog, Das EFX, DJ Red Alert, DJ Kid Capri, DJ Ron G, TLC, En Vogue, Salt-N-Pepa, Monie Love, Miki Howard, Yanni, Mesha Harlan, Gonzoe, Lost Boyz, Freddie Foxxx, Bootsy Collins, Miss Pattie and Summer, Action, Busy Bee Starsky, Big Ice and Stephanie, Hen Gee, Evil E, Quincy "QD3" "Snoopy" Jones, Ice Cube, Brother Ron, Warren G, No Name, Ras Kass, Mia Donovan, Nate Truesdell, T. Eric Monroe, Sara Sidner, Dr. Robin D.G. Kelley, Dr. Arón Montenegro, Kahlil "Cock D" Harris, Chuck Armstrong, Bernard Lee, Sr., Quanzilla and Alma, Ricky Harris, Pete Rock, Parrish Smith, DJ Premiere, Taje, Bishop Lamont, Dae One, Mykstro and Ovadose McKenny, Triple Seven, Lyndon Howard, Ramin and Mecca, Kirkpatrick "KP" Tyler, Klypso, Hokey Bowman, Sadd Dog, Jared "Honky" Morris, Greg Nalbandian, Angel "Tiny Tunes" Valentin, Silver, Riff Costello, Vito Gambino, Dorika Powake, Lester Parris, Marc Rose, Shelly Gibson-Paul, Claudette "Mama C" Rogers Robinson, Tamla Robinson, Lyric Ontiveros Robinson, Grace McKenna and the Center for Puerto Rican Studies at Hunter College, Jamaica, Queens NY, Richard Gibbs, Dennis Draith, Abigail Kende, the VIST/BROS team, Jimmy and Big Ant at the at the VA for hookin' a brotha up with all the gadgets and tech I need to help me write, and my legal team Brandon Anand, Jody Zucker, Peter Sample, Alex Spiro, and Christopher Clore. Last but never least: my fans, through all the highs and lows, and especially in the tough times, you have stayed with me and loved me, and I will always love you too, thank you.

I've lived more life than can fit in these pages. So, for those I might have forgotten, I truly apologize. Please know, it's a failure of my strained memory, not my heart. Love you! Straight ahead!

CREDITS

Kung Fu Fighting (page 26)
© Carl Douglas / Carren Music Group

Niggaz In the Pen (page 137)
© Maurice Shakur / Mutulu Music / Tupac Amaru Shakur / Dana Smith / Dana Mouse Smith Publishing

Gotta Get Mine (page 162)
© Eric Breed / Tommy Baby Music / Tupac Amaru Shakur

Nothing to Lose (page 190)
© Tupac Amaru Shakur / Randy Walker / O'Shea Jackson / Lorenzo Jerald Patterson / Kevin Rhames / Christopher Walker / Anthony D. Wheaton / Duane Thomas Nettlesby / Tracy Lynn Curry / Joshua's Dream / Universal Music Group / Gangsta Boogie Music / Ruthless Attack Muzick / Bridgeport Music Publishing / Dollarz N Sense Muzick / C.a.m. Creazioni Artistiche Musicali / Songs of Universal, Inc. / Bridgeport Music, Inc / Street Knowledge Productions Inc.

Hellrazor (original recording) (page 259)
Original Lyrics: © Val Young Andrews / Tupac Amaru Shakur / Christopher Walker / Randy Walker / Joshua's Dream

Photo Credits:

Photo 1A—Courtesy of Mopreme Shakur, Family Collection

Photo 1B—Courtesy of Sharan Golston, Family Collection

Photo 2A—Courtesy of Norris Jean Schaal, Family Collection

Photo 2B—Courtesy of Gretchen Schaal, Family Collection

Photo 2C—Courtesy of Jermaine White, Family Collection

Photo 3A—Courtesy of Carlos Ortiz Collection, Archives of the Puerto Rican Diaspora, Center for Puerto Rican Studies, Hunter College, CUNY

Photo 3B—Courtesy of Carlos Ortiz Collection, Archives of the Puerto Rican Diaspora, Center for Puerto Rican Studies, Hunter College, CUNY

Photo 4A—Courtesy of Anita Hearn Shakur ©Anita Hearn Shakur

Photo 4B—Courtesy of Anita Hearn Shakur ©Anita Hearn Shakur

Photo 5—Courtesy of Mutulu Shakur, Personal Collection

Photo 6—Courtesy of Motown Records under license from Universal Music Enterprises

Photo 7A—Courtesy of Mopreme Shakur, Polaroid caption by Mopreme Shakur ©Maurice Shakur

Photo 7B—Courtesy of Mopreme Shakur, Polaroid caption by Mopreme Shakur ©Maurice

Photo 8—Courtesy of Mopreme Shakur ©Maurice Shakur

Photo 9A—Courtesy of Mopreme Shakur ©Maurice Shakur

Photo 9B—Courtesy of Mopreme Shakur ©Maurice Shakur

Photo 9C—Courtesy of Mopreme Shakur ©Maurice Shakur

Photo 10A—Courtesy of Mopreme Shakur ©Maurice Shakur

Photo 10B—Courtesy of Mopreme Shakur ©Maurice Shakur

Photo 11A—Photo courtesy of Mutulu Shakur, Personal Collection

Photo 11B—Photo courtesy of Mutulu Shakur, Personal Collection

Photo 12—Courtesy of T. Eric Monroe © T. Eric Mornroe

Photo 13—Courtesy of T. Eric Monroe © T. Eric Mornroe

Photo 14—Courtesy of Mopreme Shakur ©Maurice Shakur

Photo 15A—Courtesy of Tracy Danielle Robinson, ©Tracy Danielle Robinson

Photo 15B—Courtesy of Mopreme Shakur, ©Maurice Shakur

Photo 16—Photo by Stefany Baclaan, © Stefany Baclaan

INDEX